VOID
Library of
Davidson College

FREGE
Tradition & Influence

FREGE
Tradition & Influence
Edited by Crispin Wright

Basil Blackwell

©The Philosophical Quarterly 1984

First published in 1984

Basil Blackwell Publisher Ltd
108 Cowley Road, Oxford OX4 1JF, UK

Basil Blackwell Inc.
432 Park Avenue South, Suite 1505,
New York, NY 10016, USA

All rights reserved. Except for the quotation of short passages for the purposes of criticism and review, no part of this publication may be reproduced, stored in a retrieval system, or transmitted, in any form or by any means, electronic, mechanical, photocopying, recording or otherwise, without the prior permission of the publisher.

Except in the United States of America, this book is sold subject to the condition that it shall not, by way of trade or otherwise, be lent, resold, hired out, or otherwise circulated without the publisher's prior consent in any form of binding or cover othe than that in which it is published and without a similar condition including this condition being imposed onm the subsequent purchaser.

British Library Cataloguing in Publication Data

Frege: tradition and influence.
  1. Frege, Gottlob
  I. Wright, Crispin   II. Frege, Gottlob
  193   B 3245.F24
  ISBN 0-631-13831-5

Printed in Great Britain by T. J. Press, Padstow

CONTENTS

Editor's Foreword		vii
Eternal Thoughts	*Peter Carruthers*	1
Fregean Thoughts	*Harold Noonan*	20
Frege's Platonism	*Bob Hale*	40
The Philosopher behind the Last Logicist	*Joan Weiner*	57
The Sense of a Name	*Michael Luntley*	80
De Re Senses	*John McDowell*	98
Frege, Sommers, Singular Reference	*Gregory McCulloch*	110
The Sense and Reference of Predicates: A Running Repair to Frege's Doctrine and a Plea for the Copula	*David Wiggins*	126
Frege's Metaphysical Argument	*Gregory Currie*	144
What does a Concept Script do?	*Cora Diamond*	158

DISCUSSION

Reference and Sense: An Epitome	*David Bell*	184
Fregean Connection: Bedeutung, Value and Truth-Value	*Gottfried Gabriel*	189

CRITICAL STUDIES

An Unsuccessful Dig	*Michael Dummett*	194
Dummett's Frege	*John Skorupski*	227
BIBLIOGRAPHY		245
INDEX		247

Editor's Foreword

This collection of papers, offprinted from *The Philosophical Quarterly* 34 No. 136, is published in celebration of the centenary of Frege's *Grundlagen der Arithmetik*. But only the contributions of Hale and Weiner are primarily given to exegesis of Frege's thought in that work. Diamond seeks to clarify the nature of the philosophical project which underlies the quest for a *Begriffsschrift*. Carruthers and Noonan are concerned with the evaluation of Frege's notion of a Thought. Currie argues that the assimilation of concept to function cannot be rendered coherent, but that this flaw in Frege's system can be contained. Wiggins attempts a running repair of Frege's semantics for incomplete expressions so as to obviate the paradox of the concept Horse. Luntley, McCulloch and McDowell are variously concerned with issues arising from Frege's semantics for singular terms. Bell attempts a unified account of the notions of sense and reference from which Frege's distinctive theses concerning those notions may flow. Gabriel seeks a better historical understanding of Frege's doctrine of truth-values as the reference of sentences.

Although Frege has his defenders in these pages, there is little cosiness of atmosphere. Few, if any, of the contributors would regard themselves as apostles of Frege. But they are united by conviction of the greatness of Frege's philosophical achievement, and of the enduring philosophical importance of the theses, concepts, and issues which he bequeathed to us. Recently a different trend in Fregean scholarship has emerged, whose principal claims are that Frege's accomplishment has been greatly overrated and that his philosophical legacy has been largely counter-productive to the growth of understanding. It seemed fitting to include a detailed critique of a major representative of this trend: Dummett's critical study of Baker's and Hacker's *Frege: Logical Excavations*. But the inclusion of Skorupski's critical study of Dummett's own *The Interpretation of Frege's Philosophy* should not be seen as an expression of editorial impartiality; Skorupski is not party to the new trend, and the Editor is not impartial.

Philosophical achievements can be measured in different ways. One important measure is the quality of the philosophy which a philosopher inspires. By this measure Frege's greatness wants no further evidence. But it is a pleasure to record the opinion that, if further evidence were wanted, it may be found in ample supply in this volume.

I should like to thank my colleagues on the Editorial Board for their assistance in the preparation of this volume, and Campbell Purton for compiling the Index.

Crispin Wright
St. Andrews
March 1984

ABBREVIATIONS

Full details of works frequently referred to in this collection will be found in the general Bibliography at the end. In the text, references to these are given thus: (Bell, p. 23). Other references are given as footnotes. Throughout the collection the following abbreviations are used.

Works by Frege

AB	"Anwendung an der Begriffsschrift"
BrL	"Booles rechnende Logik und die Begriffsschrift"
Bs	*Begriffsschrift*
FB	"Funktion und Begriff"
Ged	"Der Gedanke"
Gg	*Grundgesetze der Arithmetik*
Gl	*Grundlagen der Arithmetik*
KS	*Kleine Schriften*
NS	*Nachgelassene Schriften*
SB	"Über Sinn und Bedeutung"
WB	*Wissenschaftlicher Briefwechsel*
BLA	*Basic Laws of Arithmetic* tr. Montgomery Furth
CN	*G. Frege, Conceptual Notation* tr. T. W. Bynum
FA	*Foundations of Arithmetic* tr. J. L. Austin
FG	*Foundations of Geometry* tr. E.-H. Kluge
LI	*Logical Investigations* tr. P. Geach and R. Stoothoff
PMC	*Philosophical and Mathematical Correspondence*
PW	*Posthumous Writings* tr. H. Hermes et al.
TWF	*Translations from the Philosophical Writings of Gottlob Frege* ed. P. Geach and M. Black

Other works

FPL	Michael Dummett, *Frege: The Philosophy of Language*
IFP	Michael Dummett, *The Interpretation of Frege's Philosophy*
PI	Wittgenstein, *Philosophical Investigations*
TLP	Wittgenstein, *Tractatus Logico-Philosophicus*

ETERNAL THOUGHTS

By Peter Carruthers

I

Introduction. A Thought, as Frege understands the notion, is the sense of a context-free sentence (that is, a sentence free of all indexicality, whether explicit or implicit).[1] At various points throughout his writings – including, as is appropriate in this the centenary year of its publication, *Gl* – Frege is to be found arguing that Thoughts exist eternally. Indeed a belief in the eternality of Thoughts stayed with him through almost the whole of his philosophical career, being regarded as an essential plank in his wider views on language, mathematics and truth. I shall present, on Frege's behalf, a number of arguments which he himself does not distinguish very clearly from one another. So although I shall give, in each case, references to those passages in his writings that inspired me to produce these arguments, I shall make no attempt at detailed textual exegesis. A more fruitful approach is simply to construct the strongest possible arguments consistent with what he actually says.

Of course Thoughts are not the only entities believed by Frege to exist eternally. As is well known, he believed the same about numbers. These two beliefs essentially belong together, given his further belief that the truths of arithmetic are analytic. For an analytic truth is, presumably, true in virtue of sense; and the realm of Thoughts is the realm of sense. However, since hardly anyone today shares Frege's belief in the analyticity of arithmetic, I shall have nothing further to say about the possible bearing of his arguments upon the supposed eternal existence of numbers.

I propose to take for granted the broad outlines, at least, of the Fregean apparatus of sense and reference, as well as allowing him his belief in the objectivity of truth and necessity. I shall content myself with showing, contra Frege, that one can be broadly realist about such matters, without being committed to the eternal existence of Thoughts. Indeed I shall take it for granted that Thoughts do *exist*, thus allowing to be genuine such apparent

---

[1] Throughout I shall write 'thought' with a capital 'T' whenever I use it in the sense of Frege's technical term. When talking about particular Thoughts I shall, as an aid to the reader, use square brackets to indicate the scope of the Thought.

references to them as would occur in, 'A gave expression to the Thought [that *p*], and B wished to contradict that Thought'. The question that concerns me is not whether Thoughts exist, but whether they exist independently of us. Is it appropriate to speak of a genuinely independent *realm* of entities here, that we have to reckon with and make discoveries about, in the manner of Frege's famous comparison between the mathematician and the geographer? Or are Thoughts somehow supervenient upon human speech and activity? It is to Frege's credit that he recognised a gap here that needs to be filled. The philosophical interest of an argument establishing the existence of such abstract entities as Thoughts or numbers is strictly limited, unless it also establishes, or can be developed in such a way as to establish, that they exist eternally, or at least mind-independently.[2] I believe many who would not wish to count themselves as platonists, would be prepared to recognise a class of abstract entities whose existence somehow supervenes upon our own existence. It would be natural, for instance, to take just such a line about sentences: to allow that sentences do genuinely exist – and exist independently of whether, and when, they are uttered – but to insist that the sentence, 'It is raining' did not exist prior to the existence of a language in which it may be formulated, and never would have existed had no human beings ever existed.

I shall not, then, be concerned with the issue of ontological reductionism. As is familiar, it is one thing to claim that a certain class of entities (mental states, say) may be reduced to, or analysed into, another class (physical states); and it is quite another, weaker, thing to claim that the one class could not exist in the absence of the other. Nor shall I discuss in any detail just what the supervenience of Thoughts might consist in. However I can see, in outline, at least two possibilities. First, it may be that the supervenience of Thoughts over human behaviour and dispositions is explicable in a manner similar to Davidson's account of the supervenience of the mental over the physical.[3] Since on a Fregean approach the notions of belief and judgement will themselves involve the notion of a Thought, the impossibility of a reduction may have to do with the sort of *holism* associated with attributions of beliefs and judgements to intelligent agents. Alternatively, it may be that the relationship is, in the terminology introduced by the later Wittgenstein, *criterial* rather than truth-conditional. There may be 'loose' logical relations between Thoughts and human behaviour – certain kinds of behaviour both warranting ascriptions of

---

[2] There is a lacuna here in Crispin Wright's recent spirited defence of Frege's platonism, in that, so far as I am aware, he presents no argument for supposing numbers to be mind-independent (Wright).

[3] D. Davidson, "Mental Events", in *Actions and Events* (Oxford, 1980). Strictly speaking, Davidson's claim is that although each particular mental event *is* some physical event, nevertheless mental events cannot, in general, be reduced to physical ones.

grasp of Thoughts, and forming part of our understanding of the very notion of a Thought – but where those relations are not of such a kind as could be used in an effective reduction.

There is a strong presumption against the mind-independent existence of Thoughts, in the absence of positive arguments to the contrary. Apart from being metaphysically more conservative, the supervenience thesis would avoid all the mystery that otherwise attaches to the notions of grasping, or thinking, a Thought. Frege's major difficulty is that we are required to be *aware* of Thoughts – it being my grasp of a given Thought which is to guide my use of the associated sentence – and yet we are not aware that we are aware of them. On the supervenience thesis, on the other hand, there is no such difficulty. My grasp of the associated Thought would somehow be *manifest in* (without being constituted by) my use of a given sentence.

It will help to impose some structure on the discussion that follows, if we distinguish three different notions within the broad notion of the eternal. Let us refer to an entity that exists at all times in the actual world as "omnitemporal", to an entity that exists at all times in all possible contingent worlds as "necessary", and to an entity that exists even if there is no world and no time as "absolutely necessary". These are notions of increasing strength, with 'omnitemporal' being implied by 'necessary', and 'necessary' being implied by 'absolutely necessary', but not vice versa. And note that all three are stronger than 'mind-independent', since if an entity is omnitemporal it exists independently of the human mind, but not vice versa. On my presentation, Frege's argument from communication (§III) will attempt to establish the mind-independence of Thoughts, his argument from omnitemporality of truth (§IV) their omnitemporal existence, his argument from objectivity of truth (§V) their necessary existence, and his argument from analyticity (§VI) their absolutely necessary existence. I shall rebut all four arguments.

It will also help at this point to introduce informally the wider notion of a *proposition*, to stand alongside Frege's notion of a Thought. A Thought is, as we said, the sense of a context-free sentence. A proposition, as I shall understand it, is the sense of a type-sentence that may or may not be context-free. Frege himself held the view that the wider notion of a proposition is logically redundant. For he believed that all statements express Thoughts, it being possible to re-formulate what is said by any statement involving an indexical sentence in context-free terms, and it being the sense of this context-free sentence (a Thought), rather than the sense of the original indexical sentence (a proposition), which is the proper bearer of the truth-value of the statement. However this view of Frege's will prove to be of little importance for our purposes.

II

Eternality versus timelessness. Before we begin to consider Frege's arguments, we must face an objection which threatens to render consideration of those arguments pointless.[4] For it could be maintained that Thoughts exist *timelessly*, in a sense of 'timeless' which bears no logical relation (beyond mutual exclusion) to the three senses of 'eternal' distinguished above, but which would, nevertheless, imply mind-independence. Thus it could be claimed that it simply *makes no sense* to say of the Thought [that snow is white] that it exists now, or exists at all times. On this view, it would make just as little sense to say that a Thought exists at a particular time, as to say that a number exists at a particular place – and the sentence, 'The number 7 is (or is not) in London' is obvious nonsense. If this were correct, then any attempt to argue for a version of the thesis that Thoughts exist eternally, would clearly be misconceived. Yet we should still have enough to establish the thesis of mind-independence. For if Thoughts are *not* independent of the human mind, then there *was* once a time, prior to the existence of the human race, when they did not exist. But this conclusion, according to the timelessness thesis, makes no sense; so the premise cannot be true. (Note that we cannot derive a parallel *reductio* from the premise that Thoughts *are* independent of the human mind. For the claim that there was once a time when no humans existed but Thoughts did, need not be interpreted as implying that the Thoughts existed *at* that time. We can, rather, interpret it as follows: there was a time t when no human existed, and it was true at t that the Thought [that p] exists (timelessly).)

It is important to distinguish the thesis of *timeless* existence, expounded above, from the phenomenon of *tenseless* existence. There is certainly a way of reading, 'There are such things as dodos' ('Dodos exist'), according to which this sentence comes out true, despite the fact that dodos are extinct. Similarly, there is a way of reading, 'There is such a person as Moses' ('Moses exists'), according to which it comes out true. But tenseless existence normally stands in the most intimate logical connection with temporal existence. Thus, 'There is (tenseless) an x such that x is a dodo' both implies and is implied by, 'There is (present), was, or will be an x such that x is a dodo'. Now the distinctive thing about attributing existence to Thoughts, on the Fregean view, is that, 'There is (tenseless) an x such that x is the Thought [that p]', implies (and is implied by), 'There is, at *all* times, an x such that x is the Thought [that p]'. The thesis of timeless existence, on the other hand, claims that if the former sentence is true, then the latter sentence makes no sense at all.

---

[4] This objection was urged upon me by both Christopher McKnight and Tim Williamson. I am grateful to both for many helpful criticisms of an earlier draft.

One difficulty for the timelessness thesis is this: if Thoughts cannot sensibly be said to exist-at-a-time, how then can they be graspable-at-a-time?[5] How can a sentence like, 'Person A grasps, at time t, the Thought [that p]', not entail the sentence, 'The Thought [that p] exists at time t'? The only response to this difficulty is to deny that the grasping-relation is a genuine, extensional, relation. Construing it, rather, on the model of, 'A has, at t, a belief about x' (which of course does not entail, 'x exists at t'), it could be claimed to be an intentional relation. This is, however, a high price to pay. For part of the point of introducing the notion of sense in the first place, is that it should be put to work in explaining the phenomenon of intentionality. But now it appears that the notion of *grasp* of sense, which would have to figure in such an explanation, is itself an intentional one.

Another difficulty with the timelessness thesis is simply that it lacks intuitive plausibility. For sentences like, 'The Thought [that snow is white] always has, and always will, exist', just do not have the obvious kind of senselessness possessed by such sentences as, 'The number 7 is everywhere'. They seem, on the contrary, perfectly intelligible, if not obviously true. If they are, despite appearances, senseless, it wants an argument to show that they are. Now admittedly, what *is* true is that sentences attributing existence to Thoughts at *particular* times have an air of oddity about them, not possessed by the sort of universally quantified sentence above. Thus a sentence like, 'The Thought [that snow is white] existed in the year 2000 B.C.', does have a strange ring to it. But this will be easily explicable if it is supposed to be obvious and uncontroversial that Thoughts exist omnitemporally.[6] For in that case, the attempt to attribute existence to a Thought at some particular time, will lack any significant contrast; and the resulting ring of oddity will derive from a breach of one of the conventions of conversational implicature, rather than from literal senselessness. For one of these conventions is that you should not give less information on a certain topic than you are capable of giving (easily). Yet this is just what someone would be doing who asserted the sentence above, if it were generally accepted that it implies, 'The Thought [that snow is white] exists at all times'. "Why do you bother to say that?", one would wish to expostulate, "when for no greater expenditure of effort you could have said so much more, and when to say what you did suggested that the Thought in question did *not* exist at *other* times." Nevertheless, what would have been asserted would have been, literally, true. Moreover I shall wish to deny, myself, that the mere existence of a Thought *does* imply that it exists at all times; in which case it will be significant, after all, to assert that the Thought exists at some particular time.

[5] I owe this point to Crispin Wright.
[6] Any oddity that might be felt about the claim that Thoughts always have, and always will, exist, will be similarly explicable if it is supposed to be obvious that Thoughts have necessary existence.

If the timelessness thesis is to survive these difficulties, some argument must be found in its support. An apparently promising line would be to press the analogy between timelessness and spacelessness: just as it makes no sense to say of an abstract object, like a Thought or a number, that it occupies some particular place (nor all places), so too, it might be suggested, it makes no sense to say of a Thought – non-physical, imperceptible, and essentially changeless – that it exists at some particular time (nor at all times). But can the analogy be substantiated? The reason why it makes no sense to attribute spatial position to an abstract entity, is that it forms an essential part of our conception of what it is for an entity to occupy space (with the exception of spatial points themselves), that it be either physical, or perceptible, or both. We simply have no conception of what it would be for an entity to occupy a particular place, except in terms of its possible causal interactions with other entities (including ourselves). However these aspects of the supposed nature of Thoughts – their being non-physical and imperceptible – cannot be enough to establish the timelessness thesis. For it is at least intelligible that someone might believe there to be a class of entities – e.g., souls and their states – which are not physical (which perhaps cannot causally interact with anything physical, even), and which are imperceptible, and yet the changes in which occupy genuine positions in time. So if any feature of Thoughts is to establish their timelessness, it must be their supposed changelessness. And indeed it is true that the concept of change seems essentially connected with that of time, in something like the way that the concept of the physical is connected with that of space. Many have argued that if there were no change there could be no time, just as they have argued that if there were no physical things there could be no space. However, the nature of the essential connection is certainly not strong enough to warrant the timelessness thesis, since we can easily imagine a physical object which, while being itself absolutely changeless (in everything except relational properties), is surrounded by changing things, and which may be said to exist *through* the times of those changes. So the changelessness of any particular entity certainly does not imply that it exists timelessly.

The only other possible ground that I can see for adopting the timelessness thesis, arises purely out of a confusion between the notions of the timeless and the absolutely necessary. Suppose someone were to believe that Thoughts would have existed even if there had been no world and no time: he might take this to be tantamount to believing that Thoughts cannot sensibly be said to exist *at* any time. For if Thoughts would exist even if there were no time, how can they exist *in* time, given that there *is* time? But this is a muddle. Suppose the universe to consist simply of a single changeless sphere: then, many would maintain, there would be no time; so the sphere exists in the absence of time. Now imagine this very same sphere surrounded by changing things: is there any reason to deny that it exists *at* the times of those changes? Thus from the supposition that Thoughts would exist even if there were no time, it does not follow that they cannot be said to exist at times, given that there is time. (On the contrary, as I indicated above, I take the absolutely necessary existence of Thoughts to *entail* their omnitemporal existence.)

III

The argument from communication.[7] The argument for the mind-independence of Thoughts which is closest to the surface in Frege's writings, is also the weakest. It runs as follows:

(1) Communication between two individuals takes place only if,
   (a) the Thought expressed by the one, and the Thought grasped in consequence by the other, are one and the same, and
   (b) both know that this is in fact the case.
(2) All mental states and events are private to the individual who has them.
(C) So Thoughts must have an existence which is independent of such states.

There are in fact two rather different arguments here, depending upon whether 'private' in (2) is taken in an epistemic sense, or rather in the sense of 'inalienable'. Consider the former possibility first. Then premise (2) will claim that no one can have knowledge of the mental states of anyone besides himself. This is false. But more interestingly in the present context, even if true it would not warrant Frege's conclusion, since the existence of mind-independent Thoughts leaves him in no better position to explain the possibility of communication. For, as stated in (1b), communication only takes place if speakers know what Thoughts the others are currently *grasping*; and even if Thoughts themselves are mind-independent, the grasping relation is presumably mental. (See Currie, p. 164).

Consider then the other possibility: that premise (2) claims – truly – that no person can *possess,* or have any kind of immediate awareness of, the mental states of another. This, too, makes the argument fail, even given the truth of premise (1). It does not even follow that Thoughts cannot be *reduced* to mental states, let alone that they are not supervenient upon them. For suppose that the truth-conditions of 'A grasps the Thought [that p]' could somehow be cashed in terms of A's current mental states and dispositions. Then it could be true, as (1) requires, that A and B both grasp the very same Thought, the identity in question being explicable in terms of the kinds of mental state that constitute a

---

[7] See LI, pp. 15–17, 26, and PW, pp. 133–4, 137.

grasp of that Thought. All we should need would be to provide an analysis of Thought-identity along the following lines:

(Thought x = Thought y) iff, for all persons p (p_1 grasps x & p_2 grasps y) iff (Fp_1 & Fp_2))

(where 'Fp_1' states the truth-condition, in purely mentalist terms, of 'p_1 grasps Thought x').

IV

The argument from omnitemporality of truth.[8] Frege's second, and much more plausible, argument for the mind-independence of Thoughts, is as follows:

(1) Truth is a property of Thoughts.
(2) Possession of a property implies the existence of the thing possessing that property.
(C1) So any truth implies the existence of a Thought.
(3) Truth is omnitemporal (i.e., if something is true at any time, then it is true at all times).
(C2) So Thoughts exist omnitemporally (and hence mind-independently).

I regard the truth of (2) as uncontroversial, as is the move from (1) and (2) to (C1). My discussion will concentrate on the plausibility of premises (1) and (3), and the soundness of the move from (C1) and (3) to (C2).

Whether we accept or reject premise (1), we shall still have sufficient reason to conclude, with Frege, that any truth implies the existence of a Thought (or at least a proposition), so long as we remain within the framework of a Fregean semantics. The only other half-way plausible candidates, as bearers of truth-values, would be propositions, sentences (either token or type), statements, occurrent thoughts (acts of thinking), and beliefs. If propositions are the bearers of truth-values, we shall immediately be able to construct a parallel argument to show that any truth implies the existence of a proposition, which is of course no advance. And in the case of all the other candidates, the existence of Thoughts or propositions must still be brought into the picture in one way or another. It is only sentences-with-a-given-sense that can plausibly be maintained to be the bearers of truth-values. And in each of the other cases, it will be the Thought or proposition that constitutes the *content* of the act or state in question. If one accepts the legitimacy of the notion of sense at all, then to make a statement will be to put forward a Thought (or proposition) as true; to have a thought occur to you will be to grasp, or think, a Thought (or proposition); and

[8] See FA, p. *vi*, LI, pp. 4, 17, 25, 27–8, and PW, pp. 129, 135, 148.

to have a belief will be to adopt an attitude involving a Thought (or proposition). The general point can be put like this: the idea of truth is the idea of a *correct representation of reality*. And for anyone who adopts a broadly Fregean approach to semantics (as we have resolved to do), it is the senses of sentences – either on their own (Thoughts), or in conjunction with context (propositions); and either as such, or asserted, grasped, or believed – which constitute the essential representors of reality. So how could there exist such a thing as a correct representation (a truth), unless there also exists that which represents (a Thought, or a proposition)?

Let us now turn our attention to premise (3), to the effect that truth is omnitemporal. One conflicting thesis, that truth is, rather, timeless, may be dealt with in a manner similar to the way in which we dealt with the parallel suggestion about the kind of existence that Thoughts possess: the thesis has little intuitive plausibility – 'It always was, is, and will be true that $2+2=4$' seems to make perfectly good sense – and what plausibility it does have will be easily explicable in terms of breaches of conventions of conversational implicature. Moreover, there is a distinct lack of sound arguments to make up for the lack of plausibility.

Another ground for rejecting premise (3) would be a conviction that truth is fundamentally a property of statements, occurrent thoughts, or beliefs, rather than of Thoughts or propositions. It is certainly not the case that if a statement is true at a certain time, then it is true at all times, since it will not *exist* at all times; and of course the same goes for occurrent thoughts and beliefs. We might try to capture the thesis of omnitemporal truth in hypothetical terms only, to try to get around this problem. Thus: if a statement is true at a certain time, then if anyone *were* to make that statement at any other time, they would make a true statement. But this will run foul of examples such as the following. Consider the statement, 'No intelligent life exists prior to the year 20 million B.C.'. This is, let us suppose, true. Now an application of the hypothetical version of the thesis of omnitemporal truth, will give us the following: if anyone (i.e., any intelligent agent) *had* made the above statement in the year *40* million B.C., he would have made a true statement. This is, of course, false. (Note that if we try to get around this sort of difficulty, by adding a clause insisting that the making of the statement at the time in question be independent of the truth of that statement, then we have effectively limited the scope of the omnitemporality thesis. Not *all* truth will be omnitemporal, on this account.) So if we wish to maintain the truth of premise (3), we have no option but to insist that truth is a property of Thoughts, or at least propositions.

Yet another ground for rejecting (3), would be to deny that indexicality is always eliminable. If this were correct, then two things would follow. First, we should have to give up the idea that truth – all truth – is a property of Thoughts, or involves the existence of Thought. For if the proposition [that I am now in pain] is true, and if it were to prove impossible to capture adequately in context-free terms what is – in the circumstances – expressed by this proposition, then it would not be any Thought, but rather a proposition, that is true. Secondly, we should have to give up the thesis that truth is omnitemporal. For from the fact that the proposition above is true now, as expressed by me, it does not of course follow that it always was and will be true. However it is doubtful if this need really affect Frege's argument, if only because, since some propositions *are* Thoughts (the class of Thoughts being a sub-class of the class of propositions), the argument can go through as before so long as the scope of premise (3) is restricted to the truth of *Thoughts*. Thus consider the Thought [that there exist sabre-tooth tigers in England in the year 20 million B.C.]. If this is true, then the omnitemporality thesis tells us that it was also true in the year 40 million B.C., and indeed in any other year that you care to mention. Now how can it be the case that both (a) any true Thought implies the existence of that Thought, and (b) the Thought above was true in the year 40 million B.C., unless that Thought existed in that year? (This argument can of course be extended to show that the Thought in question exists in every year. And since a parallel argument can be constructed for falsity, we may establish that all Thoughts exist omnitemporally.)

It is worth noting that a similar argument may be used to demonstrate the omnitemporal existence of at least some propositions that are not Thoughts, specifically those in which the only form of indexicality is *tense*. For there is a thesis relating to such propositions, that has just as much plausibility as the thesis of omnitemporal truth has in relation to Thoughts, namely, the thesis of the unrestricted soundness of the truth-value links between the tenses. (There may be similar theses governing other forms of indexicality as well, but I shall not pursue this suggestion here.) According to this thesis, if the proposition [that Peter is now in pain] *is* true, then the proposition [that Peter will be in pain] *was* true (at all times in the past), and the proposition [that Peter was in pain] *will* be true (at all times in the future). And how could it be the case that both (a) any true proposition implies the existence of that proposition and (b) the proposition [that Peter will be in pain] was true in the year 40 million B.C., unless that proposition existed in that year? This argument does not yet show that such propositions exist omnitemporally. It only shows that all true future-tensed propositions exist at all times in the past, and that all true past-tensed propositions exist at all times in the future. However, since a parallel argument would also work for falsehood, we shall be able to derive the omnitemporal existence of tensed propositions so long as the principle of bivalence is endorsed relative to any particular time. And then, having demonstrated that all Thoughts, as well as some propositions that are not Thoughts, exist omnitemporally, it would seem reasonable to believe that *all* propositions exist omnitemporally.

Frege is correct: one cannot believe in the omnitemporality of truth without being committed to the omnitemporal existence of Thoughts. (Nor can one believe in the unrestricted soundness of the truth-value links between the tenses without being committed to the omnitemporal existence of at least some propositions that are not Thoughts.) But why should we not take this argument as a *reductio*, replacing the thesis of omnitemporal truth with a more modest hypothetical form, similar to that sketched above for statements? – namely, if any presently-existing Thought is true, then if anyone *were* to give expression to that Thought at some time other than the present, they would give expression to a true Thought (unless, as in some of the examples above, the Thought in question itself implies that it was *not* expressed at that time). Indeed this is surely the correct response, since the full extent of our *use* for the omnitemporality thesis lies in the weaker hypothetical form. We have no use for the thesis of the omnitemporal truth of Thoughts, except in our assessments of the truth-values of assertions of those Thoughts. (A similar point holds for the truth-value links between the tenses of tensed propositions.) Thus we make use of the fact that the Thought [that sun shines in Belfast on the 16th of June 1984] is presently true, in assessing last week's prediction by a weather-forecaster that it *would* by sunny on the 16th, as well as in justifying the counterfactual that if he *had* predicted sun on the 16th he would have been right. We have no use for the idea of the past truth of that Thought, except as it relates to actual, or possible, predictions. (Similarly, we have no use for the idea of the future truth of the Thought, except as it relates to assessments of actual, or possible, historical claims.) We thus have no need of the strong theses of omnitemporal truth, and of the truth-value links between the tenses; the weaker hypothetical forms will do.

I suggest, then, that we should reject as false the sentence, 'The Thought [that no intelligent life exists prior to the year 20 million B.C.] was true in the year 40 million B.C.', not because of any thesis about the indeterminacy of the future, but simply because it implies the existence of a Thought in the year 40 million B.C.. We should, similarly, reject as false the sentence, 'The proposition [that no intelligent life will exist prior to the year 20 million B.C.] was true in the year 40 million B.C.'. For nothing of any importance will be lost to us by giving up these sentences as false. Each consists, in fact, of two independent claims. First, that the Thought or proposition in question existed in the year 40 million B.C.; this we have no reason to accept, in the absence of an independent proof of the mind-independence of Thoughts and propositions. Secondly, that it is in fact true that no intelligent life exists prior to 20 million B.C.[9] Whether

---

[9] Dummett marks a similar distinction, in his brief discussion of eternal Thoughts, FPL, pp. 368—70. He does not, however, distinguish between the arguments from omnitemporality, and from objectivity, of truth; nor does he give either argument a proper run for its money.

or not a belief in the objectivity of such truths commits us to the mind-independence of Thoughts and propositions, will form the subject of the next section.

V

The argument from the objectivity of truth.[10] This argument proceeds first, as did the previous one, to conclusion (C1), that any truth implies the existence of a Thought (or proposition). It then continues as follows:

(3) There are objective truths about the past (and future), and about counterfactual situations.

(C2) So Thoughts (and propositions) exist at times in the remote past and future, and many would have existed even had the world been very different.

(4) Any falsehood implies the existence of a Thought (or proposition), and the principle of bivalence holds relative to any particular time and context in any particular possible world.

(C3) So Thoughts (and propositions) exist necessarily (i.e., they exist at all times in all possible worlds).

Premises (3) and (4) appear obviously true; at any rate, I propose to grant them, since I am granting Frege his general realism. And the move from (C2) and (4) to (C3) appears sound. Everything turns, I suggest, on the soundness of the move to (C2). On one way of taking the argument, this move has essentially the same form as was involved in the argument from omnitemporal truth. Thus consider, as a particular instance of (3), the true Thought [that there exist sabre-tooth tigers in England in the year 20 million B.C.]. The claim will be that since this Thought was, itself, *true* in the year 20 million B.C., it must have existed in that year. But this can now be rejected as false. We can retain objectivity of truth in relation to the past by maintaining that the Thought in question is *presently* objectively true. We can reject as false the claim that it *was* true in 20 million B.C., on the grounds that the Thought probably did not exist in that year. For the same reason we can reject as false the claim that the Thought *would have been* true if there had never been any intelligent agents. The objectivity of truth in relation to such a counterfactual possibility may be adequately captured by means of the following: the Thought [that there exist sabre-tooth tigers in the year 20 million B.C., in any world that differs from the actual world only in that it never contains any intelligent agents] is (now) objectively true. So what is quite unclear, is why it should be believed that a

---

[10] See FA, p. *vii*, LI, pp. 4, 25 and PW, pp. 129, 131–3.

truth *about* the past, or *about* a counterfactual possibility, presupposes the existence of a Thought (or proposition) *in* the past, or *in* that other possible world. What reason have we for saying anything more than that we make use of currently existing Thoughts and propositions in order to represent the past, and in order to represent how things might have been?

There are hints in Frege of quite a different sort of warrant for the move from (C1) and (3) to (C2), which is best presented by developing a certain conception of objectivity.[11] Objectivity about the present apparently requires that a Thought (or proposition; take the qualification as read for the remainder of this section) and the state of the world should settle the truth-value between them, with no further contribution required from us. Given that a sentence about something in the present has the sense that it has, and given that the world is as it is, then that sentence is already determinately true, or determinately false, independently of us; all that remains for us to do is discover, if we can, *which* it is.[12] Now try applying this idea to explain objectivity about the past, without bringing in Thoughts as independently existing entities. Thus suppose that sense is some function of presently-existing semantic intentions: then objectivity about the past requires us to picture these intentions somehow "reaching out" into the past to determine, in conjunction with the way the world was, and independently of us, the truth-value. But is this picture intelligible? How can anything reach into the past, since the past no longer exists? How can a presently-existing Thought – which exists, by hypothesis, *only* in the present (and recent past) – be made true by some long-past event? How can the relationship between a Thought and the state of affairs that renders it true, cross the boundaries of time? Frege's answer is: only by having itself *existed through* the time in question. The idea is this: it is because the Thought I now express is the very same Thought as a Thought that existed at the time I am thinking about – at which time it was rendered determinately true or false by the state of the world at that time – that I have given expression to a Thought which has, now, a determinate truth-value. We can thus conceive of the Thought about the long-past event as having picked up its determinate truth-value at the time when the event occurred, and as having carried that truth-value forward to the present.

Note that we cannot adopt quite this treatment for determinacy of truth-value about the future, nor about counterfactual possibilities. For we cannot sensibly say that a Thought may "carry its truth-value back" from the future to the present, nor from other possible worlds to this one. All that we can say is:

---

[11] See, for instance, FA, p. *vii*, where Frege argues that if nothing remained fixed for all time, then there could be no knowledge and no truth.

[12] For further exposition of this conception of objectivity, together with a critique, see my "Ruling-out Realism", *Philosophia* 1985.

the Thought that we now express will still exist in the distant future, and would have existed had things been different; and it will then, or would then, have picked up a determinate truth-value. It is doubtful whether this is sufficient for us to say that those truth-values are *now* determinate. But then our belief in objectivity in relation to the past is that much more firmly held than the corresponding beliefs about the future and about counterfactuals. (We can, however, still get an argument for the necessary existence of Thoughts, although the argument expounded here only strictly establishes their past existence, if we are prepared to insist that there will always be, and would always have been, objectivity of truth in relation to the past.)

Note also that we cannot hope to explain determinacy of truth-value about the past, without committing ourselves to the independent existence of Thoughts, by appealing to the hypothetical version of the thesis of omnitemporal truth, whose acceptance was urged in the last section. For suppose we try to explain how the Thought [that there are sabre-tooth tigers in England in the year 20 million B.C.] can be, now, determinately true, by claiming that, if that Thought *had* existed in the year in question, then it *would have* been rendered determinately true (or false). Is this hypothetical Thought itself determinately true (or false) or not? If not, then it cannot be used to explain the determinacy of the original. But if so, then just the same problem recurs: how can a merely presently-existing Thought be made true by a past event? For it can be nothing other than the fact that there *were* sabre-tooth tigers in England in that year which makes it true that, had the Thought in question existed, it would have been determinately true.

My strategy against this argument of Frege's will not be to tackle head-on the challenge of explaining how a presently-existing Thought can "reach back" into the remote past. It may indeed be that this idea cannot be made fully intelligible, thus motivating some version of anti-realism about the past. Rather, I shall argue that Frege's own position involves essentially the same difficulty. So a belief in independently-existing Thoughts at any rate leaves us no *better* placed to explain objectivity of truth in relation to the past.

If Thoughts are to enable us to bridge the gap between present and past, then we must have some conception of the identity-over-time of such entities. Now as for criteria of identity *at* a time, we might either go with Frege, and give our account in terms of sameness of information-content, or with the early Wittgenstein, and give it in terms of logical equivalence.[13] But either way, we could hardly do other than utilise the very same notion in explaining identity *over* time, since Thoughts are essentially changeless. Suppose we gave our

---

[13] For further discussion of these different conceptions of sense-identity, see my "Fragmentary Sense", *Mind* (1984).

account in terms of the weaker notion of logical equivalence (this being the simpler view to express), thus: Thought x at t_1 = Thought y at t_2 if and only if x is logically equivalent to y. Then, substituting, our attempt to explain determinacy of truth-value about the past becomes: the Thought that I now grasp is logically equivalent to a Thought that was rendered either determinately true, or determinately false, at the time in question. This requires us to be able to identify, or refer to, a past Thought, by means of the description, 'the Thought logically equivalent to the Thought I now express'. So we now have to picture the sense of this description reaching back into the remote past to pick out a particular Thought. Yet this is, of course, precisely the sort of phenomenon ("reaching back into the past") that Frege's account was designed to explain – in which case we might just as well let the past-existing Thought drop out altogether. If Frege's own account presupposes that a presently-existing description-sense can reach back into the past to pick out a particular Thought, then we may as well picture the presently-existing Thought projecting back internal relations to confront the past state of the world *directly*, so as to determine an objective truth-value.

VI

The argument from analyticity.[14] The final argument for the mind-independence of Thoughts that may be discerned in Frege's writings, runs as follows:

(1) There are truths that are true absolutely necessarily (i.e., that are true at all times in all possible worlds, and would have been true even if there had been no world).
(2) Such truths are analytic, or conceptual, truths, and are true purely in virtue of the meanings (senses) of the words involved.
(3) That in virtue of which something is true must exist at any time, and in any circumstances, in which it is true.
(C1) So meanings (senses) exist absolutely necessarily.
(C2) So Thoughts (senses of context-free sentences) exist absolutely necessarily.

This argument is, I suggest, valid. Any weakness must lie in the premises.

I propose to grant Frege the existence of the class of analytic truths, as being an essential aspect of his views on mathematics, and of his general approach to the philosophy of language. Given this, the thesis that analytic truths are

[14] See: FA, pp. *vi–vii*, LI, pp. 17, 24-5, 27, and PW, pp. 133, 135, 148.

eternal truths is extremely plausible, in either its weaker or its stronger forms. For not only are we prepared to rely upon an analytic truth – a law of logic, for instance – in reasoning about events in the remote past or future, we should also be prepared to rely upon it in reasoning about any counterfactual possibility, no matter how far removed from the real world. And indeed many have felt that God himself must have been subject to the laws of logic, even prior to the creation.

Note that we cannot reject premise (1) by deploying the sort of distinction we used in our attack on the argument from omnitemporality in §IV. For consider the statement that it *was* impossible, 20 million years B.C., that any object should have been both red all over and green all over. We cannot here distinguish between the implied claim that a certain Thought existed in the year 20 million B.C., and the claim (expressible by a merely presently-existing Thought) that a certain state of affairs obtained in that year. For in virtue of premises (2) and (3), what state of affairs could this be, except the obtaining of relations between senses? (It will be instructive here to compare the argument from analyticity with a more modern variant, namely, (1) Necessary truth is truth in all possible worlds, (2) Any truth implies the existence of a proposition, (C) So (some) propositions exist in all possible worlds. Premise (1) is in fact no more plausible than the thesis of omnitemporal truth, and may be rejected accordingly. Distinguishing between truth *about* a possible world, and truth *in* a possible world, we may express the necessity of, 'No object is both red all over and green all over' as follows: for all possible worlds w, the Thought [that no object is both red all over and green all over] is a truth about w (as opposed to a truth *in* w). And this of course gives us nothing beyond the existence of the Thought in *our* world. The distinctive feature of the argument from analyticity, in contrast, is that a necessary truth is construed as being *about* relations between sense. This apparently enables it to block the deployment of any parallel distinction.)

The account of analyticity expressed in premise (2) should appear plausible to anyone who, like Frege, believes in the objectivity of necessity, who believes that we are here concerned with a genuine class of *truths*, and who is prepared to put forward a reasonable account of our knowledge of them. For it is extremely natural to believe that there are objective, internal relations between the senses of our expressions, which can be genuine objects of discovery. And it is equally natural to believe that we must be especially well placed to have knowledge of such relations. For since sense is what is known in virtue of linguistic understanding, all that one would have to do to discover internal relations between senses, would be to think clearly about the content of our understanding. Thus in the case of at least a large class of those sentences believed to be necessarily, and objectively, true, it is hard to avoid the conclusion that such sentences are true in virtue of sense.

Premise (3), too, appears plausible. The Thought [that Jesus is a carpenter in the year 20 A.D.] is true, if it is, in virtue of the properties Jesus possessed in the year represented. So how could it be true unless Jesus, and his properties, existed in that year? Similarly then, if the necessary truth, 'No object is both red all over and green all over' holds good for the year 20 million B.C. (as indeed it does for all time), and if it is true in virtue of relations between senses, then how could those senses not exist in that year? However, if this analogy is to be sound, we have to regard the Thought [that it is impossible that any object should be both red all over and green all over throughout the year 20 million B.C.], as being true in virtue of the fact that the senses of the predicates 'is red all over' and 'is green all over' *were* incompatible in the year in question, just as the Thought about Jesus is true in virtue of the properties Jesus possessed in the year in question. But we could equally well regard it as being true in virtue of the fact that the senses of the predicates 'is red all over throughout 20 million B.C.' and 'is green all over throughout 20 million B.C.', *are* incompatible. We can thus reject premise (3), in its complete generality, without having to give up either of premises (1) and (2). We can claim that it is relations between merely presently-existing senses which constrain our talk *about* the past.

If Frege's argument is to work, then when we say that an analytic truth holds good for all times, and in all possible worlds, we have to be construed as saying something which will be true, if at all, in virtue of relations that obtain between senses at all times in all possible worlds. Thus the eternality of, 'No object is both red all over and green all over' has to derive from a truth of something like the following form:

> For all times t, and all possible worlds w, the senses of 'is red all over' and 'is green all over' are mutually incompatible at t in w.

This certainly would imply the eternal existence of sense. But we could equally well be construed as saying something which will be true in virtue of relations between merely presently-existing senses, where those relations are such that they remain invariable so long as they occur in Thoughts relating to the same objects at the same time, and so long as those Thoughts relate to the same possible world. Thus the eternality of 'No object is both red all over and green all over' could just as well derive from a truth of the following form:

> For all modes of identifying a time t, and all modes of identifying a possible world w, the senses of 'is red all over at t in w' and 'is green all over at t in w', are mutually incompatible.

Here, by quantifying over *modes of identification* of times and worlds (i.e., entities belonging to the realm of sense), we have avoided commitment to anything other than the present existence of sense. And yet we have retained enough to explain how it is that sentences like 'In the year 20 million B.C., there is an object both red all over and green all over' and 'If there had never been any intelligent agents, there would have been an object both red all over and green all over', cannot possibly be true.

One can thus believe in the existence of a class of objective analytic truths: believing that all internal relations between senses were determined, independently of us, as soon as the senses of our expressions were determined; believing, indeed, that these relations are genuine objects of discovery. And one can believe that an analytic truth is an eternal truth: constraining our talk about remote times, and about counter-factual situations, just as much as it constrains our talk about the present. And yet one can, consistently with both beliefs, believe that sense depends for its existence upon our existence: only coming to exist when we first begin to use a language in which that sense may be expressed.

VII

Conclusion. This paper has been largely negative: I have argued that Frege has provided us with no good reason for believing in the mind-independent existence of Thoughts and propositions. There remains the positive task, which falls outside the scope of my discussion of Frege, of showing just *how* these entities might depend upon the human mind. Do Thoughts reduce to some function of human activity? Or do they merely supervene on that activity? And if the latter, what is the exact nature of the supervenience relation? It is conceivable that this positive task may prove to be impossible. (Thus reductionism, at any rate, would appear to be an unpromising strategy, given the work of such modern writers as Quine and the later Wittgenstein.) If this were to turn out to be the case, then we should, after all, have a negative argument (an argument "by default", so to speak) for the independent existence of Thoughts. But it would still want an argument to show that Thoughts exist eternally. For compare: if it were to prove impossible either to reduce the mental to the physical, or to explain adequately how the mental might supervene on the physical, then we should have reason to believe that minds exist independently of bodies; but we should have no reason to believe that they exist eternally, in any of the various senses of 'eternal'. Nor can the supposed changelessness of Thoughts make the difference between the two cases, since from the fact that an entity is changeless throughout its existence, it does not follow that its existence cannot have a beginning and an end.

Thus if, as I believe, Frege's arguments for the eternal existence of Thoughts are the best available to us, and if the considerations adduced in this paper have been sound, then there is no prospect of any convincing argument for a belief in eternal Thoughts. The most that could be hoped for – were there to be repeated failure in attempts to ground a supervenience thesis – would be some reason to believe that Thoughts exist independently of the human mind. But we should then still be left with the problem of explaining how one can grasp, and be guided by, a Thought, without being aware that one is.

The Queen's University of Belfast

FREGEAN THOUGHTS

By Harold Noonan

I

Three features of thoughts frequently emphasized by Frege are the following:

(1) Thoughts are bearers of unrelativized truth-values; they are not merely true or false (or truth-valueless) relative to a context, but absolutely. In the case of a sentence containing an indexical expression the context in which it is uttered may be relevant to assessing *its* truth-value, but this will merely be because the identity of the thought expressed will be determined not just by the meaning of the sentence but also by relevant features of the context of utterance.

(2) Thoughts are psychologically real: they are the objects of the propositional attitudes and it is by reference to an agent's propositional attitudes that his rational actions are to be explained. Thus thoughts act on the material world by being grasped and taken to be true.

(3) The existence of a thought is never dependent upon that of any contingently existent object which the thought is about, i.e., which is determined as reference by any component sense of the thought. The one exception to this is the case of 'I'-thoughts. When a speaker employs the 'I' of soliloquy – as opposed to the 'I' of communication – the thought he expresses is one no one else *can* think. Thus it is one that could not be thought at all if he did not exist, and presumably, therefore, a thought that would not exist if he did not exist, since the idea of a thought existing but unavailable to be thought by any thinking being should surely be rejected (Cf. IFP, pp. 120—1). But with this one exception – whose exceptional status is never acknowledged in any unified treatment of the notion of a thought by Frege, but only mentioned when the use of 'I' is the specific topic under discussion – it holds generally that thoughts are not dependent for their existence upon that of the references determined by their constituent senses.

These, then, are three prominent features of Frege's notion of a thought, and I think that at first sight they should seem fairly uncontentious. It is just commonsense that our rational actions are to be explained by reference to our propositional attitudes – our desires and beliefs, hunches, yens and so on. So if thoughts are to be considered the objects of these attitudes their psychological reality cannot be disputed. Again, we think of our beliefs as true or false, our desires as satisfied or unsatisfied *simpliciter*, given the way the world is. So it is difficult to see how to avoid the conclusion that thoughts, *qua* objects of the attitudes, must possess unrelativized truth-values. As for the third feature of thoughts, if one denies that they possess it, while continuing to regard them as the objects of the propositional attitudes, then one has to allow the possibility that someone can be quite mistaken about the beliefs and desires he has merely as a consequence of being mistaken about the nature of the external world confronting him, i.e., that merely as a consequence of this, he can think that he has a belief or a desire of a certain kind when he does not. But this is intuitively quite implausible.

Nevertheless, despite the *prima facie* uncontentious nature of the three features listed, a number of influential arguments have recently appeared which entail, if correct, that *no* notion having these three features can be applicable in all cases.

In particular, these arguments claim that the propositional attitudes to which we give expression using sentences containing indexicals (other than 'I'), proper names, and natural kind terms (insofar as these are analogous to proper names) cannot be regarded as having such Fregean thoughts as their objects. Elsewhere I discuss the views of the defenders of "Russellian thoughts" — Peacocke, Evans and McDowell – who argue that the objects of these attitudes must be regarded as entities lacking feature (3) of Frege's notion of a thought.[1] In this paper I shall discuss the arguments of the methodological solipsists – particularly of Fodor, Perry and of Burge.[2]

II

The term 'methodological solipsism' was introduced by Putnam for the assumption that "no psychological state, properly so called, presupposes the existence of any individual other than the subject to whom that state is ascribed".[3] As Putnam goes on to say, to make this assumption is to adopt a restrictive programme which limits the scope and nature of psychology to fit certain mentalistic preconceptions, or, in some cases, to fit an idealistic

---

[1] C. Peacocke, "Demonstrative Thought and Psychological Explanation", *Synthese* 49 (1981), 187–217; Evans; and my paper given to one of the Thyssen conferences and due, I hope, to appear in the conference proceedings.
[2] J. A. Fodor, "Methodological Solipsism Considered as a Research Strategy in Cognitive Psychology", *The Behavioural and Brain Sciences* 3 (1980), 63–73; Perry; and "The Problem of the Essential Indexical", *Nous* 13 (1979), 3–21; Tyler Burge, "Individualism and the Mental", in *Midwest Studies in Philosophy* IV ed. P. French, T. Uehling and H. Wettstein (Minneapolis, 1979), and "Other Bodies", in *Thought and Object*, ed. A. Woodfield (Oxford, 1982), 97–120.
[3] "The Meaning of "Meaning" " in *Philosophical Papers, vol. II*, (Cambridge, 1975).

reconstruction of knowledge and the world. And, he adds, only if we assume that psychological states of the type allowed by methodological solipsism (*narrow*, as opposed to *wide*, psychological states) have a significant degree of causal closure is there any point in embarking on such a programme. Of course, this must be right, but there is a further point. We think of our psychological states, properly so called, in particular of our propositional attitudes, as explanatory of our intentional actions. Consequently the assumption of methodological solipsism would be merely a pointless stipulation of a new meaning for the expression 'psychological state' if reference to any but narrow psychological states were ever essential to an adequate psychological explanation of an intentional action. The methodological solipsist is thus committed to believing that this is not so, and it is this which brings him into disagreement with Frege.

To see this, we need to consider a little more carefully the distinction Putnam draws between narrow and wide psychological states. "Narrow" states are introduced as those that do not presuppose the existence of any individual other than the subject to whom they are ascribed; "wide" states do have such a presupposition. Thus *believing* that there are tables is presumably a narrow psychological state, if anything is, while *knowing* that there are tables is wide. But Putnam also implies, later in his paper, that in Twin Earth cases one shares all one's narrow psychological states with one's Doppelgänger. If I believe that *I* have toothache, however, and my Doppelgänger believes that *he* has toothache, the belief state I am in – namely, a state of believing *of* HN that he has toothache in virtue of believing something I could express in the form 'I have toothache' – is a belief state *only* I could be in, and is thus distinct from my Doppelgänger's belief state – which is one only he could be in. Therefore, since we do not differ in our narrow psychological states, these cannot be narrow. But they cannot be wide either – at least, not unless believing in the existence of tables is a wide psychological state, for they no more presuppose the existence of an individual (other than that to which they are ascribed) than it does. It may be helpful if I reformulate this point as a point about psychological *predicates* rather than as a point about psychological *states*. Consider the two predicates 'believes that there are tables' and 'believes himself to have toothache'. In one respect these predicates are alike and unlike the predicate 'knows that there are tables': *prima facie*, at least, if a subject satisfies either, it does not follow that any other individual exists. But in another respect they differ. If I satisfy either so does my Doppelgänger, but if I satisfy the predicate 'believes himself to have toothache', it follows that I also satisfy the predicate 'believes *of* HN that he has a toothache', a predicate any number of people *could* satisfy, including my Doppelgänger, but one which he does *not* satisfy (unless I am aware of the existence of Twin Earth and believe of *him* that he has a toothache). On the other hand, satisfaction of the predicate 'believes that there are tables' does not entail satisfaction of any such predicate. So we must make not merely a two-fold, but a three-fold distinction within the class of psychological predicates, and consequently also within the class of psychological states.

It thus follows that, unless the class of narrow psychological states as originally defined by Putnam is empty, his distinction between narrow and wide states is not exhaustive, and we must distinguish two versions of the methodological solipsist thesis. The stronger version is that reference to *non-narrow* states is redundant in the explanation of intentional action; the weaker version, that reference to *wide* states is redundant. Of these, only the former is in conflict with Frege's views, but it is this version that the methodological solipsists are most concerned to defend, as follows.[4] In Twin Earth cases, they say, my behaviour is identical with that of my Doppelgänger, so there is a sound inductive (not, of course, *deductive*) argument that the cause of my behaviour must be the same as the cause of his. However, since my actions are rational they have to be explicable by reference to my psychological states. These then, or at least those which are relevant to the explanation of my action, must be identical with those of my Doppelgänger. They cannot be wide states, presupposing the existence of any of the contingent individuals here on Earth, since my Doppelgänger is in no psychological state which presupposes the existence of anything here on Earth. And they cannot even be non-wide but non-narrow states distinct from those of my Doppelgänger. In particular then – and this is how the disagreement with Frege arises – any propositional attitudes relevant to the explanation of *my* actions must be ones whose objects are identical with the objects of those of my Doppelgänger's propositional attitudes relevant to the explanation of *his* actions. But some such attitudes will be ones to which I can only give expression using sentences containing indexicals, proper names or natural kind terms, and what I say using such a sentence may be true while what my Doppelgänger says using it is false, or vice versa (since Earth and Twin Earth can differ in innumerable ways so long as everything *seems* the same to me and my Doppelgänger). Consequently, if the methodological solipsists' argument is right, the objects of the attitudes to which I give expression using such sentences cannot be regarded as entities having unrelativized truth-values and thus cannot be regarded as Fregean thoughts as defined by features (1) to (3).

So goes what I take to be the principal methodological solipsist argument. But the reply to it, I believe, is very obvious. The actions which need explaining in my case are *not* identical with those of my Doppelgänger on Twin Earth. I reach for the bottle of aspirin at place p, for example, and he reaches for the bottle of aspirin at place p' and $p \neq p'$. My actions are intentional under descriptions in which singular terms occur, and so psychological explanations

---

[4] Here I am indebted particularly to Fodor and most especially to his contribution to the Thyssen conference mentioned in note 1.

of them are required under those descriptions. But so described my actions are distinct from those of my Doppelgänger.[5]

Note that I am not here arguing that my psychological states *must* be different from those of my Doppelgänger because my actions are distinct from his. That would be to give the defenders of Russellian thoughts their conclusion on a plate. Rather I am simply pointing out that the *methodological solipsist* argument from identical effects to identical causes rests on a false premiss, viz, that the only descriptions under which my actions are psychologically explicable are ones also true of the actions of my Doppelgänger. Since this premiss is false it is *permissible*, despite the inductive strength of an argument from sameness of effects to sameness of causes to say that the psychological states involved in the explanation of my actions are distinct from those involved in the explanation of my Doppelgänger's actions and consequently permissible to regard the propositional attitudes involved in the explanation of my actions as having objects with unrelativized truth-values, even where this requires them to be distinguished from the objects of my Doppelgänger's attitudes.

The methodological solipsist may reply that this is indeed permissible, but it is not necessary. However, if he allows that actions are capable of psychological explanation under descriptions in which singular terms occur, he will have to say that in the explanation of actions so described reference will have to be made *both* to narrow psychological states – those he recognises, *and* to features of the context in which the particular action takes place. But if he says this, it is not clear that he is any longer in disagreement with Frege. For it is allowed by Frege that the identity of the thought expressed by an utterance of a sentence on a given occasion will be determined jointly by the meaning, i.e. conventional significance, of the sentence and features of the circumstances of utterance. For example, if I now say, "I feel ill now", the meaning of that sentence together with the fact that *I* am saying it *now* determines the thought I express. In other words, my being in the *narrow* psychological state of believing a thought I would express by saying, "I feel ill now", together with the fact that it is *I* who am in that state *now*, determines the thought I believe. Consequently, a Fregean must allow that an explanation of my actions by reference to my attitudes to such a context-independent-truth-evaluable thought as the one I would express now by saying, "I feel ill now", can be in no way superior to an explanation that refers solely to my being in such narrow psychological states as believing a thought I could express by saying, "I feel ill now", together with the fact that it is *I* who am in the state *now*. But then, if the methodological solipsist allows that reference to something other than narrow states is needed in action explanation – and he must if he acknowledges that actions can be given psychological

---

[5] This reply to the methodological solipsist is also given by Peacocke in "Demonstrative Thought and Psychological Explanation" and by Evans, pp. 203–4. However they take it as an argument in favour of their own position; for the reason given in the next paragraph, it is not.

explanations under descriptions containing singular terms – it is utterly unclear how he can be in any substantive disagreement with the Fregean. *He* says that reference to attitudes to Fregean thoughts, where these cannot be regarded as narrow states, is not necessary to the psychological explanation of action. But the Fregean must agree, given his view of how thoughts other than those determined solely by the meanings of the sentences expressing them are determined by those meanings jointly with features of the context of utterance. For he must allow that the information conveyed by an explanation in which reference is explicitly made to attitudes to Fregean thoughts not construable as narrow states could equally well be conveyed by an explanation in which *only* narrow states and certain features of the context of action were explicitly referred to.

Of course, some philosophers will take these remarks merely as indicating the precise way in which Frege is wrong and the methodological solipsist right. For, they will say, it follows from what I have just said that we are not *ontologically committed* to Fregean thoughts by our need to give psychological explanations of intentional actions, but this is precisely what the methodological solipsist says and what any self-respecting Fregean must deny. I lack the space to go into this matter fully, but let me just say that I agree with Crispin Wright (Ch. 1, §v) that one does not show that reference to objects of a certain sort, e.g., Fregean thoughts, is merely apparent by showing how to paraphrase the sentences in question into ones in which there are no apparent references to such objects, or, to put the point in the material mode, one does not establish that there are no A's "over and above" B's by showing how to paraphrase all sentences containing apparent references to A's into ones containing only apparent references to B's. If these points are admitted, however, the inclination to think that my remarks above in some way provide the methodological solipsist with an argument against Frege will disappear.

I conclude that it is only if the methodological solipsist insists on his premiss that my behaviour is identical with that of my Doppelgänger that he is committed to a position inconsistent with Frege's. But then he is insisting on a falsehood. Of course, as I said earlier, the *weak* methodological solipsist thesis is entirely compatible with Frege's position, though not, in fact, entailed by it on the formulation of features (1), (2) and – most importantly – (3), of his notion of a thought given above.

III

So much, then, for the conflict between Frege's views and methodological solipsism. I turn now to John Perry's arguments. The aim of these arguments is to show that we must replace the Fregean notion of a thought with the two notions of a (sentential) *role* and a *piece of information*. Sentential roles are simply the meanings of (indexical) sentences, conventionally determined by the rules of the language, and so the role of an unambiguous indexical sentence is context-independent. Perry speaks of roles as *entertained*. On the other hand, the piece of information *apprehended* when the role of an indexical sentence is entertained in a certain context depends upon the context and can therefore be different when the same role is entertained in a different context. Perry suggests that we identify the piece of information apprehended when the role of a subject-predicate sentence $F(d)$ is entertained in a context C (where 'd' is an indexical) with the ordered pair consisting of the referent of 'd' in C together with the property (incomplete sense) expressed by $F(x)$. Thus if I say, "I am ill", and you say, speaking to me, "You are ill", we apprehend the same piece of information while entertaining different roles. Whereas if you also say, "I am ill" we entertain the same role but apprehend different pieces of information.

It is roles, Perry thinks, that possess feature (2) of Frege's notion of a thought, i.e., which are psychologically real. They also possess feature (3), but lack feature (1). Pieces of information on the other hand, possess feature (1), but lack features (2) and (3). Frege's notion of a thought, he thinks, is an illegitimate conflation of two distinct notions.

One of Perry's arguments for this thesis is the principal methodological solipsist argument just discussed (Perry, p. 494), and the same reply is in order. Our actions are intentional, and so psychologically explicable, under descriptions in which occur terms denoting the singular objects to which they are directed. So described, my actions are not identical with those of someone who, while entertaining the same role, is in different circumstances and acts on different objects. Reference to the roles I entertain can thus not be sufficient to provide an adequate explanation of my actions so described, whereas reference to the Fregean thoughts I believe – which are different from those of the other person who is entertaining the same roles – can be. Perry's argument thus does not demonstrate, as he takes it to, that in the case of our indexically expressed attitudes it is impossible to regard their objects as entities possessing both features (1) and (2).

Perry might acknowledge this, but reply that his view that all the work of the Fregean notion of a thought can be done by his two notions of a sentential role and a piece of information – neither of which Frege can deny to be a legitimate notion – is still correct. For, he might say, in order to explain actions under descriptions of the type just mentioned, it is indeed necessary to refer to more than the roles entertained by the agent, but one need not refer to any *Fregean* thoughts. Rather it will be sufficient to refer in addition merely to the pieces of information, i.e. thoughts-in-his-own-sense, apprehended by the agent.

But if Perry were to reply in this way it is not clear that he would any longer be in any substantive disagreement with Frege. For presumably the pair of the role entertained by a thinker and the piece of information thereby apprehended uniquely determine what Frege would call the thought grasped.[6] This answer to Perry's envisaged reply, of course, parallels the answer to the methodological solipsist given at the end of the last section. But if Perry were to reply in this way, what he said would be objectionable on other grounds also. For he would then be involved in the difficulties faced by the defenders of Russellian thoughts which I elaborated in the paper referred to in 1 above (of course, the pair of a sentential role and the piece of information apprehended on an occasion when that role is entertained has all three features of a Russellian thought). For consider someone who apprehends a certain thought by entertaining a certain role — say, he apprehends the thought that the cat in front of him is going to claw him. He responds appropriately, say, by kicking the cat. His action is intentional under a description in which a singular term for the cat occurs, a description, perhaps, of the form 'kicking that [expletive deleted] cat', and Perry, if he were to take the line now being considered, would say that in the explanation of the action so described reference will have to be made both to the role (sense) the agent entertains and to the piece of information (thought) he thereby apprehends. But now consider a counterfactual situation in which everything seems the same to the agent, but in fact he is hallucinating a cat. He presumably lashes out in exactly the same way. But now, *why* does he do so? For the piece of information he apprehended in the first situation, reference to which, on the line of reply for Perry now being considered, was necessary to the explanation of his action, is not present in the second situation (since the cat is not), and there is no reason why he must be apprehending any pieces of information or entertaining any roles in the second situation which he was not apprehending or entertaining in the first, reference to which can therefore provide an alternative explanation of his action there. So it looks as if, given that his action in the first situation could only be explained by reference to the piece of information of which the cat was a constituent which he apprehended there, his action in the second situation must be inexplicable. But this is absurd.

There are various objections Perry can make to this argument, parallel to those available to a defender of Russellian thoughts. I have discussed these in the same paper.[7] But in the end, as John McDowell has made clear to me, there

---

[6] Frege never gives a criterion of identity for thoughts which provides the notion of sameness of thought with a definite application in all cases, and Perry tells us very little about how to determine what piece of information is apprehended on a given occasion. If I think, "It was raining yesterday", is yesterday a component of the piece of information I apprehend? — or is today, but not yesterday, a component, as must presumably be the case if 'yesterday' just means 'the day before today'? So it is *consistent* with all that Frege and Perry say that a unique Fregean thought is determined by every pair of role entertained and piece of information thereby apprehended.

[7] An obvious response is that the explanation available in the first situation is not *needed* in the second because the action which occurs in the first situation does not occur in the second. I do not have the space to explain why this is an unsatisfactory reply — briefly, however, the problem is that in both situations the action is directed towards exactly the same *place* and an explanation is needed of why this is so.

is only one tenable position open to the defender of Russellian thoughts – or to Perry. What he must do is deny that in the second – hallucinatory – situation there is no psychological state of the agent not present in the first situation. In other words he must deny that the agent is in the *same* perceptual state in the second situation as in the first and that the difference between the two situations is merely a matter of the *causation* of that state. If he does this he will be able to claim that there *is* an alternative explanation of the agent's action in the second situation after all, and therefore that the absence from that situation of something – namely, the piece of information of which the cat is a constituent – crucial to the explanation of the action in the first situation does not entail the absurdity that the action has *no* explanation in the second situation. But though this is a possible position for Perry to adopt I doubt that he would be willing to do so, in view of the succeeding remarks he makes, which clearly indicate, I think, his commitment to the view that there is a common perceptual state in both veridical and non-veridical perception, and that the difference between them is merely a matter of the causation of that state.[8]

I conclude, then, that Perry's first argument against Frege fails. It is not sufficient, in explaining an agent's actions, to refer to the sentential roles he entertains. But to refer both to them *and* to the pieces of information he apprehends – just as to refer to Russellian thoughts of the type defended by Evans, McDowell and Peacocke – is to refer to more than is necessary. Some Fregean notion of a thought as something possessing features (1) to (3) appears to be precisely what needs to be added to Perry's account.[9]

Perry's second argument against Frege is equally unconvincing. It depends on the assumption that the Fregean sense of any singular term must be expressible by a definite description wholly devoid of indexicals. (That Perry is assuming this comes out particularly clearly in "Frege on Demonstratives". He writes, for example, as if this is a problem for Frege: "I can express a thought with 'Today is sunny and bright' . . . I may have no idea what day it is, and not be able, without recourse to 'today' or other demonstratives, to say anything about today at all, that does not describe dozens of other days equally well." Again he writes, as if presenting an objection to Frege, "There is no reason to believe we are on each occasion each equipped with some non-demonstrative

---

[8] "The Problem of the Essential Indexical".
[9] Of course, Perry could reply that in the explanation of action only a *sub-class* of pieces of information, i.e., thoughts-in-his-sense, need to be referred to, namely, those whose only constituents apart from incomplete senses are the agent and the time of action — indeed this fits with his suggestion in "The Problem of the Essential Indexical" that 'I' and 'now' may be the only ineliminable indexicals. He would not then be vulnerable to the argument sketched above against the defender of Russellian thoughts. But the roles an agent entertains, together with the thoughts of this type he apprehends, must determine all the Fregean thoughts he grasps, given that Fregean thoughts possess feature (3). For the reasons elaborated at the end of the last section, then, if Perry were to take this line he would not be disagreeing with Frege in any substantive way.

equivalent of the demonstratives we use and understand. This goes for 'I' as well as 'today'.") Of course, Frege never says explicitly that he requires this, and it would self-evidently be an absurdly strong requirement for him to make. Moreover, it is incompatible with his criterion of difference for thoughts, according to which sentences s and s' must express different thoughts (as uttered in a context C) if it is *possible* for someone in C to assent to the thought expressed by s while dissenting from the thought expressed by s' (indeed, Perry himself makes this incompatibility quite clear). But Perry apparently believes that Frege is committed to requiring senses to be capable of a wholly indexical-free form of expression because of his insistence on the publicity and communicability of thoughts (implicit in his suggestion that Frege's doctrine of an incommunicable sense for the 'I' of soliloquy was a reaction to the difficulty of finding a wholly non-indexical form of expression for its sense). However, this is not so. The senses of other indexicals as well as 'I' are incapable of an indexical-free form of expression, but Frege does not postulate incommunicable senses for them. Nor does he need to, because even if a sense cannot be expressed without indexicals it is still possible for it to be expressible by different people in different contexts if they use suitably related indexicals (in the case of temporal and spatial indexicals Frege draws attention to this possibility himself).

But why then *did* Frege insist on an incommunicable sense for the 'I' of soliloquy? Despite the considerations of the previous paragraph, unless some other answer than Perry's can be given to this question, some force may still seem to attach to his criticism of Frege.

Note first that it need not surprise us that Frege treated 'I' differently from 'now' and 'here'. For, as Gareth Evans has made beautifully clear, there are strong reasons for denying that the thoughts we express with the latter can be context-bound, but these do not carry over to the case of 'I' (Evans, pp. 192-6). But what *positive* reason might Frege have had for insisting on an incommunicable sense for the 'I' of soliloquy?

Colin McGinn suggests that a form of Cartesianism is the only explanation. (McGinn, Ch. 5) Frege, he surmises, "believed that I cannot really be *presented* with Dr Lauben's self at all but only (say) with his body. The reference of 'I' would then be inaccessible from a third-person perspective in much the way that a person's mental states have often been supposed to be.' He acknowledges that it would be somewhat surprising to find such a Cartesian sentiment behind Frege's views on 'I', but suggests that it seems the only way to explain his divided treatment of indexicals.

I think, however, that there is an alternative explanation. In the statement of feature (3) of Frege's notion of a thought at the beginning of the paper I treated the dependence of an 'I'-thought's availability to be thought on the existence of its subject as a consequence of its incommunicability: if no one else can think my 'I'-thoughts then if I did not exist they could not be thought at all. But actually the conclusion is independently plausible. Even if you can think my 'I'-thoughts as things are, how could you possibly do so if I did not exist? (Presumably if you could think them you could express them, but you could not express them using 'I', of course. Suppose you were to use 'You' or 'He'; then if you were talking to, or of, someone existing in your world you would be giving expression to his 'I'-thoughts, if any, not mine. If you were confronting a mere hallucination of an HN-lookalike this would not be so, but there would then be no reason to say that you were expressing *my* 'I'-thoughts rather than those of any of my innumerable possible doubles. And if you were neither hallucinating nor confronting anyone actually existing in your world, then whatever you were doing, how could it possibly count as thinking one of *my* 'I'-thoughts?) However, if my 'I'-thoughts could not be thought at all if I did not exist, then it immediately follows, given feature (3) of Frege's notion of a thought, that no one else can think them even though I *do* exist. For, of course, from *your* point of view, my existence is a contingent feature of the external world, and so, given that they possess feature (3), none of your thoughts can be dependent on it for their thinkability. Hence none of your thoughts can be identical with any of my 'I'-thoughts.

Of course, this explanation of why Frege insisted on an incommunicable sense for the 'I' of soliloquy, like McGinn's, rests on no textual evidence. But its availability is enough to make it clear that we are not *forced* to fall back on Perry's suggestion, as the only possible explanation, no matter how unsatisfactory; and, on the ground that we should not ascribe to Frege, without any evidence, an assumption which we ourselves believe to be false, I suggest that it is to be preferred to McGinn's Cartesian surmise. (See McDowell, p. 106 below—Ed.)

In sum, then, Perry's idea that Frege must be in some way committed to the possibility of an indexical-free form of expression for all senses, which is the basis of his second argument against him, is wholly unwarranted. Frege never says that he requires this of senses and indeed insists on a criterion of difference for thoughts which rules out any such requirement. Moreover, his usual insistence on the publicity and communicability of thoughts does not commit him to believing that all senses must be thus expressible, since a sense may be public and communicable even if it cannot be expressed without the use of indexicals – as Frege himself implicitly recognizes in the case of the senses of spatial and temporal indexicals. Finally, we are not, as Perry suggests, forced to ascribe to Frege an inclination to believe that public and communicable senses must be expressible by indexical-free descriptions in order to explain his view that the sense of the 'I' of soliloquy is incommunicable, for there is an alternative possible explanation of this (indeed, two alternative possible explanations, since the chance that McGinn is right cannot be excluded).

But after all this is said, I think, the feeling may still persist that whether or not Perry's *arguments* are sound ones, he has nonetheless succeeded in putting his finger on a major defect in Frege's system. For is not Frege's admission of private and incommunicable 'I'-thoughts such a defect? And even if the argument given above in support of Frege's position on this is a valid one, does that not just cast doubt on its premisses – and crucially, on its implicit premiss that all thoughts, 'I'-thoughts included, must possess the Fregean features (1) and (3)? I believe that these questions should be answered negatively: Fregean 'I'-thoughts are indeed in one sense private and incommunicable, but not in any objectionable sense. They are private and incommunicable in that only their subject can *think* them; but other people can know exactly what thoughts he is thinking when he does so, so they are not private objects in the sense spoken of by Wittgenstein. When I say, for example, using the 'I' of soliloquy, 'I have a headache', I thereby give expression to a thought you cannot think; but you can say exactly *what* thought it is which I thus express and you cannot think: namely, *the* thought (for there is only one) expressible by me using the sentence 'I have a headache'. And in identifying my thought in this way you are not picking it out by a merely *accidental* property of it (as a "private sensation" might be identified as the one contingently connected with a certain type of behaviour); given the meaning of the English sentence it is *essential* to my thought that it be thus expressible, and no other thought *could* be expressed by me in those words.

Perry's criticisms then, can finally be laid to rest. We now need to see whether Tyler Burge's arguments can be answered as easily.

IV

In the two papers cited in note 2, Burge presents a pair of arguments which are designed to establish that, as he puts it, the content of a person's thought is sometimes determined by features of his social and physical environment which can vary independently of his "physical, behavioural, phenomenalistic, and functional history". In the first paper he argues that someone who has beliefs whose contents can be reported correctly by using an oblique occurrence of the term 'arthritis' would lack all such beliefs in a counterfactual situation which differed from the actual one *only* in the way the word 'arthritis' was used by other members of his community. In the second paper he argues that someone who has beliefs whose contents can be reported correctly by using an oblique occurrence of the term 'water' would lack all such beliefs in a counterfactual situation which differed from the actual one *only* in the nature of his physical environment. In presenting these arguments he takes himself to be making explicit a line of thought which is just below the surface in Putnam's "The Meaning of 'Meaning' ", but which leads to the far more radical conclusion that features of the social and the physical environment of a speaker make a contribution to determining not just what his words mean but also what his thoughts are. In fact, however, Burge's conclusion is not just more radical than Putnam's. In being a claim about *thought* rather than *meaning* it is a claim of a completely different kind. For no one has ever claimed, of course, that meaning *by itself* determines extension (even in the case of a description wholly devoid of indexicals, like 'the first dog to be born at sea', this is obviously false); it is only meaning *together with how things are* that has ever been claimed to do so. Consequently the Twin Earth Putnam refers to in his arguments has to be located, not in another possible world, but somewhere here in the actual world. On the other hand the Twin Earth that Burge refers to in *his* arguments has to be located in another possible world, i.e., it has to be merely a counterfactual Earth, for otherwise his arguments would not have the significance for traditional views on thought content he takes them to have: they would not, for example, suggest that the thoughts entertained by someone at a certain time and place could be different in two situations merely in virtue of differences in his physical environment in the two situations of which he was totally unaware, and so they would not pose any challenge to a Fregean conception of thought.

It will be convenient to look at the discussion in "Other Bodies" first, and then turn briefly to that in "Individualism and the Mental"; the pattern of argument is identical in the two papers.

In "Other Bodies" Burge makes use of Putnam's Twin Earth thought experiment with 'water'. As already stressed, however, Burge's Twin Earth is not a distant planet, but a counterfactual state of the actual Earth, or, as I shall say, a counterfactual Earth. Otherwise everything is the same as in Putnam's discussion. On the counterfactual Earth the substance which is present in the seas and rivers is not H_2O but a superficially similar substance XYZ. This is known to the scientific community on the counterfactual Earth, just as the fact that the substance in seas and rivers is H_2O is known to the scientific community on the actual Earth; but there are some users of the term 'water' on the counterfactual Earth who are ignorant that what they refer to by this term is XYZ, and who could not, unaided, distinguish XYZ from H_2O. The counterfactual Adam is such a person. Similarly, the actual Adam is ignorant that what he refers to as 'water' is H_2O, and he could not, unaided, distinguish H_2O from XYZ. However, there is no doubt that the counterfactual Adam and the actual Adam *do* refer respectively to XYZ and H_2O when they employ the term 'water', since they use this term deferentially to their respective scientific communities, who are aware of the difference. The coununterfactual Adam and the actual Adam thus refer to different substances when they use the term 'water', the actual Adam to water, the counterfactual Adam not. Consequently, while the actual Adam has a multitude of beliefs about water to which he could give expression using the term 'water', the counterfactual Adam may have no beliefs about water, and certainly has none he could give expression to using that term. That is, none of the beliefs he could give expression to using that term are ones which it would be correct to ascribe to him in sentences in which it occurred transparently. Burge goes further. The counterfactual Adam, he claims, does not even have any beliefs which it would be correct to ascribe to him in sentences in which the term 'water' occurred *obliquely* — or at least, none to which he himself could give expression using the term 'water'. And intuitively this seems right. For as I have indicated, there may well *be* water on the counterfactual Earth; it is just that it is not where it is on the actual Earth, and is not the reference of the counterfactual Earthian term 'water'. But then if we allow that the counterfactual Adam does have *de dicto* beliefs about water (beliefs in whose description one would use the term 'water' obliquely) we get into conflict with the compelling principle that if A believes that x is F and x exists then A believes, with respect to x, that it is F (e.g. if A believes that the shortest spy is a woman and the shortest spy exists, A believes, with respect to the shortest spy, that she is a woman; if A believes that King Arthur defeated the Saxons and King Arthur exists, then A believes with respect to King Arthur that he defeated the Saxons).[10] Unless 'water', as used on the actual Earth, denotes XYZ molecules as well as H_2O molecules, then, it has to be granted to Burge that the counterfactual Adam has no *de dicto* beliefs about water, and given that on the actual Earth the scientific community employ the term 'water' to refer to what they also know to be H_2O, though well aware of the possibility of superficially similar substances which might deceive a layman, while the lay community is deferential in its use of the term to the scientific community, I submit that we have no choice but to acknowledge that 'water', as used on the actual Earth, denotes H_2O molecules solely, and that Burge is right about the beliefs possessed by the counterfactual Adam.

In fact, I think, Burge's argument still goes through even if we drop the assumption that there are scientists in the actual Adam's community who are aware that the substance commonly referred to as 'water' is H_2O. Suppose, in fact, that not just the two Adams, but everyone on the two Earths possesses exactly the same knowledge of what he refers to as 'water': it is not known by anyone on the actual Earth that the substance in seas and rivers is H_2O and it is not known by anyone on the counterfactual Earth that it is XYZ. In each community, however, the term 'water' is used to refer to the *kind* of substance to be found in seas and rivers, and the scientific members of the two communities have certain criteria for sameness of kind – the same in both

---

[10] This principle is only compelling, of course, if 'believing something *with respect to* X' is interpreted in accordance with what Chisholm has called the "latitudinarian" conception of *de re* belief. But the point is that the principle *is* compelling when so interpreted, and allowing the counterfactual Adam to have *de dicto* beliefs about water *is* in conflict with it.

communities – according to which, if they were applied, H_2O and XYZ would come out as distinct kinds of substance. If all this is so, it seems clear that on the actual Earth the reference of 'water' will be H_2O and on the counterfactual Earth its reference will be XYZ, even though the actual Earth and the counterfactual Earth now differ solely in physical respects and not at all in respect of the knowledge available to their respective communities. And it also seems clear that Burge's conclusion is still compelling: only the actual Adam, not the counterfactual Adam, has *de dicto* beliefs about water to which he could give expression using that term.

Only if we modify the features of the Twin Earth experiment still more, and suppose that the two communities are so primitive that even their most knowledgeable members possess no criteria by which they could judge samples of H_2O and samples of XYZ to be distinct kinds of substance, does it become doubtful that 'water' has distinct references in the two communities. But this has no bearing on the cogency of Burge's argument.

I think we are bound to accept, then, that in "Other Bodies" Burge does establish that the correctness of a *de dicto* belief ascription in which the term 'water' occurs can depend upon features of the physical environment of the subject of the ascription of which he is wholly unaware; and the argument in "Individualism and the Mental" establishes the same, with respect to their subject's social environment, for *de dicto* belief ascriptions in which the term 'arthritis' occurs. The only difference is that Burge now supposes that the physical environments of the actual Adam and the counterfactual Adam are identical, and in particular that they suffer from exactly the same afflictions. But on the actual Earth the physicians, to whom the actual Adam uses the term deferentially, use 'arthritis' to refer to arthritis, i.e., an ailment that only afflicts the joints; while on the counterfactual Earth the physicians, to whom the counterfactual Adam uses the term deferentially, use it to refer to a variety of rheumatoid ailments, including some that do not afflict just the joints. Consequently, the counterfactual Adam, unlike the actual Adam, has no beliefs with respect to arthritis, or at least none he could express using the term 'arthritis',and does not have any *de dicto* beliefs about arthritis he could express using that term.

Now it might seem that this is a conclusive refutation of Frege's conception of thoughts. But in fact this is not the end of the matter. If a *de dicto* belief ascription is assumed by the Fregean to do nothing more nor less than assert a relation between the subject of the ascription and a thought named by the "that"-clause, then, indeed, his position is refuted by Burge's argument. However, one can hold to Frege's conception of thoughts while denying that *de dicto* ascriptions of propositional attitudes *should* by given such a straightforward relational analysis. The challenge to the Fregean is thus to provide an account of the truth-condition of *de dicto* ascriptions of propositional attitudes which explains how Burge can be right about his examples even though the actual Adam and the counterfactual Adam in fact have *exactly* the same attitudes to *exactly* the same Fregean thoughts.[11]

One's first thought is obviously that what Burge's argument shows is merely that the truth of a *de dicto* belief ascription about water requires the truth of a *de re* belief ascription about water, e.g., that if one believes *de dicto* that water is widespread then one must believe, with respect to water, that it is widespread. But the difficulty with this is that we are willing to ascribe to people *de dicto* beliefs about non-existent natural kinds, e.g., ambrosia or unicorns, and if this requirement were generally correct as a truth-condition of a sentence of the form 'A believes that x is F', where 'x' is a natural kind term, we would be wrong to do so.

Moreover, I think it is fairly obvious that we would be unjustified in resting content with an account of the truth-conditions of sentences of the form 'A believes that x is F' where 'x' is restricted to natural kind terms. Rather, we need an account which works both for such cases and for cases where 'x' is a proper name – a name of a person, building or whatever. For both natural kind terms and proper names are rigid designators by Kripke's tests and, as I have argued in a previous paper,[12] the reason for this in the case of proper names is that we employ them in accordance with the phenomenon Putnam has drawn attention to under the title "the linguistic division of labour". Furthermore, Burge's pattern of argument can in fact be deployed to establish exactly the same conclusion about belief ascriptions in whose content clauses proper names occur obliquely as he establishes for *de dicto* belief ascriptions about water and arthritis. Suppose some children find a strange looking creature wandering around the outskirts of their house, make friends with it and give it the name 'E.T.', which then gets used in exactly the ways in which nicknames of people and pets are used, so that there is no doubt that it *is* functioning as a proper name. Suppose now that this is the actual situation and imagine a counterfactual situation in which everything seems exactly the same but in fact it is another creature from the stars that the children encounter, a distinct but indistinguishable member of the species. Then it is obvious that in this counterfactual situation, in which, though E.T. exists, the children never meet him, they have no *de re* beliefs about him, and obvious too that they have no *de dicto* beliefs about him. That is, with respect to this counterfactual situation, all such sentences as 'Eliot believes that E.T. wants to phone home' are false. For if that were true, then, given that E.T. exists in this counterfactual situation, it would have to be true also that Eliot believes, with respect to E.T., that he

---

[11] If I read him right, this is also how Peacocke views the significance of Burge's examples: see *Sense and Content* (Oxford, 1983), p. 199.
[12] "Rigid Designation", *Analysis* 39 (1979).

wants to phone home. But he does not, for he has no beliefs about E.T. at all, but only about the different extra-terrestrial whom he encounters in the counterfactual situation.

So we need an account of the truth-conditions of sentences of the form 'A believes that x is F' which works both for cases in which 'x' is a natural kind term and for cases in which 'x' is a proper name. But, of course, we have a multitude of proper names of non-existent "entities" which we have no hesitation in using when ascribing *de dicto* beliefs to those who mistakenly believe in their existence. To insist that is is a necessary condition of the truth of a sentence of the form 'A believes that x is F' that 'A believes, with respect to x, that it is F' also be true, would simply be to stipulate that all such belief ascriptions are false, whereas I take it that we should accept such a conclusion only as a last resort. (It is accepted in Evans, p. 366.) Nor does it meet the difficulty to say that this is a necessary condition of the truth of the *de dicto* belief ascription if the entity named exists in the situation with respect to which its truth is being assessed, but not if it does not. For it may be that in the counterfactual situation in which the children encounter a distinct but indistinguishable extra-terrestrial the real E.T. never existed; but we should hardly regard this as making it easier for them to have *de dicto* beliefs about him.

In two previous papers[13] I gave an account of the truth-conditions of *de dicto* belief ascriptions containing oblique occurrences of proper names which did not meet this difficulty. Nevertheless, it had two features which I think any adequate account must retain.First, it fitted in with the view that the use of proper names was subject to linguistic division of labour, and thus distinguished between *de re* and *de dicto* belief ascriptions containing proper names in a way that did not rely upon the assumption that the sense of a proper name in a community was constant from speaker to speaker. And secondly, it allowed for the truth of *de dicto* belief ascriptions containing proper names even when the individuals to whom the beliefs were being ascribed did not themselves employ those names.

What I now want to work towards is an account retaining these features while meeting the difficulty raised above.

To begin with we need an account of what it is for a community of name users to be participants in a common practice with respect to their use of a name, even though the sense of the name shifts from speaker to speaker. I suggest that this will be so, in the case of two users of the name who attach different senses to it, if one of them is deferential to the other in his use of the name, or if one of them is deferential to a third person who is deferential to a

---

[13] "Rigid Designation", and "Names and Belief", *Aristotelian Society Proceedings* 81 (1980–1).

fourth ... who is deferential to the other, or if both of them are deferential to a third person (directly or in the indirect way just indicated), or if there is a group of people who use the name with the same sense and one is deferential (directly or indirectly) to one of the group while the other is deferential (directly or indirectly) to another of the group.

According to this account, then, it is neither necessary nor sufficient for the existence of a single name-using practice with respect to a certain proper name that there be a single individual of which the name is a name. Grounding any name-using practice will be a group of individuals who use the name non-deferentially (a group of "producers" as Evans calls them) and typically such a group of people using a name of a contemporary will have a capacity to recognise that person. Two such groups could use the same name for the same individual but be quite unaware of the fact, because they recognised him in quite different ways (suppose, Evans suggests, that in R. L. Stevenson's story the Jekyll personality had also been known as 'Mr Hyde', but people did not realise that the terrible Mr Hyde and the kind Mr Hyde were one and the same). Then there would be two name-using practices involving the same individual. On the other hand, a group of people could believe that two individuals were one, and be so thoroughly confused in their identifications that there would be no ground for saying that the single name they employed was a name of one rather than the other. Then there would be a single name-using practice with respect to that name even though *no* single individual was named.

Now I can state a necessary condition for the truth of 'A believes that x is F', as asserted by myself, in the case in which the truth of the statement rests on the possession by A of a belief he could express using the name 'x'. Namely, that with respect to our use of the name 'x', A and I are participants in the same name using practice, and that A could express his belief in a statement using 'x' in the way he uses it as a participant in that practice, i.e., using quantification over Fregean senses and square brackets in the manner employed in my "Rigid Designation", that for some α, for some β, 'x' expresses α in A's idiolect, 'x' expresses β in my idiolect, A believes that [α is F], and by virtue of his association of α with 'x', A is a participant in the same name using practice as I participate in by virtue of my association of β with 'x'.

Now, however, we need to consider the case in which A does not have the name 'x' in his repertoire at all. In such a case, I think, we can say that he believes that x is F only if he could express his belief using, roughly speaking, some *translation* of 'x'. But this notion of translation cannot be cashed straightforwardly in terms of identity of sense. Rather we need to see the relationship which holds between the name 'y' in A's use and the name 'x' in B's use, when 'y' as used by A is a translation of 'x' as used by B, as derivative from a relationship between the two name-using practices in which they are participants. Suppose A and B are both deferential name users and the group to whom A is deferential associates the same sense with 'y' as the group to whom B is deferential associates with 'x'. Then it would seem reasonable for B to use 'x' obliquely in his ascriptions of those of A's beliefs he would express with 'y'. Similarly, if A's community as a whole is deferential in its use of 'y' to the use of 'x' by B's community or conversely. In either case then it would be appropriate to describe 'y' as used by A as a translation of 'x' as used by B. But if neither relationship held between the name using practices in which A and B were participants, but it was simply that as a matter of fact 'x' as used by B and 'y' as used by A named the same thing, it would seem incorrect for B to use 'x' obliquely in his ascriptions of those of A's beliefs he expressed using 'y'. Imagine, for example, that 'x' and 'y' are in fact names of a single mountain. But A's community lives on one side of it, B's on the other, and it looks completely different from the two sides so that the two communities do not realise that they are in fact speaking of a single mountain. Members of A's community who have encountered members of B's introduce the name 'x' to their community as a name of the mountain B's community calls 'x', but it is not realised, and in fact generally disbelieved, that x is y, and A is one of the disbelievers. In this circumstance it would seem absurd for B, if he discovered the identity, thereupon to ascribe to A *de dicto* beliefs about x on the basis of his assertions using 'y', and it seems evident that if such ascriptions are incorrect in this case they could not be correct if the situation was different merely to the extent that 'x' was not in A's repertoire at all.

So much then for necessary conditions of the truth of 'A believes that x is F'. But Burge's examples make it clear that these necessary truth-conditions cannot also be sufficient. I suggest that we can state sufficient conditions only by distinguishing cases. On the other hand if x does not actually exist then satisfaction of one of these conditions *is* sufficient for the truth of 'A believes that x is F'. That is, if I can say truly 'x does not actually exist', then 'A believes that x is F', as uttered by me, will be true with respect to a possible situation just in case in that situation one or other of these conditions is satisfied. (Of course, this does not require that I exist in that possible situation. If A himself uses 'x' to express his belief what is required is only that the way A uses 'x' in the possible situation and the way I use 'x' in actual fact are such as to make us participants in a common name using practice, while if A does not use 'x' what is required is only that the way in which A uses the name with which he does express his belief in the possible situation and the way I use 'x' in actual fact are such as to make the name A uses a translation of 'x' as used by me.) On the other hand, as Burge's arguments make clear, if x does actually exist then an additional condition has to be satisfied for the truth of 'A believes that x is F', namely, that A believes with respect to x that it is F. That is, if I can say truly 'x actually exists', then 'A believes that x is F', as uttered by me, will be true with respect to a possible situation just in case in that situation one or other of the necessary conditions is satisfied *and*, in consequence, A believes with respect to x that it is F. This explains why we cannot regard 'A believes that x is F' as true with respect to a counterfactual situation in which x does not exist if, in actual fact, x does exist, and it is compatible with the fact that we are happy to ascribe *de dicto* beliefs about say, King Arthur, to believers while ourselves remaining agnostic. For in such cases we know that one or other of the two necessary conditions is satisfied and that either King Arthur actually existed or he did not. And since we know we are making a belief ascription to someone in the actual world, we know that if King Arthur did actually exist the subject to whom we are ascribing the belief on the basis of his satisfaction of one of the two necessary conditions will automatically count as having a belief, with respect to King Arthur, that he was so and so.

That completes my discussion of Burge's examples. I have argued that the challenge to Frege's conception of thoughts which they pose can be met so long as we do not insist on regarding *de dicto* propositional attitude ascriptions as having a straightforward relational analysis (of the type, indeed, that Frege assumed), and I have elaborated this suggestion by providing an account of the truth-conditions of such ascriptions which fits in with a more complex analysis.

University of Birmingham

FREGE'S PLATONISM

By Bob Hale

The central concern of this paper is with an argument which may be seen as underpinning Frege's Platonism in general and, in particular, his view that there exists a range of numerical objects. I shall confine my discussion to that form of the argument which seeks to establish the existence of numerical *objects* and will not consider parallel arguments along similar lines for the existence of mathematical entities of other types – properties, relations and functions – though these form, of course, part of the full Fregean ontology. It is convenient to set these aside because the analogues of the argument for numerical objects that would give us properties, etc., depend on Frege's ascription of reference to incomplete expressions and are to that extent more controversial than the argument for numerical objects, which relies on the relatively less controversial ascription of reference to singular terms.

§I outlines the Fregean argument, drawing attention to its reliance on criteria of singular termhood of the sort proposed by Dummett. §II poses a challenge to the argument based on the language-specific character of those criteria. I argue in §III that the problem is not to be avoided by replacing them by a broadly semantic language-neutral characterization of singular terms, and in §IV that a suggestion made by Dummett, which might be thought to afford a solution, runs into severe difficulties. In §V, I set up what I hope to be an instructive parallel between our problem about characterizing singular terms and a problem in characterizing valid inference. I propose (§VI) a solution to the latter problem and an analogous solution to the former. §VII argues that the proposed solution is not, as might be supposed, viciously circular. Finally, (§VIII), I comment briefly on some other objections to the strategy of the Fregean argument.

I

Baldly stated, Frege's case for acknowledging numbers as a kind of object runs thus: if there is a range of expressions members of which function as singular terms in true statements, then there exists a range of objects corresponding to them. But numerals and other numerical expressions do so function – notably, though not of course exclusively, in arithmetical statements of the sort to which Frege gives especial prominence, i.e. arithmetical equations. Hence there exists a range of numerical objects to which reference is made in arithmetical statements.

Evidently this line of argument, whatever its merits and whatever other doubts may be felt about it, would be hopelessly circular if our only means of ascertaining that an expression functions as a singular term involved determining that it stands for an object. Perhaps, in the end, we can give no more illuminating answer to the question, 'what is it for an expression to function as a singular term?' than: singular terms are those expressions whose function it is to stand for particular objects. It remains the case that the Fregean argument just outlined clearly presupposes the availability of an answer to the different question, 'which expressions are/function as singular terms?' – i.e. of acceptable *criteria* of singular termhood, where an obvious constraint on acceptability is that their application should not involve any prior recognition of a class of objects as the referents of members of a class of putative singular terms.

Criteria expressly designed to meet this requirement have been put forward by Dummett. (FPL, pp. 57–69) The specific criteria he offers are based on the idea that there are certain simple patterns of inference distinctive of singular terms in the sense that if certain positions in the premisses or conclusion are occupied by singular terms, we have a valid inference, otherwise not. As *necessary* conditions for t to be a singular term, Dummett gives:

(1) for any sentence 'A(t)', the inference 'A(t)⊢ There is something such that A(it)' shall be valid;
(2) for any sentences 'A(t)', 'B(t)', the inference 'A(t), B(t)⊢ There is something such that A(it) and B(it)' shall be valid;
(3) for any sentence 'It is true of t that A(it) or B(it)' the inference from that sentence to 'A(t) or B(t)' shall be valid.

Though perhaps necessary, these conditions are, as Dummett points out, insufficient. In particular, whilst they exclude indefinite noun phrases such as 'a policeman' when they occur in grammatical subject or object position, as in 'A policeman struck George' and 'George struck a policeman' (since from these premisses we may *not* infer 'Someone both struck and was struck by George'), they fail to exclude such phrases when they occur as grammatical complements. Thus from 'George is a policeman' and 'Henry is not a policemen' we *may* validly infer 'George is something which Henry isn't'. Noting that these rogue cases exploit the possibility of using 'something' to express second- or higher-level generality, Dummett constructs an additional test for discriminating between these uses and imposes the further requirement that in conditions (1) and (2), the generality expressed by 'something' shall be of first-level.

These criteria, though of the general kind required, stand in need of some revision. In particular, Dummett's test for level of generality is unsatisfactory, as I have argued elsewhere.[1] However, since the problem I shall be discussing in the remainder of this paper is quite independent of their detailed formulation and derives from a feature which will certainly be shared by any revised criteria of the general sort we are concerned with, I shall omit further refinements.

II

Dummett's criteria are framed relative to a particular language – English as it happens – some mastery of which their application presupposes. Thus they equip us, at best, to recognise which English expressions function on which occasions as singular terms. This is no dispensable feature. Any attempt to generalize them by eliminating reference to the linguistic forms by which, in a particular language, (first-level) generality is expressed would require restating e.g. condition (1) so as to require that for t to function as a singular term in a sentence 'A(t)', *existential generalization* with respect to the relevant occurence(s) of t shall be valid. But this restatement of (1) assumes, in effect, that we are already equipped to recognise some sentence as the existential generalization of 'A(t)' with respect to t. Yet one entirely innocent of the general notion of singular term and as yet unequipped with criteria for picking out such terms could scarcely gain a grip on the notion of a quantifier, and any plausible criteria for picking out those expressions which function in a given language as quantifiers will surely involve prior recognition of others that function as singular terms.

Dummett's criteria avoid this kind of circularity, but do so in a way which depends upon their lack of generality or language-neutrality.[2] As stated, they presuppose understanding of various expressions which serve as logical words in English – the sentential operators 'and' and 'or', the quantifiers 'something' and 'everything' and the like. But this is to assume a *purely practical* mastery of certain aspects of English; it is *not* to assume, illegitimately, that the user of the criteria is equipped with the *general notions* of sentential operator and quantifier, or with *criteria* by which expressions may be recognised as belonging to these categories. But for anyone who seeks to base conclusions about what kinds of objects there are on the application of criteria of singular termhood, this apparently inescapable lack of language-neutrality poses a serious challenge. Objects are, no doubt, what singular terms refer to. If, however, we lack

---

[1] In 'Strawson, Geach and Dummett on singular terms and predicates' *Synthese* 42 (1979), I argued that the difficulty can be overcome without appeal to any general means of distinguishing first- from higher-level generality. A useful discussion of Dummett's criteria may be found in Wright, ch. 2. Some further difficulties, including a general difficulty over the behaviour of singular terms in opaque contexts, are best handled, I think, by restating the criteria so as to discriminate between *uses* in which they function as singular terms and other (irreferential) uses.
[2] This point is argued more fully in my *Synthese* paper (pp. 289–90).

any general, language-neutral characterization of singular terms, must not a parallel linguistic relativity affect the objects which are being thought of as their correlates? Must we not acknowledge that we can provide no general defence of the claim, say, that numbers are (abstract) objects; that the most we can properly claim is that they are treated as objects in English, or German, etc? More generally, how can we give a good sense to, much less justify, claims to the effect that there exists such and such a kind of object, as distinct from claims to the effect that there are such and such English objects, or German objects, etc? How, in short, is International Platonism[3] even possible?

We should distinguish this challenge to the Fregean argument from another which also claims to uncover an unwanted linguistic relativity in its conclusion. It is, it may be urged, certainly possible, and perhaps even quite likely, that different languages diverge over the ranges of singular terms they contain. We may suppose that such discrepancies are unlikely to be significant between languages as closely related as, say, English and German. But between languages that are remote from one another – English and Hindi, say – it seems perfectly possible that the divergence should be considerable, and that some languages should contain, but others lack, a vocabulary of singular terms for abstract objects, or abstract objects of a particular kind.

This second challenge is quite distinct from the first, which notes the inescapably language-specific character of workable criteria of singular termhood and challanges us to give grounds for thinking that this does not, after all, debar us from speaking of objects in some unitary, language-neutral sense. Provided that the Platonist can satisfactorily answer the first challenge, he can, I think, meet the second without much fuss. At least, it is clear in outline how he may respond to it. If, but only if, he can meet the first challenge, he will be entitled to claim that objects enjoy an existence independent of our or anybody else's thought and talk about them, and that it is only our epistemological access to them which is mediated by language-specific criteria of singular termhood. But then the availability of a range of singular terms standing for objects of a certain kind cannot be a necessary condition of their existence. If, then, a particular language lacks a range of singular terms found in other languages, it is that language which is the poorer, not the realm of (non-linguistic) objects. The crucial question is: how can the first challenge be met?

III

Immediately after arguing that it is "essential, if Frege's whole philosophy of language and the ontology that depends upon it are to be even viable, that it

---

[3] I borrow this apt expression from Crispin Wright, who gives a forceful exposition of the problem (*loc. cit.*).

should be possible to give clear and exact criteria, relating to their functioning within language, for discriminating proper names from expressions of other kinds" (FPL, p. 58), Dummett acknowledges further that "if Frege's philosophy of language is sound, the category of proper names is to be recognized within every conceivable language. But the principle on which they were distinguished, if formulated in such a completely general way, could only relate to the kind of sense which they had, that is, to the general form of the semantic rules governing them."

We may see in this latter thought – that any general characterization of the category of singular terms must be given in terms of the kind of sense belonging to expressions of that category – the germ of an answer to the threat of ontological nationalism. Just how might such an answer run?

One suggestion which we must reject, though Dummett's words may seem to encourage it, is this. Suppose that a completely general characterization of singular terms, relating to the kind of sense belonging to them, can be given. Then we may have, after all, a general, i.e. language-neutral, criterion. So the threat of unwanted ontological nationalism simply lapses.

This suggestion is too simple. If this were the kind of general principle Dummett has in mind, then it would be a complete mystery why he should seek to develop criteria of the sort we have been discussing; for any such language-specific criteria would then be simply redundant. And in any case, this suggestion goes flat against Dummett's own claim that decisive tests for singular termhood "can only relate to the correctness or incorrectness of certain simple patterns of inference, recognition of which may again be left at the intuitive level" (FPL, p. 58). For if recognition of their (in)correctness is to be justifiably left at the intuitive level, such patterns of inference must be specified in terms of the linguistic forms of a particular language of which he who is to apply the tests has the requisite mastery. There can be no question of formulating the tests in some international formal language (e.g. that of first-order quantification theory) – obviously, for then they could only be applied by one who already possesses criteria by which to determine which expressions of a given natural language belong to the various categories found in the formal language. The present suggestion conflates two questions we should keep apart:

(1) What is it for an expression to function as a singular term?
(2) How are expressions which do so function to be recognised as such?

Dummett's criteria are to be taken as an answer to the second question; his lately quoted remark must be understood as addressed to the first.

The suggestion I wish to explore is rather this. We can answer the first question by providing a general, language-neutral account of the role or function of singular terms, which is, however, of no use as a criterion for picking out singular terms in any particular language. We can answer the second by providing detailed criteria which are, however, unavoidably language-specific. But these language-specific criteria are so related to the general account that we are justified in regarding the expressions picked out by different sets of criteria for different languages as singular terms in a unitary sense, so that the charge of ontological nationalism is unfounded.

IV

There is little warrant for ascribing this suggestion to Dummett, and more for supposing that, in so far as he addresses our question, he would favour a different answer. After presenting his criteria of singular termhood for English, he explains that his

> purpose has been to make it plausible that sharp criteria could be given, which were not *ad hoc* in the sense of relying on highly contingent features of the language to which they were applicable, and were of the general kind that Frege's theory requires. (FPL, p. 69)

Evidently Dummett perceives the need for generality but is banking on achieving it by ensuring that criteria of singular termhood, whilst inevitably framed relative to some particular language, should exploit only features of that language which it may justifiably be held to share with all other languages. What are the prospects for a resolution along these lines? As Wright points out (Wright, p. 64), if this suggestion is to work, it is essential that someone should be able, having grasped Dummett's criteria for a particular language, to recognize their counterparts for any other language without needing to fall back on explicit, language-neutral criteria for the identification of existential quantification and the like. Where there are firmly established conventions of translation between the languages in question, this will present no problem. But the crucial issue concerns our capacity to recognize the adequacy of the relevant conventions. And we may seriously doubt, Wright contends, that a field linguist could reasonably convince himself of the correctness of a particular translation of 'something' into a radically foreign language without, in effect, appealing to the distinctive role and characteristics of existential quantification. Perhaps this doubt can be relieved, but it is serious enough to make it worthwhile to develop my alternative suggestion.

V

There is a parallel between our present concern and the task of characterizing valid inference. Just as we need to distinguish the questions (1) and (2) above (§III), so we should distinguish between asking:

(3) What is it for an inference to be valid?
(4) Which inferences are valid and how are they to be recognized as such?

And just as we can supply a general answer to question (1) – singular terms are, roughly, those expressions used to refer to particular objects – so we are ready with a general answer to question (3) – an inference is valid just so long as it is not possible for its premisses all to be true but its conclusion false. Like the answer to (1), this answer to (3), though inevitably stated in a particular language, is language-neutral: making no reference to the devices of any particular language it can apply, as intended, to all inferences in no matter what actual or possible language they may be formulated. But, as with our answer to (1), this answer to (3) achieves generality at a price – it does not, unless supplemented by further semantic information of a language-specific kind (i.e. about the truth-conditions of the various types of sentence belonging to the language), afford any means of identifying the valid inference patterns of any particular language.

In one respect, the parallel I am drawing is less than perfect. When we turn to question (4), we find that the situation is more complicated than it is with respect to question (2). For whilst we seldom, if ever, outside of philosophical enquiries, explicitly address ourselves to the question whether a given expression is, in a certain context, functioning as a singular term, the question whether a given inference is valid is one that confronts us frequently in every field of intelligent activity. Equipped with something like the general notion of validity embodied in the principle of truth-preservation, the intelligent non-professional resolves such questions largely unaided by any generally applicable criteria or tests of validity. We may like to regard his answers as grounded in untutored logical intuition – or, less mysteriously and less misleadingly, simply as exercises of his practical grasp on the logically relevant aspects of the meanings of the sentences involved in the inference he evaluates. However we choose to put it, it is clear that his judgment that a given informal inference is (in)valid will, if it deserves to be taken seriously, draw upon his knowledge of facts about the meanings of its constituent sentences. Such informal assessments of particular informal inferences are partial answers to question (4).[4]

For more comprehensive and systematic answers we naturally turn to formal logic. It is not evidently impossible in principle – though the gap between principle and practice is clearly enormous – that a fully comprehensive, though not of course effective, characterization of the valid inference patterns of a

---

[4] In a way closely akin to that in which instances of Tarski's T-schema are partial definitions of the truth-predicate for a specified language.

particular natural language should be developed.[5] Such a characterization would unavoidably involve reference to the inferentially significant expressions or constructions of that particular language and would thus be language-specific. Logic proceeds differently, turning away from the overwhelming complexity of natural languages and investigating validity by means of formal languages and systems based upon them (though a natural language remains in use as a metalanguage). This difference complicates but does not in any essential respect undermine my parallel. It is true that formal characterizations of the class of valid inferences of a certain well-defined type achieve generality and neutrality with respect to particular natural languages simply in virtue of being couched in terms of a formal language in which any inference of that type framed in any natural language may, by means of judicious construal, be formalized. But, so far from obviating the need for exploitation of our knowledge of the contributions of inferentially significant words or constructions, the procedure of characterizing the valid inference patterns of natural languages indirectly through the medium of a formal language actually doubles it. The recognition of a particular informal inference as valid via its identification as an instance of a valid inference pattern belonging to a given formal logic involves the exercise both of knowledge of the senses of inferentially relevant devices employed in the informal inference (in identifying it as an instance of the formal inference pattern in question) and of knowledge of the senses of the logical constants which supplant them in its formalized counterpart (in its recognition as a valid inference pattern).

It may be objected to this last claim that it simply ignores the familiar point that, with respect to a specified formal system, the class of valid inferences may be characterized purely formally, without recourse to the intended senses of the logical constants, as those inferences $X \vdash A$ such that A is deducible from X, the criteria for an array or sequence of formulae to be a valid deduction being themselves purely formal. The claim on which this objection rests is of course indisputable, but it lacks the significance the objection supposes it to possess. Firstly, and quite generally, we standardly seek to provide, in addition to a purely syntactic (proof-theoretic) characterization of validity for the system, a characterization in semantic (model-theoretic) terms and treat the latter as the more fundamental of the two, with the former answerable to it (Dummett1). We so treat it because the formal semantic characterization stands in a more direct relation to our arguably basic extra-systematic notion of validity (i.e. guaranteed truth-preservation) than does its syntactic counterpart. And this affords one reason to view the connection between informal and formal

---

[5] Paradox may be a problem, as much here as in the case of the truth-predicate for a natural language. Perhaps the best we can expect is an indefinitely extendable but never exhaustive characterization of validity for successively larger fragments of the language in question.

inference as mediated by the standard formal semantics of the system which involves a determination of the senses of the logical constants. Secondly, and quite independently, if the proof-theoretic validity of a formal inference pattern is to be a reason for deeming a given informal inference valid, we require assurance that the latter may properly be regarded as an informal instance of the former. Now it is true that we may, and indeed perhaps generally do, make the required connection without explicit appeal to the thought that the sentences of the informal inference have the same form of truth-conditions as the corresponding formulae. But if we are to avoid appeal to this thought, we must appeal instead to accepted informal readings of the formal operators, where the senses of these informal readings are taken for granted. My proposed parallel thus remains intact; the possibility of indirectly characterizing valid inference via formal systems complicates but does not undermine it.

It should, perhaps, be stressed that the contrast I make between the general notion of validity and detailed characterizations of valid inference is not to be identified with the familiar contrast between semantic (model-theoretic) and syntactic (proof-theoretic) characterizations of validity for a given (formal) language or system. Whether such a characterization is effected in syntactic or semantic terms, it will, in one way or another, involve reference to the inferentially relevant features of sentences and will thus be language or system relative.[6] Thus when we claim that a sentence A is formally deducible in a certain formal system from a set of sentences X, we standardly write $X \vdash_S A$, appending a subscript reference to the single turnstile. Similarly, when we claim that A is a semantic consequence of X, we write $X \vDash_S A$ rather than plain $X \vdash A$ thereby acknowledging that our claim is relative to a certain formal semantics. If a formal language is taken to be a purely formal object given by listing its primitive symbols and formation rules only, then it is, admittedly, improper to express this point by saying that the syntactic and semantic consequence relations are language-relative. For different formal systems – S4 and S5, say – may share the same formal language in *that* sense and yet we have e.g. $MLp \vdash_{S5} Lp$ (and $MLp \vDash_{S5} Lp$) and $MLp \nvdash_{S4} Lp$ (and $MLp \nvDash_{S4} Lp$). If, however, as we surely may, we take a formal language to comprise in addition, a definition of proof (or deduction), then we may quite properly describe the syntactic consequence relation as language-relative. And if we understand by a language not a purely formal object given by its syntax, but, as we are again free to do, that *plus* an interpretation (i.e. a detailed set of rules fixing the truth-conditions of its sentences, including a definition of the appropriate class of

---

[6] This point is made by Susan Haack, *Philosophy of Logics* (Cambridge, 1978) ch. 2, who takes a similar view of the relationship between informal and systematic validity to that adopted here, though she does not distinguish, as I think we should, between the general extra-systematic notion of validity and particular assessments of informal inferences.

models), then we may quite properly speak of the semantic consequence relation as relative to a language. There remains a clear distinction between detailed syntactic or semantic characterizations of validity effected with respect to a formal language and the general, extra-systematic conception of validity which underlies them.[7]

Whilst, for reasons some of which I have just touched upon, we are usually careful in formal talk of validity to flag the turnstiles with subscripts denoting the appropriate formal system, when making ostensibly parallel claims about informal inferences we generally omit any such reference. We say e.g. that the inference:

> Most boys like girls and most boys like games ⊢ Some boys like girls and games

is valid, rather than valid-in-English. Why is that?

Well, it could simply be that the seemingly necessary relativization to English is left out because it may safely be taken as read. And certainly in one sense the reference to English must be understood, since it is possible, however unlikely, that typographically the same sentences are sentences of some other language in which the second is not a logical consequence of the first. But there are, I think, deeper reasons behind the omission. The first of these concerns a hitherto unmentioned reason for relativizing formal consequence claims to well-defined formal systems. One reason why it is important to keep track of what follows from what in S5, say, as opposed to T or S4, is that we may be interested in which of these (and possibly other) modal logics most adequately formalizes informal modal argumentation. We may view various modal logics as rival characterizations of logical consequence in its modal aspect in informal reasoning, but there is no need to assume that there is just one correct modal logic for this reason to weigh with us. It may be, as some[8] have argued, that different modal logics fit different areas of modal discourse – it will clearly be equally important to keep track of consequence in different formal systems. Plainly, this reason for relativizing formal consequence claims is not applicable to their informal counterparts.

---

[7] It is, of course, possible to view, for example, the standard model-theoretic semantics for modal logics as a purely mathematical device in terms of which purely mathematical questions as to completeness, etc., may be raised and answered. From this point of view, it is a misleading accident that terms like 'true at w', 'possible world', etc., which suggest some connection with truth and possibility, are employed. And from this standpoint, of course, much of what I have said about syntactic characterizations being answerable to semantic ones would require considerable amendment. The bearing of formal characterizations of validity on informal inferences would now depend entirely upon the acceptability of our informal readings of the formal operators.

[8] E.g., E. J. Lemmon, "Is there only one correct system of modal logic?", in *Aristotelian Society* Supp. Vol., 23 (1959).

Secondly, I think we feel some resistance to appending the qualification 'valid-in-English' because, roughly speaking, we feel that to insert it would carry the suggestion, which we should repudiate, that the very same inference, though valid-in-English, might be invalid-in-French, German, etc., in the way that the inference MLp⊢Lp, though valid in S5 is invalid in S4, T, etc. The apparent inconsistency here – between, on the one hand, the acknowledgement that reference to a particular language must be understood in informal claims about validity and, on the other, our wish to reject any such relativization – is, I think, only apparent. Reference to English, say, must be understood if the inference we are declaring to be valid is to be correctly identified; our wish to extrude reference to English is grounded in the conviction that the validity of the inference, once identified, is not a fact about English as opposed to French, German, etc. In short, we believe, as Strawson once put it, that "logical statements framed in one language are not just about that language".

I hope I have made sufficiently clear the sense in which this belief might be true. The next question – which runs nicely parallel to our crucial question about Platonism – is: What, if anything, justifies such a belief?

Again there is some temptation to appeal here to considerations about translation. Thus Strawson:

> The important thing to see is that when you draw the boundaries of the applicability of words in one language and then connect the words of that language with those of another by translation rules, there is no need to draw boundaries again for the second language. They are already drawn. This is why (or partly why) logical statements framed in one language are not just about that language (Strawson, p. 12).

And the appeal to translation confronts the same kind of difficulties as noted previously. When we consider languages between which there are well-entrenched conventions of translation, the suggestion seems to work smoothly enough. But again the crucial issue is how we recognize the adequacy of the conventions. The trouble is, of course, that we are apt to take it as a criterion of adequacy of a proposed translation scheme from L_1 to L_2 that under it valid inferences of L_1 go over into valid inferences of L_2 and vice versa. I shall try a different line.

VI

We have, on the one hand, a quite general, language-neutral conception of valid inference, encapsulated in the principle that valid inferences are those in which truth is necessarily preserved. We have, on the other, detailed though perhaps incomplete characterizations of validity, in syntactic or semantic terms, which are, however, language-specific. How are they related?

The role of the truth-preservation principle is, I suggest, largely *regulative*: it constrains us, quite simply, once we have settled the meanings (or at least the truth-conditions) of the sentences of L, to recognize as valid exactly the L-inferences in which truth cannot fail to be preserved, and thereby guides our construction of any detailed characterization of L-valid inferences. That is, any proposed characterization of validity for any particular language L is answerable to this general regulative principle. It is in this sense that acceptable characterizations of validity for different languages are characterizations of the same thing.

To resume the other half of my parallel: what general, language-neutral account of singular terms can be given, and how is it related to criteria of singular-termhood framed relative to particular languages?

Frege ascribes both sense and reference to expressions of *all* logical types. The function of the sense of an expression of *any* type is to determine its reference. Hence it does not suffice, in order generally to characterize the kind of sense belonging to a singular term, to say that it is that in virtue of which it has some particular entity as referent. What is *distinctive* of the *kind* of sense belonging to a singular term, on Frege's view, must be that it determines a reference of a certain kind – the kind in question being, of course, *objects*. That is, for Frege, our general conception of the category of singular terms will run something like this.

> (S) A singular term is any expression whose sense embodies a means of identifying a particular object as the referent of that expression.

In view of the controversial character of Frege's doctrine that reference is always in virtue of sense, and the serious doubts that may be raised about the viability of the notion of sense itself, it is desirable to enquire how a general characterization in more neutral, and so more austere, terms might run. (S) in effect embodies both a conception of the function of singular terms, which is not peculiarly Fregean, and a distinctively Fregean view of how that function is discharged. Excising the latter, we are left with the bare principle:

> (S') A singular term is any expression whose function is to identify a particular object.

How is (S') related to specific criteria of singular termhood for particular languages? Briefly, I suggest it bears to them the same kind of regulative relation as the principle of truth-preservation bears to characterizations of validity for different languages. That is, in choosing criteria of singular termhood for a particular language, we are guided by, and our proposed criteria are answerable to, some such general conception as (S') formulates. And because this is so, we may regard different sets of criteria for different languages as serving to pick out singular terms in a unitary sense. And this, in turn, entitles us to resist the addition of an ontologically nationalistic qualification to the conclusion of the Fregean argument for numerical objects.

VII

An obvious objection to this suggestion is that (S′) employs the notion of *object*, and does so quite blatantly. Does this not mean that the whole enterprise is, in the end, viciously circular? I shall argue that it does not – but much depends on the *kind* of circularity in question, since one kind of circularity must, I think, be admitted, but is arguably non-vicious, while a different kind, which would be vicious, is avoidable.

(1) It is true that we can, in the end, give no *general* account of what a singular term is other than that it is an expression whose function is to stand for an object. And it is true (or at least, so the Fregean must insist) that we have no *general* conception of an object other than that of the referent of a (possible) singular term. But it is a familiar point that in investigations of a conceptual nature, a level may be reached where we are no longer able to explain conceptually derivative notions in terms of conceptually more basic ones, but must be content to exhibit connections between (equally) fundamental notions. Taking the notions of object and singular term to be such a pair, we may deny that the admitted circularity is vicious, or at least demand some additional reason for thinking it to be so. Certainly one standard reason for holding explanatory circles to be vicious – that they effectively preclude acquisition and application of the terms in the circle – does not apply in this case. For we can give *criteria* of singular termhood not involving the notion of object.

(2) The alleged circularity may be held to consist in the fact that on the one hand our Fregean argument presupposes the availability of independent criteria of singular termhood, whilst on the other, we have been able to produce no better answer to the question 'what is a singular term?' than: an expression whose function is to refer to an object.

It may be countered that if the criteria proposed were of such a kind that their application involved a prior ability to discriminate between objects and entities of other kinds, this circularity would indeed be vicious. But this is not so. It remains the case that in the *application* of our criteria, no independent ability to recognize certain entities as objects is called upon. This is really just the point that our general conception of singular terms, formulated as (S′), *regulates* our construction of criteria but does not *replace* them.

It may be replied – surely with some justice – that this merely exhibits the somewhat indirect character of the circularity, but does nothing to show that it is harmless. Granted that we make no *direct* appeal to the idea that certain expressions stand for objects in ascertaining, by means of the criteria, that they are singular terms, it remains the case that, if pressed to explain or justify our preference for these criteria, we shall be obliged to fall back on the claim that expressions satisfying those criteria serve to effect reference to objects.

This shows, I think, that the Platonist cannot here both eat his cake and have it (i.e. admit circularity of the second kind but argue that it is harmless). But it does not leave him defenceless. The distinctively philosophical tasks of devising criteria of singular termhood and of proposing and defending answers to the question 'what kinds of object are there?' are not tasks which we approach empty-handed, with no idea of which expressions function as singular terms and thus stand for objects. Nor, of course, do we approach them with complete, definitive answers. We approach them with – and it is hard to see how we could approach them without – some intuitive convictions to the effect that such-and-such expressions, at least, function as singular terms, standing for objects. Such intuitive convictions, which need not be unshakeable, play an indispensable part in any attempt to devise and evaluate explicit criteria of singular termhood. We can no more approach that task without some idea of which expressions ought to be classified as singular terms than we can construct a grammar for a natural language without some idea of which combinations of marks or sounds ought to be classified as sentences of that language. And a similar point applies to the task of devising explicit criteria for the evaluation of inferences.

The Platonist argument can now be restated in a way which both reveals it as innocent of the kind of circularity threatened and displays more clearly the kind of pressure it exerts upon us. We have, on the one hand, the general conception of an object as the referent of a (possible) singular term. On the other, we accept a wide range of expressions as functioning as singular terms (and so as standing for objects). With these undoubted cases of singular terms as our yardstick, we devise explicit criteria of singular termhood. By these criteria (kinds of) expressions lying outside the range of those unquestioned cases qualify as singular terms also. And expressions of these further kinds function as singular terms in true statements. Thus unless it can be demonstrated (without appeal, obviously, to the question-begging assumption that the problematic singular terms do not stand for objects) that our criteria are unacceptable, we have no good reason to refuse to admit the existence of kinds of objects corresponding to them.

VIII

The Platonist conclusion may, of course, be resisted, and the Fregean argument for it, with which this paper has been exclusively concerned, challenged in other ways. I end with a few brief and, I regret, somewhat inconclusive comments on some anti-Platonist moves which relate directly to the strategy of the Fregean argument as I have presented it.

Dummett (FPL, Ch. 14, *passim*, esp. p. 505) contends that pure abstract objects are creatures of language in such a way or sense that the "realistic conception of reference" for abstract singular terms eventually breaks down. The nub of Dummett's argument for this conclusion is that there is no kind of statement concerning the supposed referents of, say, numerical singular terms which plays the same role vis-a-vis those terms as what he calls recognition-statements (e.g. 'This is Buckingham Palace') play in relation to singular terms standing for concrete objects. Being so placed as to be able to make a true recognition-statement is being in a position to identify some object as the referent of a singular term. Dummett toys with the idea that arithmetic identities one of whose terms is a standard numeral (e.g. '120 = 5!') may be seen as playing such a role. But his final view is that this is insufficient to warrant the extension of the realistic conception of reference to numerical singular terms. Whilst we may in some sense be said to identify 120 as the value of the function n! for the argument 5, there is no such thing as identifying an object as the referent of the standard numeral '5', say. "The recognition of the truth of a numerical equation cannot be described as the identification of an object external to us as the referent of a term, precisely because there is no sense in which it requires us to discern numbers as constituents of the external world." He concludes that "pure abstract objects are no more than the reflections of certain linguistic expressions, expressions which behave, by simple formal criteria, in a manner analogous to proper names of objects, but whose sense cannot be represented as consisting in our capacity to identify objects as their bearers" (FPL, p. 505).

This argument is essentially the same as that by which Dummett earlier seeks to show that Frege's ascription of reference to incomplete expressions is unjustified (FPL, Ch. 7, esp. p. 243). The difference is just that these incomplete expressions are said to fail to accord with the paradigm of reference afforded by singular terms because understanding an incomplete expression does not require any capacity to identify an entity as its referent, whereas here *abstract* singular terms are said to fail to accord with the (narrower) paradigm afforded by *concrete* singular terms, on the same ground.

Full discussion of this argument, and in particular of whether, in view of its crucial employment of the notions of identifying or being confronted with an object external to us, it effectively begs the question against the Platonist, requires another paper.[9] One point may, however, be made quite briefly. It is not merely the case that certain kinds of e.g. numerical expressions behave, by simple formal criteria, in a manner *analogous* to proper names of objects. The expressions in question undoubtedly satisfy Dummett's own criteria of singular termhood. Hence he may not have it both ways: he must *either* admit that these

---

[9] For discussion of the matter, see Wright ch. 2, Section x.

criteria are *inadequate* (in which case the onus is on him to explain, in some non-question-begging way, why they are and to indicate how they should be amended) *or*, retaining those criteria, he must sever the connection, on which the Platonist case relies, between being a (genuine) singular term and standing for an object. Either course will, it seems, involve rejecting some crucial elements of Frege's overall philosophy of language, including some (e.g. the treatment of logical categorization of expressions as prior to ontological questions) which Dummett himself appears to endorse.

Another objection, along similar lines, couples the thought that our broadly formal criteria of singular termhood outstrip the notion of genuine reference with the claim that what makes for the uncontroversial character of the range of uncontroversial singular terms on which the Fregean argument relies is that their presumed referents are capable of causal interaction if not with us directly then at least with other entities to which we stand in more or less indirect causal relations. If, as the Fregean argument would have us believe, any attempt to characterize, by means of broadly formal criteria, the smallest class including all uncontroversial singular terms will lead to the admission of, e.g. numerals, as singular terms then what this shows is not that numbers are genuine objects but that the best formal criteria we can devise fail to remain faithful to the notion of genuine reference. The weakness of the Fregean strategy is that it appeals to a range of uncontroversial singular terms but offers no account of what underlies their acceptance as such. The objection fills this gap; but what fills the gap provides also a ground for rejecting the Fregean conclusion.

This is not the place for a full discussion of this objection.[10] But it is worth pointing out that it is not free from difficulties of its own. In particular, we may ask: what account is to be given of those ostensibly true arithmetic statements involving what are, by our best formal criteria, numerical singular terms? There seem to be three possible positions the objector may occupy:

(1) Pure arithmetic statements are not genuine truths at all, but are false or, perhaps better, truth-valueless.
(2) They are true, but their form is misleading. Some reductive paraphrase is to be accepted.
(3) They are true. No reductive paraphrase is to be given. But the apparent singular terms in them are not genuine, so no referential account of their truth-conditions is to be accepted.

Option (1) is clearly unattractive. Option (3) is scarcely less so, especially when it is seen that this position involves not only rejecting the most natural semantic account of the truth of true singular arithmetic statements but, worse still, threatens to sever their inferential links with existentially quantified

---

[10] It is discussed in Wright, ch. 2, Sections xi and xii.

sentences. For it is not just that a proponent of (3) must resist saying that e.g. '7 > 5' is true just in case <7,5> belongs to the relevant set of ordered pairs; he will also, it seems, have to reject the influence from '7 > 5' to '$\exists x > 5$' – unless he is prepared to hold that the existential quantifier bears an entirely different sense when it binds numerical variables. Option (2) may thus seem to offer the best prospects. How good these are clearly depends on the availability of credible reductive paraphrases backed by reasons to think them better reflections of what the world contains than their originals.[11]

University of Lancaster

---

[11] I am particularly indebted to Crispin Wright, Stephen Read and Peter Mott for searching discussion of an earlier version of this paper.

THE PHILOSOPHER BEHIND THE LAST LOGICIST

By Joan Weiner*

In "Frege: The Last Logicist", Paul Benacerraf highlights two important features of Frege's work. One is the peculiarity, from a contemporary perspective, of Frege's enterprise, and the other is the influence of Frege's mathematical background on this enterprise. Benacerraf points out, quite rightly, that Frege is not a contemporary of ours and that any careful reader of Frege's *Gl* will see that Frege's concerns do not seem to be current philosophical concerns. The appropriate way to read Frege's works, Benacerraf argues, is to take into account their historical context. And, in his paper, Benacerraf tries to read Frege in this way. A part of the historical context, of course, is that Frege was trained as a mathematician, not a philosopher. Benacerraf leans heavily on this in his reading of Frege's work. He argues that Frege's motivation for writing *Gl* was primarily mathematical and that Frege viewed *Gl* as "only incidentally a philosophical work" (p. 33).

Although this approach seems promising, Benacerraf's reading is surprisingly unsatisfying for, on it, Frege's work seems less deep and interesting than it is generally taken to be. I want to argue that Benacerraf's reading is not only unsatisfying but wrong. But although I think it wrong, I also think that Benacerraf's paper merits careful examination. For Benacerraf's reading seems to spring from an understanding of, and attempt to grapple with, certain fundamental tensions in Frege's view. Careful attention to those passages which seem to contradict the thrust of Benacerraf's reading will provide a key to understanding how Frege viewed his work and the sense in which some of Frege's writings can be viewed as responses to fundamental tensions in *Gl*.

The upshot of Benacerraf's reading is that Frege's motivation is really very simple. Frege's project, Benacerraf says, is to prove the heretofore unproved (but provable) truths of arithmetic. And the motivation for undertaking this project is straightforwardly mathematical – Frege is simply interested in giving some new proofs. But while it is entirely plausible that someone might have this motivation for undertaking the project just described, it is less plausible that

---

* I would like to thank Burton Dreben, Warren Goldfarb, Mark Kaplan, Hilary Putnam, and Thomas Ricketts for discussion and comment on previous versions of this paper, which was written during a term of funding by a UWM Graduate School Research Committee Award.

this description could account for the project and motivations of the writer of *Gl*. How can it be viewed as a work of mathematics? It is not, after all, a book of proofs. *Gg* is a book of proofs – in which Frege attempts to prove heretofore unproved truths of arithmetic. Benacerraf has surprisingly little to say about this odd situation. He says only that *Gl* is a "sketch" (Benacerraf, p. 34) of a substantive answer to Frege's mathematical questions. But what work could such a sketch do for Frege?

There is an obvious first strategy for answering this question. There were no ready-made tools available to Frege from which proofs of the basic truths of arithmetic could be derived. For, since he wanted to prove all the unproved truths of arithmetic, no tools of arithmetic could provide the basis for his proofs. And there was no set of truths which was generally regarded by mathematicians as underlying the truths of arithmetic. Frege is generally regarded as having invented and used tools provided by his formal logic and set theory. The obvious strategy, then, is to try to read *Gl* as an attempt to make the nature of these tools clear.

But this will not work. For none of these tools is really explained in *Gl*. Frege's formal logic had been developed in his *Bs*, and there is no attempt in *Gl* to make it any clearer. Furthermore, the tools of set theory were available in Cantor's work (to which Frege alludes – see e.g., FA, p. 108). Had Frege's project been to define the number one and the concept Number in terms of logic and set theory, and to use the resulting definitions to prove the elementary truths of arithmetic, it would have sufficed to add a brief discussion of Cantor's set theory to his *Gg*. There would surely be no important role for *Gl* to play. This constitutes some evidence that Frege did not see himself as engaged in the project just described.

It may seem that the only problem with the above story is its focus on the notion of set. After all, Frege denies that he is using the notion of set to explicate that of number. He claims (FA, p. 38) not to understand the notion of set, and says that he would not recognize a definition of Number in terms of set as an answer to his questions. Thus one might argue that Frege viewed himself as giving a definition of Number in terms of a different mathematical notion, that of the extension of a concept. *Gl*, then, could be seen as an attempt to make clear the nature of this notion and the sense in which Number can be defined using it.

The problem with this reading is that Frege does not give a formal theory of extensions of concepts. The only mathematical feature of extensions of concepts which he exploits is extensionality. In this respect, Frege's extensions of concepts are no different from sets. And, if *Gl* is to be read as an explication of the role of the notion of extension of a concept in the definition of Number, it would not appear to be a work of mathematics. It seems, at this point, that there really is no mathematical role for *Gl* to play.

The lack of a serious role for *Gl* is not the only puzzle which arises from taking Frege's motivation to have been solely mathematical. Since it seems clear that he did not view his work as an attempt to exhibit links between arithmetic and some other branch of mathematics (e.g., set theory), he must have had some motivation beyond the desire to give some new proofs. What other mathematical worry might he have had? Benacerraf indicates (p. 23) that Frege's worry concerns the truth of the elementary propositions of arithmetic. But it is unclear how Frege's proofs could be taken as establishing the truth of these propositions, for the basic propositions from which he attempts to prove them were not standardly accepted as mathematical truths. Would not Frege be obliged to prove these basic propositions from still more basic (and clearly true) propositions? Which, if any, truths do not require proof? And what is our justification for thinking such truths are true? Although one might argue that a mathematician need not answer such questions, it is clear that Frege did attempt to answer them. He wanted, in particular, to be precise about what counts as a finished proof. Furthermore, he claimed that a proof is not complete unless those definitions in it which require justification are justified, and therefore needed an account of definition, and definability, in order to provide the desired precise concept of mathematical proof.

The most troubling puzzles concern Frege's understanding of definition. There is, of course, the question of when to stop defining, just as there is the question of when to stop proving. But this is relatively minor compared to some of the questions which must be answered if Frege's work is to be read as primarily mathematical. For there is a sense in which Frege's actual definitions of the number one and of the concept Number do not look like mathematical definitions. The problem is not simply that the terms used in the definitions appear to be philosophical rather than mathematical, but that the justifications of the definitions appear to be philosophical rather than mathematical. For Frege justifies his definition of the number one, not with any proofs or discussions of mathematics, but with a great deal of discussion of the philosophical notion of concept as well as the meaning of ordinary sentences (e.g., "All whales are mammals", "There are four horses"). If this discussion is to be viewed as part of some proof, then even Frege's notion of proof seems peculiarly unmathematical. Furthermore, his definition of the number one is not even determined by the truths of arithmetic.

Most of the questions raised above are not explicitly considered in Benacerraf's paper. However, Benacerraf does include an extensive discussion of related tensions in Frege's understanding of proof and definition, and also argues that Frege can have no response to some of the tensions in his notion of definition. I think that, on Benacerraf's reading, Frege can indeed have no response to these tensions. But there are other readings of Frege's work. In the next section I will sketch a reading on which there is no mystery about the role of *Gl* in Frege's overall project. In the following section I will discuss Benacerraf's criticisms of Frege's notion of definition and argue that it is possible to find answers to them in Frege's writings.

II

Frege's philosophical motivation for defining the number one is, he claims (FA, p. 3), that this project is required (on his view) for determining whether the truths of arithmetic are analytic or synthetic, a priori or a posteriori. His formulation of the analytic/synthetic distinction, of course, is somewhat different from Kant's. This, however, was not meant as a rejection of the Kantian picture, but as a reconstrual of the Kantian distinction. Frege saw this as an important detail involved in patching up what he saw as some problems with Kantian epistemology.

These problems arise, in part, from the role of logic. Frege's most fundamental assumptions about the nature of logic – that logic is concerned with the laws of thought in a normative, not psychological, sense, and that the laws of logic are the most general laws of all thought and not part of any particular science – seem to have been inherited directly from Kant's Logic.[1] The laws of logic are the general laws according to which one should judge if one wants to judge rightly (as Kant might say: *Logic*, p. 16) or truly (as Frege might say: *PW*, pp. 2—3). One problem Frege saw was that the traditional Aristotelian logic (which Kant thought was correct) did *not* set out those laws correctly. And the substitution of Frege's logic for Aristotelian logic had consequences for the Kantian analytic/synthetic distinction as Frege understood it.

Frege took Kant's analytic/synthetic distinction, along with the a priori/a posteriori distinction, to be a means of categorizing our knowledge according to its sources.[2] In the first of these categories (analytic) lies knowledge which is justified, if we understand the concepts involved, merely by virtue of the rules without which thinking is impossible. In the second category (synthetic a priori) lies knowledge which is possible only with the aid of pure intuition, but for which sense experience is unnecessary. Finally, in the third category (a posteriori) lies knowledge which cannot be justified without appealing to sense

---

[1] It is very revealing to compare Frege's comments on the nature of logic with Kant's. See, for instance, I. Kant, *Logic*, tr. Robert S. Hartman and Wolfgang Schwarz (Indianapolis and New York, 1974), pp. 15—16, and Frege, "Logic" in *PW*, p. 4 and "Logic", *PW*, p. 145. The passages from Frege's work come from two separate, unpublished, works. The editors estimate that the former was written some time between 1879 and 1891 and the latter in 1897. For similar passages in Frege's published work, see the preface to *Bs*, in particular, *Conceptual Notation* in *Conceptual Notation and Related Articles*, tr. and ed. Terrell Ward Bynum (Oxford, 1972), pp. 103—4.

[2] For a more detailed explication and defence of such an interpretation see Philip Kitcher, "Frege's Epistemology", *The Philosophical Review*, 88 (1979).

experience. An analytic proposition, then, was one which could be known through the mere form of reason. But knowledge of a synthetic proposition must have either pure intuition or sense experience as source. Kant's point, Frege says (FA, p. 102) is to show that there are synthetic judgments a priori; i.e., that we can make judgments for whose support experience is not needed but, since they are not justifiable immediately by our understanding of the concepts involved, for whose support something else is needed. Thus when Frege says in the conclusion to *Gl* that Kant did a great service in drawing the analytic/synthetic distinction (FA, p. 101) but that he drew it too narrowly (FA, p. 99), and also when Frege earlier claims only to be making clear what Kant meant by analytic and synthetic (FA, p. 3), he is talking about the failure or success of Kant's distinction in marking off sources of knowledge.

Of course, for Frege and, on this reading, for Frege's Kant, both the analytic/synthetic and a priori/a posteriori distinctions have to do with justification. And, as Benacerraf notes, Kant's own formulation of the analytic/synthetic distinction (unlike that of the a priori/a posteriori distinction) concerns the content, not justification, of propositions. Nonetheless, it is easy to find evidence that Frege did in fact take Kant's analytic/synthetic distinction to have something to do with justification. For instance, it is clear from the discussion of Kant in §12 of *Gl* that he takes Kant's claim that arithmetic is synthetic a priori to be a claim that pure intuition is "the ultimate ground of our knowledge of such judgments". Frege not only quotes from Kant's first *Critique*, but many of his remarks echo passages from it. Thus when he rewords Kant's analytic/synthetic distinction in an attempt to draw the line between those judgments which can be made merely on the basis of understanding the concepts involved and those for which some additional support (i.e., "truths of some special science", FA, p. 4) is needed, it does not seem unreasonable to take this as Frege's version of such passages as this:

> It would be absurd to found an analytic judgment on experience. Since, in framing the judgment, I must not go outside my concept, there is no need to appeal to the testimony of experience in its support.[3]

This sketch of Frege's understanding of the Kantian distinction will allow us to motivate Frege's reconstrual of it. It is important to note, first, that many of Kant's remarks seem to indicate that he would have been committed to categorizing many of the truths of Frege's new logic as synthetic. In particular, many such truths will not be of subject/predicate form, and cannot be true by virtue of the predicate concept's being contained in the subject concept. In addition, the results of Frege's logic certainly seem to extend our knowledge,

---

[3] I. Kant, *Critique of Pure Reason*, tr. Norman Kemp Smith (New York, 1929), A7/B12.

and Kant seems to indicate that our knowledge can be extended only by synthetic truths (*Critique*, A8 B12). But Frege could not take any truths of the new logic to be synthetic. For this would be inconsistent with his understanding of the essential aims of logic. Frege took his logic to provide a unified account of how the parts of a proposition contribute to determining its truth or falsity – it is meant to be nothing other than a means of setting out the formal rules of all thought, the rules which make the use of the understanding possible. Such rules can hardly be counted as synthetic or as truths of a special science, for they must underly all knowledge. Given the aims of *Bs*, Frege has no choice but to take its results to be analytic. Thus he needs to reconstrue the Kantian analytic/synthetic distinction. Not surprisingly, he characterizes analytic judgments as those which follow from logic and an understanding (or analysis by means of definitions) of the concepts involved. In this way, he can claim to be saying what Kant meant by "analytic" and "synthetic". After all, in a passage which Frege cites (FA, p. 100), Kant seems to hint that analytic truths can be seen to be true from the principle of contradiction (logic) alone, while for synthetic truths some additional support (i.e., another synthetic proposition) is necessary (*Critique*, B14).

On this understanding of Frege's use of "analytic" and "synthetic" and of the role of *Bs*, we can give a philosophical motivation for his overall project – that of defining the numbers and proving the basic truths of arithmetic – as well as an explanation of the role of *Gl*. The philosophical motivation for Frege's project is to show that the truths of arithmetic are analytic.[4] It should be clear that proofs of the basic truths of arithmetic are necessary for this. After all, none of the truths of arithmetic appear in *Bs* as basic logical laws. Furthermore, definitions of the numbers will be necessary. For if the truths of arithmetic are to be justified by logic and the definitions of the terms involved, then all definable non-logical terms which occur in propositions of arithmetic, including the numerals, must be defined. (All numerals, of course, are non-logical terms – none appears in the notation of *Bs*.)

Accordingly, since Frege's aim is to show that the truths of arithmetic are analytic, he will need to define the numbers and prove the basic truths of arithmetic using only these definitions and the laws of logic. That is, he will need to produce a work of mathematics with a philosophical punchline. There is, then, an obvious role for *Gl* to play. The *Gl* can be viewed as setting out the philosophical picture within which *Gg* establishes the analyticity of the truths of arithmetic.

It would, however, be a mistake to view Frege as straightforwardly setting up a philosophical picture in *Gl* and arguing that, on this picture, the project of *Gg*

---

[4] It seems clear that Frege was antecedently convinced that the truths of arithmetic are analytic, i.e., immediately justified by the laws which make thinking possible. See, for instance, FA, p. 21.

will be of philosophical interest. Indeed, Frege does not set up a very complete picture at all. For Frege views his work as a contribution to a philosophical tradition which does not need to be spelled out by him. Unlike Frege, however, most members of this tradition considered it highly implausible that the truths of arithmetic could be analytic. Part of Frege's purpose, in writing *Gl*, was to give such people reasons for thinking the truths of arithmetic are analytic and the numbers definable. Thus, in Ch. I of *Gl*, Frege argues that the available arguments for taking the truths of arithmetic to be synthetic (in particular, Kant's and Mill's) are unsatisfactory. Frege then goes on to begin the work of defining the number one. In the process, he tries to show that our use of number words presupposes no special science, but only the laws which make thought possible. His aim is to convince his readers that the only concepts involved in our understanding of the use of the numbers are those which underly all language and thought. If successful in this, Frege will have provided philosophers with a powerful motivation for working through *Gg*.

This reading of Frege's project not only provides a role for *Gl*, but also eliminates some of the mystery about Frege's apparent lack of accounts of provability and definability. For, on this reading, *epistemological* constraints will determine the point at which it is permissible to stop proving or defining. And, if Frege can give acceptable definitions of the numbers and use them to prove the truths of arithmetic from the laws of logic, he need not even explicate these constraints. However, the strangeness of his actual definitions remains. Some of Benacerraf's deepest points concern the constraints which govern Frege's definitions and I would like to examine these in some detail.

III

Benacerraf says that, for purposes of defining the numbers, Frege "allows that different definitions, providing different referents . . . might have done as well" (Benacerraf, p. 30). Frege wants to give a definition of, for instance, the number one on which all those propositions which are standardly taken as truths of arithmetic will continue to be true. That is, any definition on which "$0 \neq 1$" is false will be unacceptable. But this constraint allows considerable leeway. Benacerraf's point is that Frege seems to be aware of the fact that there are alternative definitions which will meet this constraint, and seems to think that the choice between these alternatives is arbitrary. In fact, many of Frege's definitions seem to be arbitrary in this way. Another example is his discussion of defining "the True" and "the False". Benacerraf notes that Frege admits that the roles these terms must play do not determine whether the two truth-values "are themselves courses-of-values and if so, which ones" (p. 31). Benacerraf then quotes a passage in which Frege says "it is always possible to stipulate that an arbitrary course-of-values is to be the True and another the

False" (BLA, p. 48). Benacerraf goes on to say "Of course it does not make mathematical difference. But *that* it makes no mathematical difference is an important philosophical point concerning what we must construe definitions such as Frege's to accomplish." (*ibid.*) And earlier, "The moral is inescapable. Not even reference needs to be preserved" (p. 30). But this is misleading. Although our use of the word 'reference' may be largely due to Frege, its contemporary use is very different from Frege's use of '*Bedeutung*' (either in *Gl* or later). I will argue that Frege thought that, before *Gl* and *Gg*, our word 'one' and numeral '1' had no reference. That is, there was no reference to be preserved (or not preserved) by Frege's definitions. I will argue for this by returning to some of the problems Benacerraf sees for Frege's notion of definition.

An account of definition and definability is necessary, Benacerraf claims, in order to give accounts of proof and provability – which Frege also needs. There is obvious reason for thinking that Frege needs such accounts, whether we view his project as mathematical or as philosophical. For it seems that he requires that the truths of arithmetic be proved from primitive (unprovable) truths. Thus it may seem that, if we do not have a general account of what it is for a truth to stand in need of proof, we also have no general criteria for deciding if a proof of an arithmetical truth is finished (i.e., is a proof from primitive truths).

However, this does not necessarily follow. Although no general account of primitiveness has been given, we do know what some of the primitive truths are. The laws of logic, for instance, must be primitive truths, since every proof must be subject to them. And if Frege can give recognizable proofs of all the truths of arithmetic from recognizably primitive truths, a general account of primitiveness would be unnecessary. At first glance this seems to be exactly what Frege is doing. Frege's aim is to show that the truths of arithmetic are analytic and he tries (beginning with *Gl* and finishing in *Gg*) to show that all truths of arithmetic can be proved using only the general laws of logic and purely logical definitions of the numbers. Since *Bs* clearly demarcates the boundaries between logic and everything else, such a proof is easily identifiable.

But there is at least one apparent weakness in this story. If all definitions were primitive truths, then Benacerraf's criticism would carry no weight at all. However, Frege indicates at several points in *Gl* that definitions sometimes require justification. So it might seem that Frege must give criteria for identifying primitive definitions and hence criteria for determining when a definition is justified. Thus Benacerraf's claim that Frege can give no adequate account of definition seems significant. And most of Benacerraf's strongest criticisms are directed at Frege's understanding of definition.

While Frege gives no explicit account of the notion of definition, he says a great deal about it both in *Gl* and in his later philosophical papers and correspondence. Benacerraf's criticism of Frege's understanding of definition is based on two conditions of adequacy which he derives from these passages. His argument is that definitions which satisfy these conditions cannot play the role required of Frege's definitions of the number one and the concept number. The first condition is that the definition must not lead to contradiction. The other condition of adequacy is more problematic. This is that a definition must prove fruitful. I will argue that the fruitfulness requirement, as Benacerraf understands it, cannot hold of mathematical definitions, as Frege understands them. Thus if Frege's project is primarily mathematical, Benacerraf's interpretation of the fruitfulness requirement is wrong and his criticism of Frege's work is unconvincing. But since this criticism depends on understanding Frege's project as mathematical, it will also be unconvincing if Frege's project is taken to be epistemological.

Benacerraf derives the fruitfulness condition on definitions from the following passage:

> Definitions show their worth by proving fruitful. Those that could just as well be omitted and leave no link missing in the chain of our proofs should be rejected as completely worthless. (FA, p. 81)

Benacerraf interprets this to mean that if a definition does not provide the means for proving something which would not be provable without it, then the definition is not admissible (Benacerraf, p. 28). I will argue later that Benacerraf's reading of this passage is very nearly right for definitions which are to play epistemological roles, but that the admissibility must be understood as admissibility for *philosophical* purposes. However, the requirement Benacerraf describes cannot be taken as a general requirement for the admissibility of definitions, for it is easy to show that mathematical definitions, on Frege's view, need not meet such a requirement. In fact, I will argue that if the passage in question is understood as Benacerraf understands it, it explicitly contradicts virtually everything else Frege says about definitions. I will then go on to argue that Benacerraf's central criticisms are direct consequences of this misreading.

It is not at all obvious that Benacerraf's interpretation of Frege's fruitfulness requirement is correct in any sense. While Benacerraf's interpretation of this requirement follows from a plausible reading of the passage he cites, there are other plausible readings. In fact, Frege does not say explicitly that a definition is not admissible unless it is necessary for some proof in the passage Benacerraf cites or anywhere else in *Gl*. And Frege's other comments in *Gl* do not support Benacerraf's interpretation. For instance, there is at least one other passage in *Gl* which might be taken as a statement of the fruitfulness requirement. Frege says in the introduction:

> Even I agree that definitions must show their worth by their fruitfulness; it must be possible to use them for constructing proofs. (FA, p. IX)

And Frege's claim here, that it must be *possible* to use a definition in a proof, is very different from the fruitfulness requirement as Benacerraf understands it: that the definition must be *necessary* for some proof. Furthermore, in later writings Frege explicitly contradicts Benacerraf. The following passage from a 1914 paper "Logic in Mathematics", is typical:

> In fact it is not possible to prove something new from a definition alone that would be unprovable without it. When something that looks like a definition really makes it possible to prove something which could not be proved before, then it is not a mere definition, but must conceal something which would have either to be proved as a theorem or accepted as an axiom. (*PW*, p. 208)

Of course, this is not conclusive. Benacerraf might want to argue that Frege must have dropped the fruitfulness requirement after writing *Gl* but before writing the above passage. I will argue that this passage does not contradict anything Frege says about mathematical definitions in *Gl* and that there is a great deal of evidence that Frege's views on definition did not change.

It may be useful to begin by discussing Frege's example of a fruitful mathematical definition in *Gl*. This example is the definition of the continuity of a function (FA, p. 100). The definition itself is simply the statement that 'f is continuous at x' is to be true just in case $\lim_{y \to x} f(y) = f(x)$. Now it should be clear that this definition does not satisfy the fruitfulness condition as Benacerraf understands it, for any theorem in whose proof this definition figures can also be proved without use of the definition. Consider, for instance, the Intermediate-Value Theorem. This theorem can be stated as follows: Suppose that f is a real-valued function which is continuous on the interval $[a,b]$. Suppose also that $f(a) \neq f(b)$ and that Y is any number between $f(a)$ and $f(b)$. Then there exists a number X such that $a < X < b$ and $Y = f(X)$. Now since the assumption that f is continuous on $[a,b]$ is necessary and since the notion of continuity is not primitive, the definition of continuity figures in the proof of this theorem. And the above statement of this theorem could not be proved without using this definition. However, it does *not* follow that the Intermediate-Value Theorem could not be proved without the definition of continuity, for the theorem could be restated without any use of the word 'continuous'. It would be necessary only to substitute, for the condition that f is continuous on $[a,b]$, the condition that for any number c, in the interval $[a,b]$, $\lim_{y \to c} f(y) = f(c)$. It should be clear that a proof of this version of the Intermediate-Value Theorem would require no use of the definition of continuity. Similarly, any other theorem in which the word 'continuous' appears can be restated so as to be provable without any use of the definition of continuity. Thus it seems to follow that, according to Benacerraf, this definition does not satisfy Frege's fruitfulness requirement.

Benacerraf's most obvious response would seem to be to deny the above claim that the definition of continuity amounts to nothing more than the claim that 'f is continuous at x' is to be understood as an abbreviation for '$\lim_{y \to x} f(y) = f(x)$'. And it seems that Benacerraf has made this response, for he says:

> Definitions are not *simply* conventions of abbreviation, for if they were, the requirement of fruitfulness cited above would make little sense. (Benacerraf, p. 28)

It is not entirely clear how strongly 'simply' should be read, but it is clear that there is an important sense in which mathematical definitions, for Frege, *are* simply conventions of abbreviation. The following remark, for instance, is typical:

> No definition extends our knowledge. It is only a means for collecting a manifold content into a brief word or sign, thereby making it easier for us to handle. This and this alone is the use of definitions in mathematics. (FG, p. 24)

Thus, as far as mathematical definitions are concerned, Benacerraf seems to be wrong about what Frege regards as a fruitful definition.

There is also a sense in which the definition of continuity does satisfy the passage from which Benacerraf derives his interpretation of the fruitfulness requirement. In that passage Frege says that definitions which

> could just as well be omitted and leave no link missing in the chain of our proofs should be rejected as completely worthless.

If we understand this literally, the definition of continuity is not worthless. For, as they are stated, the proofs in which the notion of continuity figures do depend on this definition. If the definition were omitted without any restatement of the relevant theorems, there would be gaps in all such proofs. Of course, this may seem to make Frege's fruitfulness requirement entirely trivial – it simply amounts to saying that whatever mathematicians find useful for constructing proofs is fruitful. But it is not at all clear that Frege meant there to be any importantly non-trivial fruitfulness requirement for mathematical definitions. Whenever Frege actually enumerates conditions for the admissibility of definitions (in *Gg*, for example) this requirement is not even mentioned. Furthermore, for all its apparent triviality, this requirement does eliminate one sort of apparent definition which Frege does not want to consider a proper definition. He briefly mentions these in the introduction to *Gl*:

> Besides, even mathematical textbooks do at times lapse into psychology. When the author feels himself obliged to give a definition, yet cannot, then he tends to give at least a description of the way in which we arrive at the object or concept concerned. These cases can easily be recognized by the fact that such explanations are never referred to again in the course of subsequent exposition. For teaching purposes, introductory devices are certainly quite legitimate; only they should always be clearly distinguished from definitions. (FA, p. viii)

The trivial fruitfulness requirement described above does distinguish these introductory devices from definitions, for descriptions of how we arrive at an object or concept cannot figure in mathematical proofs.[5]

At this point, it should be clear that most of these remarks do not seem to apply to Frege's definitions of the number one and the concept Number. Frege wanted to prove all truths of arithmetic from primitive truths – truths which require no proof. Frege argued that the elementary propositions of arithmetic were not primitive truths. The purpose of giving definitions of the number one and the concept Number was to make it possible to prove the truths of arithmetic from primitive truths. In fact, Frege wanted to show that the truths of arithmetic could be proved from the primitive truths of logic. It is clear that,

---

[5] It should be clear from the above that taking mathematical definitions to be mere abbreviations does not directly contradict anything Frege says about fruitfulness in *Gl*. However, it is less clear that Frege can be read as having held this view of mathematical definitions in *Gl*. Thus it might be useful to consider the evidence that Frege's views on this subject did not change.

The first reason for thinking that Frege's views on definition (and, in particular, on mathematical definition) did not change is that many passages on definition from Frege's later works seem to be nothing more than explicit versions of passages from *Gl*. I will give two examples. First, in a letter to Hilbert, Frege says:

> Every definition contains a sign (expression, word) which previously has had no reference and which is given a reference only through this definition. Once this has happened, one can make out of this definition a self-evident proposition which is then to be used like an axiom. (FG, p. 7)

And, in one of the essays which grew out of this correspondence, he says,

> In mathematics what is called a definition is usually the stipulation of the reference of a word or a sign. A definition differs from all other mathematical propositions in that it contains a word or sign which hitherto has had no reference but which now acquires one through it. (FG, p. 23)

These passages seem to be reasonable ways of spelling out the following passage from *Gl*:

> The definition of an object does not, as such, really assert anything about the object, but only lays down the meaning (*Bedeutung*) of a symbol. After this has been done, the definition transforms itself into a judgment. (FA, p. 78)

Secondly, Frege says in his essays on the foundations of geometry:

> I demand from a definition of a point that by means of it we be able to judge of any object whatever – e.g., my pocket-watch – whether it is a point. (FG, p. 63)

without some such definitions, it would not be possible to prove what Frege wanted to prove – for no arithmetical terms appear in the notation of Bs. This is a sense in which Benacerraf's version of the fruitfulness requirement seems to hold on proposed definitions of the number one and the concept Number. However, this seems explicitly to contradict the passage from "Logic in Mathematics" in which Frege claimed that nothing new could be proved from a definition. Thus, unless there is some way for Frege to reconcile his general comments on the nature of definitions with the role played by his actual definitions of the number one and concept Number, there are serious problems. I will argue that such a reconciliation can be found in Frege's writings and that from a mathematical standpoint, his definitions of the number one and the concept Number *are* mere stipulations of the referent of a word. I will also argue that this is partly a result of Frege's rather strange understanding (to twentieth century analytic philosophers) of 'reference' (*Bedeutung*). For on Frege's view, few of the words we use in everyday contexts have reference. Among these referenceless words are such basic mathematical terms as 'one'

> It is not unreasonable to think that this may have been what Frege had in mind when, in *Gl*, he says that a definition of direction is deficient because
>> it will not, for instance, decide for us whether England is the same as the direction of the Earth's axis. (FA, p. 78)
>
> More generally:
>> If we are to use the symbol a to signify an object, we must have a criterion for deciding in all cases whether a is the same as b. (FA, p. 73)
>
> Thus there is some reason to believe that Frege's later explicit claims that definitions are no more than arbitrary abbreviations are implicit in *Gl* as well.
>
> There is another compelling reason for thinking that Frege's views on definition did not change, namely, that Frege explicitly says so in many of his later writings. For instance, in the first paper on the foundations of geometry (from which several of the above quotations were taken) Frege says:
>> The usage of the words 'axiom' and 'definition' as presented in this paper is, I think, the traditional and also the most expedient one. (FG, p. 25)
>
> And, lest one think that Frege had only just decided to use 'definition' in the traditional way, it may be useful to consider some of Frege's more vehement remarks. In his second paper on the foundations of geometry, Frege chastises Korselt for using 'definition' in a non-traditional sense. He says there:
>> Whoever wilfully deviates from the traditional sense of a word and does not indicate in what sense he wants to use it, whoever suddenly begins to call red what otherwise is called green, should not be astonished if he causes confusion. And if this occurs deliberately in science, it is a sin against science. (FG, p. 58)
>
> It does not seem likely that Frege viewed gimself as having sinned against science. And thus it does not seem unreasonable to assume that Frege viewed his use of 'definition' in *Gl* to have been in accord with the traditional sense. Finally, later in the second article, Frege indicates that he is still using 'definition' in the traditional sense. For, after some pages in which he describes definitions and their uses, Frege says:
>> What I have said holds true if we understand the word 'definition' as it has traditionally been understood in mathematics. (FG, p. 78)
>
> Because such passages occur throughout Frege's writings and because Frege never explicitly claims to have changed his notion of definition, I assume that Frege understood 'definition' in the same way throughout his career. I think that this assumption is further warranted by the fact that it *is* possible to give a unified account of Frege's early and later remarks on definition.

and 'number'. In order to understand how this works, it is necessary first to be clear about some of the ramifications of Frege's notion of definition.

IV

Frege is very clear about what a definition must do. A definition of an object-name, for Frege, must be given by a description which (provably) picks out one and only one object – the object picked out by such a description is the referent of the word which is to be defined by it. In *Gg*, for instance, Frege says that a particular property can be taken as a defining property for zero

> only when we have proved that there exists one object and only one object with the required property.[6]

Concept definitions are subject to similar requirements. A definition of a concept-word must be given by a description which determinately holds or does not of each object. The objects which fall under the concept are to be precisely those which satisfy the description. Frege says:

> A definition of a concept (of a possible predicate) must be complete; it must unambiguously determine, as regards any object, whether or not it falls under the concept (whether or not the predicate is truly assertible of it). Thus there must not be any object as regards which the definition leaves in doubt whether it falls under the concept; though for us men, with our defective knowledge, the question may not always be decidable. (TWF, p. 159)[7]

Frege's requirements on definitions and defining expressions are very strict, but it is not at all clear that this should create any problems. After all, while he claims to be using 'definition' in the traditional mathematical sense, it is easy enough to regard it as a technical mathematical term rather than as standing for

---

[6] In "Translation of Parts of Frege's *Grundgesetze der Arithmetik*," in TWF, p. 145. It is important to note that the use of the word 'one' in the statement of this criterion of adequacy for definitions does not in any way make Frege's definition of the number one (or its justification) circular. To say that, for instance, a description, D, picks out exactly one object is simply to make a claim of the following logical form: $(\exists x)[Dx \& (y)(Dy \leftrightarrow y = x)]$. Thus the criterion of adequacy can be stated without any use of the word 'one'.

[7] It should be emphasized that it does not follow that all knowledge is based on definitions. Frege accuses Korselt of inferring this from Frege's requirements on definitions and Frege responds by saying:

> The question of whether a given stone is a diamond cannot be answered by the mere explanation of the word 'diamond' itself. But we can demand of the explanation that it settle the question objectively, so that by means of it everyone well acquainted with the stone in question will be able to determine whether or not it is a diamond. (FG, p. 63)

Frege also indicates that some of the necessary knowledge might be obtainable only through the senses.

our ordinary notion of definition. However, his use of 'definition' cannot be isolated from his uses of 'reference' and 'admissibility for science'. It seems to follow, ultimately, that these too must be regarded as strange technical terms. For the requirements which must be met by arguments that a certain term is admissible for scientific use or has reference are closely related to Frege's requirements on defining expressions. For instance, it seems that, in order to justify the claim that a particular term is admissible for scientific use, one must produce an equivalent expression which meets the requirements on defining expressions. Frege says:

> So long as it is not completely defined, or known in some other way, what a word or symbol stands for, it may not be used in an exact science. (TWF, p. 160)

Of course it does not follow that we need a defining expression for the term in order to establish this. After all, we might know in some other way what the term stands for. What, then, are the general requirements on knowing what a term stands for? Let us begin by considering concept-expressions. If we are to be justified in claiming to know that a concept-expression is admissible for scientific use, we must at the very least have criteria for determining whether or not the concept it stands for holds of particular objects. It seems that Frege would require that these criteria meet the requirement for a defining expression – that they determinately hold or do not hold of each object. For he says:

> But if we ask, under what conditions a concept is admissible in science . . . The only requirement to be made of a concept is that it should have sharp boundaries; that is, that for every object it either falls under that concept or does not do so. (PW, p. 179)

If our criteria admit vague boundary cases, they do not determine a concept which has sharp boundaries; that is, a concept which, according to Frege, is acceptable for scientific use. Consequently, either we are not justified in claiming to know what the concept-expression stands for or the expression does not stand for a concept which is admissible in science. In either case, the term is not admissible for scientific use. The analogous requirement seems to hold on claims that object-names are acceptable for scientific use. Frege says:

> In logic it must be presupposed that every proper name is meaningful; that is, that it serves its purpose of designating an object . . . For instance, 'the A' would be a name that was in this way inadmissible for scientific use if it were formed by means of the definite article from a name of a concept under which either no object or more than one fell. (PW, pp. 179—80)

Thus if we know what it is that a particular object-name stands for (if the object-name is admissible in science) we must have criteria which pick out exactly one object. Finally, it also seems that, for Frege, a term is admissible in science just in case it has a reference. He says

> In scientific use, a proper name has the purpose of designating an object; and in case this purpose is achieved, this object is the reference of the proper name. The same thing holds for concept-signs, relation-signs, and function-signs. (FG, p. 55)

While Frege's actual words do leave open the possibility that, in non-scientific contexts, we might plausibly say that a concept (object) expression stood for a concept (object) with vague boundaries, there is no evidence that Frege himself would have accepted this. He never, for instance, indicates that the objects and concepts of science are in any way special or strange for their precise boundaries, although he often indicates that scientific terms are special (or, at least, different from ordinary terms) because of their precision (see, in particular, the early papers on Bs). It seems more likely that Frege would say that, in our ordinary discourse, some of our terms are vague and ambiguous than that he would say they denote vague concepts.[8] But even if he admitted that a term might refer to a vague concept, he would still have to make a distinction between those terms which could be viewed as having reference for ordinary purposes but not for scientific purposes.[9] Thus, even if a term ordinarily denotes some vague concept or object, we would have to say that, for

---

[8] Since Frege rarely talks about the consequences of this for ordinary language, it is difficult to make claims about what Frege would say. However, I think it is pretty clear that Frege would not allow us to say that there are vague concepts. He says, in § 62 of Gg that concepts without sharp boundaries are not concepts at all, but "inadmissible sham concepts" (TWF, p. 145). In § 56 (TWF, p. 139), he gives the following description of vague concepts:
> If we represent concepts in extension by areas on a plane, this is admittedly a picture that may be used only with caution, but here it can do us good service. To a concept without sharp boundary there would correspond an area that had not a sharp boundary-line all round, but in places just vaguely faded away into the background. This would not really be an area at all; and likewise a concept that is not sharply defined is *wrongly termed a concept*.

And, later in the same section, he adds,
> Has the question 'Are we still Christians?' really got a sense, if it is indeterminate whom the predicate 'Christian' can truly be ascribed to, and who must be refused it?

[9] Note here that I say "even if". I do not believe that Frege would admit that a term might refer to a vague concept. I do not believe that Frege made a distinction between those terms which could be viewed as having reference for ordinary purposes but not for scientific purposes. As a matter of fact, it seems quite likely that Frege meant there to be one and only one way to understand 'reference' (*'Bedeutung'*) and that this is what I have described as "reference for scientific purposes". Frege's comment in "On the Foundations of Geometry" (FG, p. 62) that "A sign without determinate reference is a sign without reference" is a typical remark. However, the point I wish to make here is that, even if Frege were to distinguish between ordinary reference and reference for scientific purposes, the significant notion of reference would be the latter. For, when he discusses the status of the number one, Frege must be discussing reference for scientific purposes. And he says (FG, p. 62)
> A word without a determinate reference has no reference so far as mathematics is concerned.

scientific purposes, the term has no reference. Since, in fact, Frege is uninterested in ordinary language but only in scientific language (see, again, the early papers on *Bs*), there seems no harm in understanding 'reference' for our purposes as the strict sort of reference for scientific purposes described above. To have reference in this sense is simply to be admissible for scientific use.

Of course, this sense of 'reference' is somewhat different from most current ways of understanding the term. In particular on this view very few of our everyday or scientific terms have reference. Nevertheless I believe this is how Frege ultimately came to understand '*Bedeutung*'. To see what this notion of reference comes to, it will be useful to consider the consequences for arithmetic. According to this view, 'one' and 'number' were not acceptable for scientific use before Frege's work and, for scientific purposes, must be viewed as having had no reference until then. The problem is that our use of these words does not determine the sort of criteria described above. To see that this is true, it is important to remember that we are starting only with accepted propositions of arithmetic and mathematical practice, for this exhausts the evidence which can be derived from our normal use of these words. Any claim to knowledge of what 'one' and 'number' stand for must be based on this. And it is clear, at least by now, that neither the accepted propositions of arithmetic nor mathematical practice suffices to determine the required criteria. It is highly implausible, for instance, that Mill and Frege would have disagreed on any truth of arithmetic. Yet Mill claims that numbers are properties of physical objects while Frege claims that they are not. More recently, some mathematicians have worked with different models for the truths of arithmetic. Thus our ordinary everyday knowledge of arithmetic – even the knowledge a mathematician has of arithmetic – does not determine criteria which will allow us to say, in Frege's sense, that 'number' stands for a proper concept.

This consequence points up the strangeness of Frege's criteria. In spite of his objections, mathematicians had used 'one' and 'number' for some time without any difficulty and without any definition of the sort Frege required. His formulation of definitions of these words did not change actual mathematical practice. Thus it makes little difference for scientific practice whether or not a word is, in Frege's sense, acceptable for scientific use.

The point, of course, is that philosophical, not scientific, criteria determine, for Frege, what is acceptable for scientific use. His assumption is that every legitimate science must have a proper epistemological foundation. His purpose in making sure that 'one' and 'number' stand for acceptable concepts or objects is neither to show that some previously accepted mathematical results are actually false (true) nor to enable mathematicians to prove new results. Frege's real purpose is to make clear, from within his epistemological perspective, how it is that we can have knowledge of truths of arithmetic. As he argues in the first chapter of *Gl*, our ordinary use of 'one' and 'number' does not make this clear.

However, it does not seem entirely clear that giving criteria for determining whether or not something is a number (or whether or not something is the number one) should enable us to see the source of the justification of claims about numbers. In order to see how this is supposed to do this work, it is important to see what is involved in making clear the reference of a term.

On Frege's view, there are two sorts of means for making clear what a term stands for: definitions and hints. He says:

> It is not possible to give a regular definition of everything; for it must be our endeavour to go back to what is logically simple and as such cannot properly be defined. I must then be satisfied with indicating by hints what I mean. (TWF, p. 151)

Hints, of course, are less satisfactory than definitions. Hints cannot be used in scientific investigations and require a certain amount of cooperative understanding if their use is to be successful. Hints are only acceptable alternatives to definitions if the term in question is logically simple and cannot be defined. All other terms must be defined and, moreover, defined from primitive terms ("it must be our endeavour to go back to what is logically simple"). The relation between Frege's epistemological concerns and this understanding of what is required to make clear what a term stands for stems from the epistemological features of primitive (logically simple) terms. For Frege assumes that the source of our knowledge about primitive elements (i.e., those things which are denoted by logically simple terms) will be obvious.[10] Thus there are epistemological reasons for defining a term even when there is no doubt about what it stands for. Frege says

> The real importance of a definition lies in its logical construction out of primitive elements. And for that reason we should not do without it, not even in a case like this. The insight it permits into the logical structures . . . is a condition for insight into the logical linkage of truths. (FG, p. 61)

This insight into the logical linkage of truths, along with our access to the source of the justification of claims about primitive elements, will help us to determine the source of our justification of such things as the propositions of arithmetic. For, if all non-primitive terms in a proposition are defined from logically simple terms, then the original proposition can be derived from a proposition containing only primitive terms. Since the source of our knowledge about primitive elements will be obvious, the source of our knowledge of this new proposition will be obvious. Finally, since the original proposition is derivable from the new proposition, the source of our knowledge of the original

---

[10] For instance, the basis of Frege's argument in *Gl* that 'number' and 'one' are not primitive is that we do not immediately recognize the source of our knowledge about numbers and one.

proposition will be the same as the source of our knowledge of the new proposition. Hence, to find the ultimate grounds of our knowledge of some proposition, it will suffice to determine the primitive terms from which its terms can be defined. The implicit picture is that any science is based on a small number of logically primitive terms from which all other terms can be defined (or, into terms of which all other terms are analysable). Frege says:

> To be sure, that on which we base our definitions may itself have been defined previously; however, when we retrace our steps further, we shall always come to something which, being a simple, is indefinable, and must be admitted incapable of further analysis. And the properties belonging to these ultimate building blocks of a discipline contain, as it were *in nuce*, its whole contents . . . Now it is clear that the boundaries of a discipline are determined by the nature of its ultimate building blocks. (FG, p.143)

Thus when Frege asks for a definition of some term of some science, he is not only asking what the term stands for, but also what the fundamental building blocks of that science are. The purpose of finding these is to determine its ultimate grounds.

Unfortunately, all this talk about the analysis of complex scientific terms seems at odds with the passages discussed earlier on definitions. For it is not at all clear how arbitrary abbreviations can consist of this sort of foundational analysis of a term. Frege says:

> My opinion is this: We must admit logically primitive elements that are indefinable. Even here there seems to be a need to make sure that we designate the same thing by the same sign (word). Once the investigators have come to an understanding about the primitive elements and their designations, agreement about what is logically composite is easily reached by means of definition. Since definitions are not possible for primitive elements, something else must enter in. I call it explication. It is this, therefore, that serves the purpose of mutual understanding among investigators as well as of the communications of the science to others. (FG, p. 59)

But this appears to fit in neither with the view of definitions as arbitrary abbreviations nor with the view of definitions as consisting of analyses of the terms which are to be defined. For the view expressed in this passage seems to be a view of defining as a part of the building of a science from the foundations up. But it is not clear how a term can be simultaneously analyzed and constructed out of foundations. It would seem either that the term is already (implicitly or explicitly) constructed out of primitive terms, in which case the analysis consists of merely elucidating what is already there (and hence it is not being constructed), or that the term is being constructed initially from primitive terms, in which case there is no antecedent content to be analyzed. *Neither* of these stories seems to fit in with Frege's project of defining the number one. Frege cannot be creating a new science by constructing a definition of 'one' from primitive terms, for there already is a science of arithmetic. But Frege also cannot be merely elucidating the content of 'one' by constructing, in primitive terms, a description which picks out what 'one' already stands for. For the truths of arithmetic do not determine a particular object for which 'one' must stand.

Frege's reaction to these incongruities can be found in one of his later papers, "Logic and Mathematics", although there are hints at this answer in earlier works. Frege says there:

> Now we shall have to consider the difficulty we come up against in giving a logical analysis when it is problematic whether this analysis is correct. Let us assume that A is the long established sign (expression) whose sense we have attempted to analyse logically by constructing a complex expression that gives the analysis. Since we are not certain whether the analysis is successful, we are not prepared to present the complex expression as one which can be replaced by the simple sign A. If it is our intention to put forward a definition proper, we are not entitled to choose the sign A, which already has a sense, but we must choose a fresh sign B, say, which has the sense of the complex expression only in virtue of the definition. The question now is whether A and B have the same sense. But we can bypass this question altogether if we are constructing a new system from the bottom up; in that case we shall make no further use of the sign A — we shall only use B . . . If we have managed in this way to construct a system for mathematics without any need for the sign A, we can leave the matter there; there is no need at all to answer the question concerning the sense in which – whatever it may be – this sign had been used earlier . . . However, it may be felt expedient to use sign A instead of sign B. But if we do this, we must treat it as an entirely new sign which had no sense prior to the definition. (PW, pp. 210—11)

This, of course, is a description of Frege's project of defining the number one. Frege *is* building a science from the bottom up. But Frege is not building an arbitrary science from the bottom up – he is building a science which can replace arithmetic. The strategy for constructing such a science is as follows. First, Frege has already argued that arithmetic is based on two fundamental terms, '1' and 'number', that is, that all terms of arithmetic are definable from these terms. Consequently, any proposition of arithmetic is logically equivalent to a proposition whose only arithmetical terms are '1' and 'number'. Frege's next step is to

(i) define two terms, G and H, say, such that whenever, in what has been regarded by mathematicians as a true proposition of arithmetic, all occurrences of '1' and 'number' are replaced by G and H respectively, the resulting proposition will be true, and

(ii) using these terms, give correct (i.e. gapless) versions of all proofs of arithmetic in his constructed science.

Once the first of these tasks is accomplished it will be relatively easy to accomplish the second. For Frege need only translate all propositions in the arithmetical proof into logically equivalent propositions in which the only arithmetical terms are '1' and 'number' and then replace '1' and 'number' with G and H, and rectify any relevant gaps. The result will be a logically valid proof in Frege's constructed science. And there is nothing particularly special about the symbols '1' and 'number'. Thus mathematical practice would not be appreciably altered by replacing '1' and 'number' with G and H. In this sense, then, Frege's constructed science can replace arithmetic. In fact, Frege's new science might even be called 'arithmetic' without doing violence to the activities of mathematicians. Furthermore, once arithmetic is replaced by Frege's science, '1' and 'number' need not be regarded as terms which had a sense prior to Frege's work, for arithmetic will have been thrown out altogether. Consequently, G and H might themselves be replaced by '1' and 'number', provided that these are regarded as defined terms of Frege's newly constructed science.

In addition to constructing his new science so that it can replace arithmetic, Frege wants to construct this science in a way which will make clear its epistemological roots. In particular, Frege's object is to get definitions of G and H in purely logical terms. Thus the truths of Frege's new science will be logical truths. The truths of Frege's science which seem, from the perspective of pre-Fregean arithmetic, to be primitive and irreducible truths of arithmetic will be provable in *Bs*. If mathematicians are now regarded as proving results in Frege's new science, then Frege will have provided epistemological foundations for arithmetic.

While Frege is not commonly taken to be engaged in the sort of project described above, this sort of project should not be entirely unfamiliar to the reader. Consider, for instance, some of Carnap's comments about explication in the introduction to *Logical Foundations of Probability*. He says there

> The task of explication consists in transforming a given more or less inexact concept into an exact one or, rather, in replacing the first by the second.
> Perhaps the form 'explicans' might be considered instead of 'explicatum'; however, I think the analogy with the terms 'definiendum'

and 'definiens' would not be useful because, if the explication consists in giving an explicit definition, *both the definiens and the definiendum in this definition express the explicatum, while the explicandum does not occur.*[11]

Frege's definitions of 'one' and 'number' are explications in this sense. 'One' and the complex expression which Frege uses to define it have the same sense, but they have the same sense only in virtue of the definition. The definition does not consist of an analysis of what was previously understood by 'one', it should be viewed as nothing more nor less than an abbreviation. While the purpose of Frege's definitions is to provide foundations for arithmetic in the sense described above, the fact that Frege's definitions are formulated for this purpose is only a part of a hidden agenda; it is in no way a part of the actual definition.

V

I have argued that Frege's attempt to define the number one should be viewed as a central part of an epistemological project. I have also argued that, if we view Frege's definition of '1' as part of such a project, Frege's notions of definition, of defining, and of reference begin to look very strange indeed. For it follows from this picture that the numerals had no reference before Frege's work. It follows, as well, that the propositions of arithmetic had no truth values before Frege's work. These very strange consequences may seem to constitute a *reductio* of my reading of Frege (particularly given that I have seen fit to criticize Benacerraf for giving a reading on which Frege's project fails in too obvious a way). However, I think it is important to realize that the claim that the numerals had no reference, and the propositions of arithmetic no truth-values, before Frege's work is not obviously a mistake. This claim is only obviously wrong on our contemporary understanding of 'reference' and 'truth', and I have argued that it is wrong to assume that Frege understood such philosophical terms as we do today.

The apparent problem with the consequence I have drawn arises only if we see Frege as engaging in an attempt to show how words hook into the world, and if we view the reference relation as this connection. But I think that this perspective is mistaken. Frege's philosophical motivations, as I understand them, have little to do with establishing a link between words and the world. Indeed I would argue that, for Frege, the question of how words hook into the

---

[11] Rudolf Carnap, *The Logical Foundations of Probability* (Chicago, 1962), p. 3. Cf. Michael Resnik, *Frege and the Philosophy of Mathematics* (Ithaca, 1980).

world is not even formulable except in an entirely trivial sense.[12] On my reading, showing that a term has reference amounts to showing either that it is (epistemologically) primitive or that we have what amounts to the appropriate sort of definition of this term from primitive terms. One purpose of showing that a term has reference is to exhibit the epistemological foundation of the science in which it is used. The other is to guarantee that there is no ambiguity or vagueness in our understanding of the term. I claim that these possibilities exhaust the role of reference in Frege's picture. If this is right, it should not be surprising that many propositions lack truth values. For Frege thought that the definitions given by mathematicians of his day were simply inadequate and should not be used in proofs. In Frege's view, these mathematicians really did not know what they were talking about. Thus it is not difficult to see how Frege might have taken the propositions formulated and "proved" by these mathematicians not to have truth-values. Frege seems to have similar worries about everyday propositions. He says in *Gg* (TWF, 139) that the question 'Are we still Christians?' has not even a sense unless it is determinate to whom the predicate 'Christian' can truly be ascribed (i.e., unless we have criteria which determine a definition in Frege's sense). By these standards, the vagueness and ambiguity of most everyday terms will render most ordinary propositions truth-valueless.

Benacerraf began his paper by criticizing the tendency of many late-twentieth century philosophers to read Frege's work as if it had been written by a late-twentieth century philosopher. His central point is that Frege is not one of us. In this I think he is entirely correct. But there is a sense in which Benacerraf errs by not taking this advice seriously enough. The Frege described by Benacerraf does not really seem very foreign to someone with a late-twentieth sensibility, just a mathematician who failed in his overall project but who, in the process, made very interesting contributions. But this Frege fails at a very superficial level – there seems to be an obvious and irresoluble tension between the role of his definitions of the number one and concept Number and his understanding of definition and definability. I have tried to show that if we abandon the assumption that Frege's work is primarily mathematical, a careful examination of this tension suggests a coherent and exciting interpretation of Frege's work. Of course, as we have seen, on this interpretation Frege's concerns seem very different from those of philosophers today. Benacerraf is almost certainly right to claim that if Frege's position is logicism, Frege was the last logicist. But I think it highly unlikely that Frege was Benacerraf's last logicist.

The University of Wisconsin-Milwaukee

[12] I argue this in Weiner, *Putting Frege in perspective* (Doctoral Dissertation: Harvard University, 1982, Ch. V.)

THE SENSE OF A NAME

By MICHAEL LUNTLEY

Names have sense and each name has a unique sense attached to it. These Fregean theses are the subject of this paper and I shall argue that each is correct.

The notion of sense has fallen into disrepute in many quarters, mainly as a result of confusion over the metaphors used in discussing the concept. For example, sense is the *mode of presentation* associated with a name; and sense *determines* reference, which suggests an overtly active role for sense as something which is used in applying names to objects. It is as if the sense of a name were a map one had to defer to in using a name correctly. I shall remedy such confusions in what follows. Perhaps the most fundamental confusion at this general metaphorical level occurs with respect to the question, 'What kind of entity is the sense of a name?' Too often it has seemed that sense must be some *extra* thing attached to a name over and above its referent when it should have been apparent, as it now more commonly is, that sense is not a *thing* at all. Sense is to do with the concept of understanding (cf. FPL, p. 90ff.); it is the knowledge a speaker must possess in order to use a name correctly. So the thesis that names have sense comes to the claim that an account of what it is for a speaker to use a name correctly must include reference to some particular knowledge that the speaker has. Such knowledge would be, for example, knowledge of the *criterion of identity* for the bearer of the name, in the way in which Frege introduced that notion (*Gl* §62). The thesis that each name has a unique sense would then seem to be the claim that a speaker's grasp of the use of a name consists in his grasp of a uniquely determining criterion of identity for the name's bearer. Doubts about the plausibility of such a thesis have run the notion of sense for names into disrepute. Such a thesis is what is questioned when, on taking the relevant criterion of identity as some definite description, it is noted that, with respect to any given name, competent users of the name may associate with it different definite descriptions. Thus examples such as the Gödel/Schmidt case (cf. Kripke 1, p. 83ff.) are easily constructed to show that if our understanding of names functions in a manner like that suggested, then it would seem that we should all be talking at cross-purposes with such names, when patently we are not. Manoeuvres designed to avoid this problem are easily criticised and rapidly lead to the view that a "description theory of names" is wholly discredited.[1]

I dislike the identification of the thesis that names have sense with the label 'description theory of names' not because I take it to be false that a criterion of identity for a name's bearer must, if stateable, be stateable as a definite description, but because it too easily invites comparison with the "Cluster Theory" of names. More importantly, the label encourages an individualistic notion of sense, the belief that Frege's views on this matter involve conceiving of language as the intersection of the several speakers' idiolects. It is precisely the lack of any guaranteed community of sense, as the notion is caricatured in the so-called "description theory" and, perhaps, as it is found in Frege, that has lead to the disparagement of sense in general. The account of sense to be presented below will seek to remedy this defect.

I

The thesis that names have sense may be characterised thus:

> Names have sense iff an account of what it is for a speaker to have mastered correct use of a name consists in an account of a certain body of information that speaker has.

What body of information would suffice here? One thought, which has been promoted into a theory of sense for names by McDowell (see McDowell), is that what the speaker must know of any name 'NN' is that

> 'NN' stands for NN.

This thought, whether or not it be employed in a McDowellian austere theory of sense, is, I take it, in one way or another, acceptable to any theorist of names. Someone who holds a causal theory of names, that is, someone who holds that there is no useful role for any cognitive notion like sense at all in an account of the functioning of names, would surely still accept that the successful user of the name 'Hesperus' knows that

(1) 'Hesperus' stands for Hesperus.

Where a causal theorist will differ from McDowell is in the significance which he assigns to such facts. The causal theorist will accept that a competent user of the name 'Hesperus' knows the above fact but, unlike McDowell, will not take this as constitutive of his competence with the name. We might then rephrase the above preliminary thesis to accommodate this minimal constraint on what the knowledge must be in a theory of sense for names:

---

[1] See, for example, Simon Blackburn's disparagement of a Fregean theory of proper names in "Thought and Things", *Aristotelian Society Supp. Vol.* 53 (1979).

T Names have sense iff an account of what it is for a speaker to have mastered correct use of a name consists in an account of what it is for the speaker to know, of some name 'NN', that 'NN' stands for NN.

I can now state my central claim. Contrary to causal theories of names, there is indeed something to be said about what it is to know that 'NN' stands for NN. This is a complex cognitive state, the characterisation of which just is what a theory of sense provides; and, *pace* McDowell, characterisation of this state is neither as simple nor as austere as he suggests.

Following McDowell, some simple distinctions must be observed if T is not to reduce to triviality. It is, of course, true that clauses like (1) state the referent of the name 'Hesperus' and do not *state* its sense. However, T only requires that *knowledge* of such a clause is knowledge of the sense of 'Hesperus'. That is, for any competent speaker of the language, S, we must distinguish the following cognitive states:

(2) S knows the referent of 'Hesperus'

and

(3) S knows that 'Hesperus' stands for Hesperus.

(2) is a case of knowledge of *things*; (3) is knowledge of *truths*. Knowing the referent of a name is knowledge of things, whereas knowing that a name has a particular referent is knowing its sense. Clearly S may be as characterised in (2) without being as characterised in (3). Although he may know the thing Hesperus, he may know it under another name, perhaps 'Phosphorus', or by no name at all. Furthermore, we must take care to distinguish (3) from the distinct cognitive state:

(4) S knows that " 'Hesperus' stands for Hesperus" is a truth.

This should be easy. One can be in a state such as (4), knowing that 'p' is a truth, without knowing that p. For example, 'p' might be a sentence of a foreign language not understood by the subject yet known to be a truth because reported by a reliable witness. Commoner cases abound when one is ignorant of the meaning of a constituent of the embedded sentence. In such cases it is highly unappealing to say that, as well as knowing that 'p' is a truth, I also know that p. However, although the distinction between (3) and (4) is incontrovertible, reflection upon it serves to elicit a strong prima facie reason why we need a theory of sense for names.

The point is that the distinction between (3) and (4) relies on the possibility that the subject in question fails to grasp the sense of the embedded sentence, or some part thereof. In other words, if (4) is already true of S then what more is necessary, in order that (3) come to be true of him, is that he come to *understand* the sentence, " 'Hesperus' stands for Hesperus". But in order to understand that sentence, S must, of course, understand 'Hesperus'. And now, if *all* there is to say about such understanding is – as McDowell holds – what is said by (3), we wind up in a position where nothing more illuminating can be said about the knowledge which carries S from (4) to (3) except that (3) comes to be true of him. This seems to me utterly unsatisfying. There must surely be some substantial account of what it is to know of some name 'NN' that it stands for NN. Just such an account is the task of a theory of sense for names.

It might be denied that there is any task at all here for either of two reasons. Either one assumes that knowing that 'Hesperus' stands for Hesperus is simply a case of knowing of some object immediately given that it is called 'Hesperus'; or one supposes that although there is something more that may be said about what it is to recognise an object as the bearer of a name, no descriptive analysis is possible of the kind of knowledge attributed by (3), which is founded on our possession of certain irreducible perceptual skills for recognising immediately and non-inferentially that x is NN. I take the second to be McDowell's position.[2] By the phrase 'immediately given' in the first objection I mean to capture the thought that one may be acquainted with an object without being acquainted with it, as Frege would say, under a mode of presentation. This depends on how we understand this Fregean metaphor and I shall come to that shortly. More perspicuously, it might be said that, on the first objection, no further characterisation of the knowledge attributed to S by (3) is required, for his knowledge is essentially dependent upon his perception of Hesperus in a way that makes it true that (3) comes to something like:

(5) S knows that 'Hesperus' stands for *that*,

where the fact that he picks out the object demonstratively is meant to capture the idea that S has some bare acquaintance with the object. I find this notion extremely difficult to capture but, at the same time, it is widespread. It is what Evans was getting at when he spoke of the idea that one may think of an object in a particularly intimate way or that the subject be *en rapport* with the object.[3] I shall use the expression 'bare acquaintance with an object' to capture this idea. The fundamental point behind the thesis that names have sense is then that there is no such thing as bare acquaintance with objects. This is another way of putting the point that S's knowledge in (3) is cognitively complex. I do

---

[2] See the remarks about perceptual capacities in McDowell, p. 165f.
[3] Evans, p. 65. The idea of *rapport* goes back at least to Kaplan's "Quantifying In", *Synthese* 19 (1968), if not indeed to Russell. The notion goes under the name of 'direct cognitive contact' in J. Kim, "Perception and Reference without Causality", *Journal of Philosophy*, 74 (1977). The notion is also, I take it, part-and-parcel of the idea that, in one sense of the phrase, *de re* thoughts are thoughts where the object concerned is *part* of the content of the thought; cf. Woodfield's foreword to *Thought and Object*, ed. A. Woodfield (Oxford, 1982) and the papers therein. I shall not, except for a few passing remarks, have anything further to say about the nature of the representative content of thought; it would involve tackling too much in one go. However, in so far as the account of a name's sense given below is not a static notion as of one description or set of descriptions, then it does bear upon how we treat the notion of representative content.

not think McDowell intends his theory to entail the possibility of bare acquaintance with objects, but I am not sure whether his account of irreducible perceptual capacities for recognising an object as the bearer of a name really avoids it. The position I shall defend will make use of this notion of perceptual capacities but will add a further constraint on their intelligible ascription to someone which will serve to rule out the bare acquaintance thesis. We can perhaps best approach the issue of the cognitive complexity of (3) through a brief recapitulation of Frege's thought.

II

On a Fregean theory of sense a fuller characterisation of (3) is available. Where we have some descriptive phrase, e.g., 'the star that rises in the evening', which gives the sense of the name because it uniquely determines, [4] at least for S, the referent, then we may more fully describe the state referred to in (3) as[5]

(6) S knows that 'Hesperus' stands for the star that rises in the evening.

This, of course, is to follow Frege's advice that in *oratio obliqua* a name stands for its sense, not its referent. Reflection upon (6) serves to de-mythologise this doctrine. It is not that names suddenly stand for queer entities called "senses", but that they stand for normal objects, though in a more roundabout manner. The star that rises in the evening is as respectable an object as Hesperus and is, indeed, the same object. But that the sense which S gives to 'Hesperus' serves to enable him to refer to Hesperus is a contingent fact which cannot be assumed by semantic theory. To say that in *oratio obliqua* 'Hesperus' stands for its sense is just to say that we must assess the truth of S's thought about Hesperus, not by appealing to Hesperus directly, but by the means by which the sense purports to determine the object. We use the description, knowledge of which constitutes the speaker's grasp of the sense of the name, in order that we may say what we mean when we ascribe to S the knowledge given in (3); that is, in order that we may distinguish it from the knowledge ascribed in (4).

These remarks dispel the objection that on Frege's account of *oratio obliqua*, the assertion that Fa and the belief that Fa are about different things, for the object of the belief is the thought expressed by 'Fa' – dependent on the sense of

---

[4] As with 'mode of presentation', I shall return to consider what it means to say sense *determines* reference.

[5] That we have to use a definite description to verbalise the sense does not mean that the knowledge constitutive of the sense of the name *equals* knowledge of that definite description; the knowledge is a complex capacity which may be manifested in several ways.

'a' – whereas the assertion, in order for there to be communication, has to be taken to be about a. Provided the subject has correctly grasped the sense of 'a', however, his thought will be about a, the only restraint being that we judge of the correctness of his thought by appeal to this object under the description which characterises the sense he gives to the name. If we want to know whether someone believes something true of some object, it is no good referring to that object in a manner which would not be recognised as a reference by the subject in question. That much is obvious, but also encapsulates the point of taking names, in *oratio obliqua*, to refer to their senses and not their usual referents. When we no longer think of sense as a queer sort of entity we need no longer think of this doctrine as a queer sort of confusion. Of course, if the subject has failed to grasp the sense of 'a' correctly, then in asserting that Fa he may possibly have a true thought without making a true assertion. That, in such cases, we are more interested in the correctness of the assertion than of the particular thought which the subject idiosyncratically expresses by his words, does not tell against the idea of sense *per se*, but rather in favour of a public and objectively testable notion of sense. In making assertions we bare our thoughts to the scrutiny of public accountability and the need for communication requires that we have our thoughts assessed not only for truth but also for correctness of expression. It is not enough that I have true thoughts about the present Prime Minister by referring to her as "Tina" in a private idiolect; I must also, if I am to communicate my thoughts, respect the common stock of names and senses.

Such a Fregean theory of sense seems to involve what McDowell and others are at pains to deny (see e.g., McDowell p. 166), namely, that we have need of a "route" from name to bearer – a criterion by which we pick out the object. Is this not an extravagance? Assuming that our principal interest is in assessment of assertions by appeal to the object, rather than in assessment of an individual's thought by appeal to the sense he gives to a name, why should we not do away with sense altogether, except in explaining cases of private idiolects? This is a fairly common thought, but once we understand the metaphors "route" and "mode of presentation" correctly, I do not think that it can be sustained without support from the notion of bare acquaintance with particulars. We can approach this matter in the following way. There does *seem* to be a sense in which no more needs to be said about (3). For a semantic theory it is sufficient that we state what the speaker knows and not be sidetracked by questions of *how* he came to know it. However, if knowledge of the form of (3) is to be constitutive of a speaker's capacity to use a name correctly, and if that knowledge is not to be construed richly in the crudely Fregean manner of (6), it is necessary that what that knowledge is can be explained without treating its object as a Fregean thought. We are thus led directly to the notion of bare acquaintance with objects.

III

Let us ask whether, on a non-Fregean account of (3), S could have that knowledge which is essential for a correct use of 'Hesperus' without possessing the knowledge expressed in (2), knowledge of its referent? It seems, on the contrary, that the knowledge in (3) entails knowledge of the referent of the name. This entailment is required in order that the second occurrence of 'Hesperus' in (3) should stand for Hesperus itself and not a Fregean sense, as in (6). Now it might be thought that the knowledge in (3) could be had without knowledge of the thing Hesperus, for all that is required is that the speaker's knowledge be such as to enable him to derive, for any utterance containing 'Hesperus', the corresponding truth-condition containing Hesperus. Surely, the objection might go, such a requirement is met simply by invoking (3), regardless of whether S knows Hesperus at all. The knowledge in (3) would suffice in the case of utterances like 'Hesperus is bright' for S to derive the truth-condition,

Hesperus is bright.

Why, then, should it be thought that (3) entails (2)? The answer is that without this entailment we are unable to distinguish those cases where S's knowledge is of a kind with (4) from those of a kind with (3). For, if all that matters in our description of those of S's cognitive states which constitute his understanding of the language is that he be able to derive appropriate truth-conditions for a given utterance, then knowledge of the form of (4) will suffice. With such knowledge S will be able, upon hearing an utterance containing 'Hesperus', to derive the appropriate truth-condition containing Hesperus. But as we have already noted, the knowledge in (4) may be had even when the subject does not *understand* the sentence involved.

All this serves to emphasise that the ability to derive truth-conditions alone is not enough for understanding a language. S also needs to know the point of making the derivation licensed by his knowledge in (4). We can grant him some such knowledge if we grant him knowledge of the thing Hesperus. So we have arrived at an answer to the question I posed for McDowell's theory, and for non-Fregean theories generally. Such theories may distinguish (3) from (4), without saying that in (3) S knows the sense of 'Hesperus', by saying that in (3), and not in (4), S knows Hesperus, the referent of the name. And by saying that S knows the referent of 'Hesperus' I mean only this: that S has the capacity to differentiate and discriminate Hesperus-like sensory stimulations; that is, he has the ability to pick out this thing as a determinate, possibly recurring, feature of his experience. The question then is whether or not *such* knowledge, as expressed in (2), can be cognitively simple. McDowell certainly thinks it can (this is the point of his notion of irreducible perceptual capacities) and I take it to be constitutive of causal theorists' low regard for (3) that they also take (2) to be cognitively simple. That (2) is cognitively simple is, as I mean it, the thought that one's knowledge of this object is a matter of bare acquaintance. Seeing (3) as entailing (2) is, in effect, to re-read (3) along the lines of (5).[6]

But now, if knowing the sense of a name, (3), implies knowing its referent, (2), it would appear that this conception of sense is, despite its austerity, a very strong one. We would not normally expect that a person could only be said to understand a name if he knew its referent. Knowing the referent is not a necessary condition of knowing the sense. This is the case on Frege's account of names; one might know the sense of 'Hesperus' without knowing Hesperus. The ability to determine whether assertions using the name were true or false, based on the knowledge that they are to be justified by appeal to the object, whatever it is, referred to by 'the star that rises in the evening', need presuppose no knowledge of the object itself. On such an account knowing the sense of a name is knowing a *method* whereby the truth of assertions containing the name may be assessed; it does not imply that one need actually have applied that method: "In grasping the sense, one is not certainly assured of a reference". (TWF, p. 22) Of course, Frege was also willing to allow sense for empty names; Evans puts the problem clearly:

> It is really not clear how there can be a mode of presentation associated with some term when there is no object to be presented ... it certainly does not appear that there can be a way of thinking about something unless there is something to be thought about in that way. (Evans, p. 22)

However, this is to place too great an emphasis on Frege's metaphor of *presentation*. Having developed the point on which the demand for a theory of names rests (the question of the cognitive simplicity of (3) and (2)), let me now state how I propose to cash out the metaphor of mode of presentation before building upon it to show that (2) cannot be cognitively simple. I propose to take mode of presentation as follows:

> *MP*: the mode of presentation of an object is that (those) feature(s) knowledge of which would need to be called upon in defence of an identification of an object as bearer of the name 'NN' if that identification were to be challenged.

---

[6] The question whether or not we have bare acquaintance with objects, or whether (2) is cognitively simple, is allied to the question of the truth of what Evans calls Russell's Principle, namely the idea that in order to think of an object one must know which object one is thinking of (cf. Evans, Chs. 3, 4). Peter Carruthers ("Understanding Names", *The Philosophical Quarterly*, 33 (1983)) denies bare acquaintance with objects for what seems to be the same reason as the one I give below. He fails to see the significance I see in this partly because he takes sense in a very individualistic and, seemingly, mentalistic imagining way, both of which I deny. Cf. his discussion of whether two people understand each other in using a name (pp. 26—7) where this seems to mean "have the same ideas/descriptions before the mind"; nothing so occurrent or static as this is, I believe, relevant.

I thus do not interpret 'mode of presentation' as the view, or perspective, with which one is presented with an object, something embodied in the static occurrent character of one's experience at the time of presentation. It seems to me that only if the metaphor is so interpreted is there good cause to object to the dispositional notion of mode of presentation given here.[7] So, for example, it is not that the sense of 'Mrs. Thatcher' presents Mrs. Thatcher to a competent speaker of the language and user of that name in a particular way, nor that it *determines the referent* in a manner which suggests that we come equipped with the sense of the name and employ it, like a map grid, to determine the object it picks out. Rather, the point is, that in the identification of, and reference to objects, no such *processes* are involved at all. However, *if* such a term refers to a publicly accessible feature of our environment, there must be some criterion by which such reference can be defended, if need be, and the competent user of the name must be cognizant of this.

Before turning to an examination of (2) and showing how the knowledge expressed there must be cognitively complex and include reference to the object's mode of presentation as outlined above, let us note one last *prima facie* difficulty with the thought that (3) entails (2) and that (2) is a matter of bare acquaintance. If knowledge that 'Hesperus' stands for Hesperus involves a bare acquaintance with Hesperus, then knowledge that 'Phosphorus' stands for Phosphorus should involve a bare acquaintance with *it*. But then, as Hesperus *is* Phosphorus, it would appear that the right-hand side of the clauses,

(7) 'Hesperus' stands for Hesperus,
(8) 'Phosphorus' stands for Phosphorus,

should be interchangeable *salva veritate*, and indeed that the results should be equally serviceable in a theory of meaning. Plainly this cannot be so, and any theory must deny the possibility. But on what grounds can we make this denial if (3) entails (2)? If S's knowledge of (7) and (8), plus bare acquaintance with the thing which is both Hesperus and Phosphorus, does not entail knowledge of either

(9) 'Hesperus' stands for Phosphorus

or

(10) 'Phosphorus' stands for Hesperus,

this must be because S's knowledge of the object, when called 'Hesperus', and his knowledge of the same object when called 'Phosphorus', somehow have distinguishing features. It must be the case that knowing it as Hesperus

---

[7] It is at this point that my account will diverge from, for example, C. McGinn, *The Subjective View* (Oxford, 1983). One divergence is brought out if I say that I take indexical modes of presentation as cognitively complex, just as with (2) and (3), and this is a consequence of not taking mode of presentation and representative content as occurrent descriptions of an experience but more in the dispositional way above.

involves qualitative differences in S's cognitive state from his knowing it as Phosphorus. Whatever these differences be, they suggest themselves as strong candidates for characterisation of the senses of the two names. That is, if S's knowledge of (9) and of (10) does not follow in the above circumstances, he cannot have a bare acquaintance with the object.

Two responses might be made to this. First, might not S's failure to know (9) and (10) be explained by his possession of two distinct and irreducible perceptual capacities for recognising the thing as Hesperus and for recognising it as Phosphorus (McDowell, p. 164)? Discussion of this objection will occupy the rest of this paper and I defer it for only one moment longer. Secondly, might not the difference between S's relevant cognitive states be not a qualitative one in the character of S's knowledge, but a neurophysiological one in the workings of two processes of recognition? This objection would postulate a difference in the causal account of how the two knowings take place rather than a difference in what S knows in the two situations. It would explain S's failure to derive (9) and (10) from his knowledge of (7) and (8) not in terms of a lack of knowledge somewhere along the line, but rather in terms of the fact that his neural machinery is such that no such derivation is made.

Dissatisfaction with the prospect of being faced with a "causal theory of logic" here is not the only cause for misgivings. If a theory of meaning is to explain both the linguistic behaviour of the speakers of the language and what they know as masters of the language, then it hardly suffices to pass over the fact that speakers do not derive (9) and (10) without specifying a cognitive account of why they do not. The present objection presupposes that speakers' not making the derivation shows that they do not know that Hesperus is Phosphorus. But the point is that unless an advantage is to be conceded to a rich Fregean theory of sense, the entailment of (2) by (3) ensures that, in knowing the object, speakers *do* know that it is one object. The point of (2) is that S has a bare acquaintance with Hesperus, *not* with Hesperus-under-such-and-such-description, as in a Fregean theory. Of course, one can know Hesperus and Phosphorus without realising their identity if one knows the object under, as it were, different aspects (and by different aspects here I mean something capturable by the definition of mode of presentation above; for example, one's knowledge of the object is taken to be differentially defendable when known as Hesperus and when known as Phosphorus). But once again, this is to introduce qualitative differences into the relevant cognitive states and so provide the ingredients for a richer theory of sense.

IV

Frege would not have understood (2) in the way that seems intended by someone who rests a denial of sense for names on the notion of bare acquaintance. He did not allow that we can have bare acquaintance with the referent of a term without knowing it under some description or criterion of identity. For Frege, propositional knowledge, like (3), is the basic form of knowledge. This is not to deny the *de re/de dicto* distinction, as it is commonly drawn, although it is perhaps to deny some of the uses for which it has been intended. Frege allows us to distinguish between believing that spies wear brown hats and believing of a man in a brown hat that he is a spy, so long as we do not construe the latter belief as *irredeemably de re*. Ultimately it is just a more discriminating *de dicto* belief than the former.

What then are we to make of (2)? We require an account of what it is for S to know the referent of 'Hesperus' when, as I put it above, this knowledge comes to:

> (11) S has a capacity to differentiate and discriminate Hesperus-like sensory stimulations in a way that constitutes an ability to pick out this thing as a determinate, possibly recurring, feature of his experience.

The possession of such capacities constitutes the irreducible core of McDowell's account of our knowledge of the bearer of a name. Although I accept the importance of such capacities, the point which I wish to make is that they are cognitively complex in a manner enjoining a rich theory of sense. One way of considering the question "How rich need a theory of sense be?" would be to ask whether, in the knowledge constitutive of the sense of the name, we require "knowledge to the effect that the bearer of the name may be recognised thus and so" (McDowell, p. 165). In support of the claim that this requirement is stronger than need be McDowell says,

> One can have the ability to tell that a seen object is the bearer of a familiar name without the slightest idea *how* one recognises it. The presumed mechanism of recognition might be neural machinery – its operation quite unknown to its possessor. (McDowell, p. 165)

McDowell is claiming here that, for a great many cases, we simply possess perceptual capacities to recognise, non-inferentially, that such and such a particular is the bearer of a certain name. I think this claim is true, and non-trivially so, but we must be careful to see what is involved in it. Certainly, the following must be granted without exception:

> P1 We have capacities to recognise particulars without that recognition involving any conscious inference on the part of the agent.

P1 is unexceptionable because it only rules out the operation of a *conscious* inference in recognition of a particular. This point might be put by saying that a subject's capacity to *recall* nothing more than extremely sketchy and inaccurate descriptions of an object has no bearing on whether or not he has the capacity to *recognise* the referent of the name when confronted with it. A second claim which McDowell would make about these capacities might be put like this:

> P2 Such capacities are genuinely cognitive capacities: that is, nothing need be involved beyond bringing such a capacity to bear in order that knowledge might issue from the relevant sensory confrontation.

Any legitimate querying of P2 would, I think, have to arise from an argument to the effect that, for genuine knowledge to issue from the operation of such a capacity, its operation would need to be *justifiable*; and that such justification would have to consider whether or not the object satisfied certain predicates and whether, in some manner, perceiving that it satisfied such predicates was constitutive of successful operation of the perceptual capacity. Accordingly, such a critique of P2 would also be a critique of:

> P3 We have capacities to recognise particulars without that recognition involving any *unconscious* inference on the part of the agent.

It is P3 that would be the most likely target of anyone critical of the "bare" perceptual capacities necessary if a rich theory of sense is to be avoided. Of course, if we deny P3 it would be open to us to say that those features of the object involved in the unconscious-inference-based recognition of it are exactly the features knowledge of which constitutes the information which is, on a rich theory, taken as the sense of a name. But I want to resist such a move. The onus is surely on the critic to say what he means by 'unconscious inferences' and once we see how to constrain such capacities in a manner that captures the definition of 'mode of presentation' above, motivation for the critic's point will evaporate. I shall therefore assume that P3, and *a fortiori* P2, hold. What I do contend is that, as an account of our knowledge of particulars, P1–P3 are insufficient. A fourth claim is necessary which acts as a constraint on the intelligible ascription of such perceptual capacities to people:

> P4 Possession of a capacity to recognise some particular as the bearer of a name 'NN' requires that there be further propositional knowledge which would be required for a successful defence of a recognition of the object if that recognition were challenged, and that the agent be cognizant of this further information.

Before arguing for P4 and thereby introducing the framework for a rich theory of sense, I shall first clarify the role possession of such capacities is supposed to play.

V

The proposal is that on some, and perhaps many, occasions of someone's recognising an object as the bearer of the name 'NN', this is a matter of the subject simply recognising without inference that the object is so. However, there are two quite separate but related questions that need to be clearly distinguished when invoking such perceptual capacities as irreducible acts of cognition. In the first place there is the question of whether or not we possess capacities to recognise objects non-inferentially in the sense of P1—P3, and in this sense I think we do. Furthermore, possession of such capacities is important in understanding the workings of natural language. So, if we accept that we possess such capacities we may conclude that for the *operation* of such a skill we do not need to employ the whole, or some part, of a list of criteria for a name's application when, for example, we recognise Hesperus. We may agree that knowledge of the thing Hesperus can be had without the need that such knowledge *proceed in any way* via knowledge that the bearer of the name has been recognised thus-and-so. In so far as this gives content to Evans's thought cited above that there cannot be a way of thinking of an object when the name is empty, I agree with him. However, this is not yet to make a criticism of the rich conception of sense. We still have to ask what it is that S knows when he recognises Hesperus. Granted he may *arrive* in state (2) without applying a list of criteria; does this mean that he knows the thing Hesperus *simpliciter*, in some irredeemably *de re* sense of having a bare acquaintance with it? Such a conception of our knowledge of particulars is, I think, unintelligible for the following reason. Although the recognitional act may proceed non-inferentially without invoking knowledge of criteria for a name's application, we have to ask whether it makes sense to speak of such recognition if the subject is not sensitive to the knowledge which can be used to defend its operation if challenged. We may reject the idea of sense as knowledge which serves in an inferential process every time we recognise a particular; but is it intelligible to suppose that such recognition can occur *and generate knowledge* without the subject's knowing what would count as a defence of his recognition? If we find that the desired recognitional capacities are intelligible only on the assumption of S's possession of further supporting knowledge, although operational without such knowledge being activated, then such knowledge introduces material for the construction of a rich theory of sense. I see no way of avoiding P4.

We are at present concerned only with capacities for recognising particulars and not with capacities for recognising states of affairs. What would it be like for someone to have a capacity to recognise something as the bearer of the name 'NN' but not be sensitive to the information required by P4? Clearly all of us, most of the time and with a large proportion of the names we regularly employ, have the ability to respond non-inferentially to sensory stimulation in the manner "That's NN". Such identification is in many cases totally unreflective. Similarly, there is no reason why we should not allow that someone could acquire such an unreflective ability to recognise Hesperus when it appears in the evening. Indeed, it is likely that many people possess such a skill. What is not so plain is that if S is one of these people so endowed, then his ability thus to identify Hesperus tells us *what* he knows when he knows that a presented object is Hesperus. Possession of the skill to recognise this heavenly body may explain *how* S acquires the knowledge he has when he recognises it, but it does not tell us what he knows when he knows Hesperus. If it is insisted that what he knows is Hesperus, nothing more or less – he simply has a bare acquaintance with the object – then it becomes doubtful whether we are crediting him with information that is public and shareable; whether, that is, he has *knowledge*. This is because it is unclear how we can grant him knowledge of an objective feature of the environment without his possession of something over and above a bare acquaintance with it. It is one thing to say that S's identification of Hesperus is unreflective and that there is nothing, as it were, between him and the object of his knowledge. It is another thing to say that he thereby has a bare acquaintance with the object. If such a conception is insisted upon, it is difficult to see how such recognition could be constitutive of *knowing* that the object is Hesperus rather than a mere stipulation that such-and-such portion of the subject's present experience is to be called thus. Even taken as such a stipulation, this has to be restricted to the subject's *present* experience. It would not be possible to attribute to him the complex determination to call such-and-such a *kind* of experience by the name 'Hesperus', for without acknowledging some identifying criteria, at least in the sense of P4, the subject has surely failed to give any content to the thought that he has identified a determinate and possibly recurrent portion of experience.

The point here bears on Wittgenstein's remarks in the *Philosophical Investigations* in developing the celebrated "diary" example. Wittgenstein is considering the possibility of a person's giving a private ostensive definition of a term 'S' for a pain. The passage is generally misinterpreted as one or another form of scepticism. The idea that Wittgenstein is here concerned with scepticism as to how the diarist could tell that a future pain was of the kind originally dubbed 'S', is probably not so popular any more;[8] but the view that the argument still involves some version of scepticism seems prevalent. Both Kenny and Hacker take the point to turn on a scepticism about whether the diarist can know, when he turns to enter 'S' in his diary at a later time, that he is using 'S' with the same meaning.[9] Instead of a scepticism about knowledge of the object, we have here scepticism about knowledge of meaning. Kripke's recent foray into Wittgensteinian exegesis seems to suffer from the same mistake as Kenny and Hacker (Kripke2). Even this more sophisticated scepticism cannot be the right interpretation for, as Wittgenstein says, in

---

[8] Cf. R. Fogelin, *Wittgenstein* (London, 1976), who still takes the argument in this way.
[9] A. Kenny, *Wittgenstein* (London, 1976); P. M. S. Hacker, *Insight and Illusion* (Oxford, 1972).

considering the idea that by concentrating on the meaning of the sign he might "impress on himself" the connection between sign and object:

> ... "I impress it on myself" can only mean: this process brings it about that I remember the connection *right* in the future.

He then concludes (my italics),

> But *in the present case* I have no criterion of correctness, One would like to say: whatever is going to seem right to me is right. And that only means that here we cannot talk about 'right'. (PI §258)

Scepticism about how one could know one was using 'S' with the same meaning on a later occasion is misplaced for, as Wittgenstein clearly says, the idea of a wholly private ostension bestows *no meaning at all*, not even in the present case. The reason why Wittgenstein is persuaded of this is, I think, the reason why P4 is an unavoidable constraint on the ascription of perceptual capacities for the recognition of particulars; namely, that unless there are identifying criteria to which the use of a name is answerable, there are no constraints upon the use of the term at all. It is not simply that unless S's perceptual capacity for recognising Hesperus conforms to P4, we have no guarantee that he will not, on a future occasion, claim to recognise, say, Sirius as Hesperus; but further, we cannot know to which determinate portion of his present experience, if any, he is attempting to refer. 'Hesperus' might just be a term for a characterisation of his total experience rather than for some stable recurrent feature of it. So, like Wittgenstein, I am not pressing a point about P4 that depends on S's ability to *re*-identify Hesperus. It is a matter of his ability to identify *it* at all.

Similarly, if I were to say, 'There's Margaret Thatcher' and yet not show any interest or ability in how the utterance might be defended, but just repeat 'There's Margaret Thatcher', the worry would not be simply that there may be more Margaret Thatchers in this world than one might suppose and you not know to which I was referring; the point is that until the capacity I thereby exercise is responsive to knowledge of the sort outlined in P4, you have no means for knowing whether I am using the term to refer to a stable portion of our experience. To say that you know that I am using the term in such a way that

> 'Margaret Thatcher' stands for Margaret Thatcher

is simply not to the point. For until more can be said about *that*, nothing has been said to show that I am using it to refer to the same recurrent feature of experience for which everyone else uses it. Indeed, nothing has been said to show that I am using it to refer to an *object* at all. That we do all use it for a recurrent thing in experience is a function of our shared grasp of the information which gives content to P4. You might, of course, know at least that I know that

" 'Margaret Thatcher' stands for Margaret Thatcher"
is a truth, but *that* is a different matter.

The requirement for knowledge under P4, then, is a requirement without which our perceptual capacities for identifying particulars could not be seen as picking out objects, but only as responsive to total characterisations of experience at the time of the operation of the capacity. Knowledge under P4 is required in order to credit the user of a term 'NN' with the notion of an *object* as its bearer, that is, with the use of the term as a name. It is not that, without P4, objects would be represented in thought in a purely subjective way, but that *objects* would not be represented in thought at all. Again, we do well to note that the present account of sense, in saying that such knowledge constitutes the way an object is represented in thought, does not entail that in thinking of an object one need have, as it were, all this knowledge before one's mind. The temptation to think in such a way comes from thinking of the representative content of thought as a sort of mental image or picture, and of sense as a picture associated with a name with which one searches in one's experience for a bearer to match. Rather, we must see sense, as also the general notion of the representative content of thought, as a web of knowledge consisting in a complex of dispositions and capacities. One may indeed know directly, via perceptual skills, that a presented object is Hesperus; but the lack of a search and comparison procedure (or even of any conscious awareness of criteria by which the identification was made) has no bearing on the representative content of one's thought: "That's Hesperus".

VI

It might be thought that the added constraint of P4 only serves to show that names have sense and not that every name has a unique sense. There is a limited point to this. As already noted, it is fair to observe that Frege's notion of sense seems to require a picture of language as the intersection of the several speakers' idiolects. Whilst it might be thought that the constraint of P4 serves to show that any speaker who has a competent grasp of the use of a name must also have some body of information to which his use of the name is responsive, is this enough to show that the semantic role of a name in a language is determined by some *one* such body of information? Is there any particular way in which one *must* think of the object which is the bearer of some name?

I think we can substantiate the strong claim that every name has a unique sense. But again part of the problem resides in the metaphor "way in which one thinks of an object". To be sure, there need not be one unique way in which everyone thinks of Margaret Thatcher, in the sense of some unique set of mental images or whatever. But then Frege would not wish us to take 'way in which one thinks of an object' like *that*. However, it seems to me that Evans, although dissenting from the idea that there is one particular way in which one thinks of an object, has provided an answer to this point (Evans, Ch. 11). The issue turns on the social character of meaning. There is a division of linguistic labour in our grasp of sense for linguistic units which allows that, though the knowledge used by many speakers to defend the identification of some particular as the bearer of a name may not be information which is common to, or thought particularly germane by, other speakers, it is so linked through communal intercourse with the knowledge possessed by *producing members* of a name-using community that we are assured a common reference.[10]

For example, suppose someone hitherto unfamiliar with the name-using practice with 'Margaret Thatcher' has the referent of this name pointed out to him in a crowd. A few minutes later he may recognise the referent as Margaret Thatcher and his knowledge used in defence of this recognition may be no more than, "The lady looks so-and-so" and "The lady looking so-and-so was introduced to me as Margaret Thatcher by so-and-so". His use of the name, although defensible only by means of some rather sparse sensory cues, is parasitic upon knowledge shared by a wider community and ultimately responsible to the producers of the name-using practice. These are the people to whom Evans refers when he says "the expression does not become a name for x unless it has a certain currency among those who know x — only then can we say that x is *known as NN*". (Evans, p. 376) The use of a name serves as an identification cheque drawn upon this particular group of speakers. We may indeed have different and not particularly uniquely determining dossiers of information which we call upon in defence of claims based upon perceptual capacities for recognising particulars as bearers of names: for example, if we both claim to have recognised Margaret Thatcher, I may appeal to a particular tone of voice and you to a certain hairstyle. Nevertheless, our dossiers converge in that they are generated by our intercourse with a shared practice brought into being by those whose position in the genesis of the practice gives them the right to decide whether or not someone really is Margaret Thatcher. With the case of proper names in ordinary language there are not, I believe, any such determinate groups. There are no determinate answers to, for example, the question whether the person we currently call "Margaret Thatcher" would still be the bearer of that name were it suddenly discovered that she had been adopted at birth. Although there are producers for the name using practices of our language, there are not, I think, determinate ways of authenticating producers. But this is something natural language can well do without.

So although the knowledge a competent user of a name may call upon in defence of a recognition of the bearer of a name may be somewhat idiosyncratic, what makes his use a *competent* use is that this knowledge provides him with a

---

[10] P I take the term from Evans, pp. 382f.

licence to draw upon the common stock of knowledge which constitutes *the* sense of the name. The speaker's grasp of the sense of a name is more or less competent as he is more or less immersed in this common fund of knowledge. (It is knowledge he is immersed in, not a nexus of causal chains.) It is important also to note that the connection of the, as it were, preliminary dossiers, normally sufficient to defend a claim to have recognised a particular, with the somewhat shifting but communally accepted stock that is taken to determine the reference of a name, typically depends upon the assumption of the object's spatio-temporal continuity with the object known as NN by the producers of the practice. Again, the observation is due to Evans (p. 279). For example, one would not be credited with a capacity for recognising Margaret Thatcher if the information required under P4 did not include information which allowed one, on grounds of spatio-temporal continuity, to distinguish cases of recognising Margaret Thatcher from being presented with a perfect impersonator.

If this is right, then we have, in the constraint of P4, grounds for accepting a rich theory of sense for names; and we also have grounds for saying that not only do names have sense, but each name has a unique sense. The constraint of P4 alone allows us to make sense of ascriptions of perceptual capacities for distinguishing *particulars* in our experience. That being so, there can be no grounds for disallowing that the knowledge required under P4 is just the sort of knowledge Frege would have recognised as constituting what McDowell would call a rich theory of sense for names. It is the knowledge required in order that our perceptual capacities issue in public items of knowledge. To insist that sense is public because everyone has the knowledge S has in (3) misses the point; a rich theory is needed precisely in order that we be able to say what that cognitive state is and how it differs from (4).

Names, then, have sense because knowledge answering the requirement of P4 is needed if our recognitional capacities are to be capacities for recognising *things* rather than subjective characterisations of a whole experience. Each name has a sense in so far as a speaker's grasp of the use of the name is competent just to the extent that he grasps the knowledge possessed by the producing members of a particular name-using practice. Names only lack a unique sense in so far as such producers form an indeterminate group.

Linacre College & New College, Oxford

DE RE SENSES

By John McDowell

1. It is commonly believed that a Fregean philosophy of language and thought can represent an utterance, or a propositional attitude, as being about an object only by crediting it with a content that determines the object by specification, or at least in such a way that the content is available to be thought or expressed whether the object exists or not.[1] To resist this restriction would be to hold out for the idea that utterances and thoughts can be essentially *de re*; and that idea is supposed to be incapable of being made to fit within the framework provided by the theory of sense and *Bedeutung*.

I believe that this picture of the possibilities for Fregean theory is quite wrong. Gareth Evans has argued that Frege himself is positively committed to *de re* senses for singular terms, and at least to some extent recognizes the commitment; and Evans has given the outlines of a perfectly Fregean account of some sorts of *de re* sense.[2] My purpose in this paper is not to repeat or embellish Evans's positive considerations, but to criticize a theoretical structure within which they are bound to seem incomprehensible.

2. What supposedly rules out accommodating the essentially *de re* within Fregean theory is a certain conception of the contrast between *de re* and *de dicto*. I shall follow Tyler Burge's exposition, which is the most explicit and thoughtful that I know.[3]

At the level of logical form, the contrast is between *de dicto* attributions of, say, belief, which relate the believer to a "complete" (343) or "completely expressed" (345) proposition, and *de re* attributions, which relate the believer to a *res* and something less than a "complete" proposition. Underlying this semantic distinction is an "epistemic" distinction (345–6): this is between beliefs that are "fully conceptualized" (345: *de dicto*), and beliefs "whose

---

[1] This latter formulation cannot be right where the object's existence is necessary absolutely, or necessary relative to the fact that the thought in question is being expressed or entertained at all (e.g. the *Bedeutung* on an occasion of 'now', and perhaps 'I': but see Evans, pp. 249—55). But having noted this, I shall ignore it: the issue I want to consider is whether Fregean theory can accommodate *de re* thoughts outside that area.
[2] Evans, Chs. 1, 6, and 7.
[3] See Burge2: page references in my text will relate to this article.

correct ascription places the believer in an appropriate nonconceptual, contextual relation to objects the belief is about" (346: *de re*).

It would be a merely terminological question whether one should say that there are no propositions but "complete" ones, so that *de re* attributions involve no propositions; or whether in connection with *de re* attributions one should recognize propositions of a different kind: "Russellian propositions", which are not "completely expressed" but contain objects as constituents along with "expressed" items that are less than "complete" propositions.[4] The second choice brings out neatly why Fregean theory cannot countenance the essentially *de re*, conceived on these lines. In Fregean theory, utterances and propositional attitudes have thoughts as their contents, and thoughts are senses with nothing but senses as constituents: "we can't say that an object is part of a thought as a proper name is part of the corresponding sentence" (PW, p. 187).

3. Burge's fundamental intuition is this: if a propositional attitude (or utterance) is essentially *de re*, that is in virtue of the fact that a context involving the *res* itself enters into determining how the attitude (or utterance) can be correctly ascribed.[5]

But why should the essentially *de re*, conceived in conformity with this intuition, be deemed inaccessible to Frege? Frege writes:

> If a time indication is conveyed by the present tense one must know when the sentence was uttered in order to grasp the thought correctly. Therefore the time of utterance is part of the expression of the thought. (LI, p. 10)

Again, in connection with 'yesterday' and 'today', and 'here' and 'there', he writes:

> In all such cases the mere wording, as it can be preserved in writing, is not the complete expression of the thought; the knowledge of certain conditions accompanying the utterance, which are used as means of expressing the thought, is needed for us to grasp the thought correctly. (*ibid.* See also pp. 27–8.)

He is writing of thoughts which are not completely expressed by words abstracted from contexts of utterance, but he is precisely *not* conceding that the

---

[4] "Russellian propositions" in view of, e.g., p. 103 of *The Philosophy of Logical Atomism*, in *Russell's Logical Atomism*, ed. D. Pears (London, 1972). Burge remarks (343): "In Russellian propositions, the relevant *res* are not expressed but shown." His own formalizations of *de re* attributions do not group their relata, aside from the believer, into Russellian propositions, but a trivial notational change would make them do so.

[5] Burge does not discuss utterances, but the extrapolation is natural. My formulation avoids another merely terminological issue, about the word 'content'. One might count Russellian propositions (if one believed in them) as a species of content; alternatively, one might tie content to "complete" propositionality, so that an attitude's *de re* character would come out in the fact that its content falls short of a whole proposition. Burge's preference is for the second of these: see n. 2 (p. 119) of his "Other Bodies", in *Thought and Object*, ed. A. Woodfield (Oxford, 1982), 97—120.

thoughts are not completely expressed, *simpliciter*. So where Burge speaks of a *res*-involving context partly determining the shape of a correct *de re* attribution, it is not clear why this cannot be transposed, in the light of this passage from Frege, into a conception of how such a context contributes to the expression of a fully expressible but nevertheless *de re* thought.

It is sometimes supposed that the "thoughts" of this passage cannot be classically Fregean thoughts. This idea is a response to Frege's allowing that if one utters a sentence containing 'yesterday' one can express the same thought as one could have expressed on the day before by uttering a sentence containing 'today'; the idea is that this same thought would be, not a Fregean thought, but a Russellian proposition, containing the day in question as a constituent.[6]

However, if Frege had intended to alter his use of '*Gedanke*' so radically as to encompass these Russellian propositions, he would surely have remarked on it. (That is putting it mildly, since the alteration would undermine the fundamental point of his notion of sense, which includes thought: namely to capture differences in cognitive value. One can take opposing "cognitive" attitudes simultaneously to one of these Russellian propositions. See Perry, pp. 482–5) If there were no alternative explanation of what Frege is driving at, we might be forced to suppose that he has slipped inadvertently into a non-Fregean use of '*Gedanke*'. But there is an alternative explanation. Evans has suggested that Frege's idea is this: if one "keeps track of" a day as it recedes into the past, thinking of it successively as *today, yesterday, the day before yesterday*, and so on, that enables one to hold on to thoughts about it – thoughts that preserve their identity through the necessary changes in how they might be expressed.[7] These "dynamic thoughts" are not Russellian propositions; not just any mode of presentation of the day in question would demand the appropriate capacity to keep track of it, so a dynamic thought is not determined by the sheer identity of its object.[8]

---

[6] David Kaplan takes this view in his unpublished "Demonstratives" (at least in the 1977 version); so also (by implication) John Searle, *Intentionality* (Cambridge, 1983), p. 229. On this reading, Frege's remarks would amount to suggesting that if we give due weight to the expressing role of "accompanying conditions", we can allow that even Russellian propositions can be completely expressed. If accepted, this would disrupt Burge's apparatus; but it would not vindicate the possibility of a genuinely *Fregean* approach to the *de re*.

[7] See G. Evans, "Understanding Demonstratives", in *Meaning and Understanding*, ed. H. Parret and J. Bouveresse (Berlin and New York, 1981), 280–303, pp. 291–5. One can take opposing "cognitive" attitudes to one of these "dynamic thoughts", but not simultaneously, and there is a perfectly Fregean explanation of how it happens: by losing track of the object, one loses track of the thought.

[8] Note how Evans's reading of the passage answers Colin McGinn's query, McGinn, pp. 61–3: if, as Frege allows, a 'yesterday'-utterance and a 'today'-utterance, or a 'here'-utterance and a 'there'-utterance, can express the same thought, why not an 'I'-utterance and a 'you'-utterance? The answer is that an 'I'-utterance and a 'you'-utterance could not be connected by expressing a single dynamic thought. This preempts McGinn's speculatively Cartesian answer to his query (pp. 63–4).

4. If we had only the linguistic expression of thoughts to consider, it would be somewhat mysterious why Burge assumes – contrary to the apparently reasonable line that Frege himself, as we have seen, seems to take – that contextual factors must be extraneous to the expressive capacities of context-sensitive utterances. An explanation emerges from Burge's treatment of the "epistemic basis" for his semantic distinction between *de re* and *de dicto*.

He writes (345–6):

> The rough epistemic analogue of the linguistic notion of what is expressed by a semantically significant expression is the notion of a concept. Traditionally speaking, concepts are a person's means of representing objects in thought. For present purposes, we may include as concepts other alleged mental entities that the empiricist tradition did not clearly distinguish from them – for example, perceptions or images – so long as these are viewed as types of representations of objects. From a semantical viewpoint, a *de dicto* belief is a belief in which the believer is related only to a completely expressed proposition (*dictum*). *The epistemic analogue is a belief that is fully conceptualized.* That is, a correct ascription of the *de dicto* belief identifies it purely by reference to a "content" all of whose semantically relevant components characterize elements in the believer's conceptual repertoire.

Given that conceptual content is made up of *means* of representation in thought, a belief's being fully conceptualized can mean only that it has a fully propositional content exhausted by some collection of thought symbols; and it would follow that there is no room for contextual factors to contribute to determining how such a belief may be correctly ascribed. This makes Burge's picture of the relation between conceptual content and context obligatory; and, applied to the linguistic expression of thought, with a plausible equation between conceptual content and what can be completely expressed, it generates Burge's curious deafness to what Frege seems to be trying to say in the passage that I have quoted.

But Burge makes this look inexorable only by a patent slide; from concepts as parts or aspects of the *content* of a representational state, such as a belief, to concepts as *means* of representation. In the former sense (which is non-Fregean, but for present purposes only harmlessly so), concepts would indeed be analogous to *what is expressed* by words, as Burge says. In the latter sense, they would be analogous to *what does the expressing*: to the words themselves.

Once this conflation is discerned, the direction of argument can reverse: it is not that an independently compulsory division between content and context undermines Frege's wish to make a different use of the concept of expression, but rather that the evident coherence of Frege's remarks, with the same plausible equation between 'conceptual content' and what can be 'completely expressed', shows that Burge's picture of the relation between context and content is unwarranted. There is no more reason to accept that contextual factors are extraneous to the content-determining powers of a conceptual repertoire than there is to accept, in face of Frege, that what is expressed by a context-sensitive utterance cannot be partly determined by the context in which it is made. So for all that Burge shows, a conceptual repertoire can include the ability to think of objects under modes of presentation whose functioning depends essentially on (say) the perceived presence of the objects. Such *de re* modes of presentation would be parts or aspects of content, not vehicles for it; no means of mental representation could determine the content in question by itself, without benefit of context, but that does not establish any good sense in which the content is not fully conceptualized.

It would be illuminating to consider why it is so tempting to conflate mental content with means of representation, but for my purposes here it is enough to point out that it is a conflation. Writers on Frege typically assume without much argument that a Fregean sense, of the sort suitable to be the sense of a singular term, must be available to be expressed whether or not it determines an object.[9] Burge supplies an explicit argument, whose premisses are, first, the plausible thesis that we can make room for existence-dependence in, say, beliefs only by giving contextual factors an essential role in determining their correct attribution; and, secondly, the separation of content from context. Failing an alternative, it seems fair to suppose that something like Burge's argument lies behind the usual assumption about the possibilities for Fregean theory; indeed something on the lines of Burge's division of content from context is a near orthodoxy in writers on these matters, usually without Burge's self-consciousness about it. But this division of content from context is recommended only by a conflation.[10]

5. A *de re* sense would be specific to its *res*; perhaps Frege is simply drawing out the implications of this, as applied to a sort of *de re* sense whose instances present a thinker as himself, when he writes that "everyone is presented to

---

[9] There are passages where Frege seems to say this. But given the plausible connection of the concept of *Bedeutung* with the concept of semantic value, the idea of a sense that determines no *Bedeutung* is very difficult: see Evans, pp. 22–8; and the passages can be neutralized by adverting to peculiarities in Frege's use of the notion of fiction: *ibid*. pp. 28–30. Contrary to something implied at p. 197 of Christopher Peacocke, "Demonstrative Thought and Psychological Explanation", *Synthese* 49 (1981), 187–217, Frege's apparent attribution of senses to empty singular terms is quite distinct from his doctrine that senses have only senses, not *Bedeutungen*, as constituents (and much more peripheral to his position).

[10] Evans's rebuttal of Perry's "Frege on Demonstratives" (see "Understanding Demonstratives") turns on the lack of any basis for Perry's assumption that Fregean senses for singular terms must be "descriptive". This complaint is quite correct; but it risks being met with incomprehension as long as the framework which holds the assumption in place is not challenged.

himself in a special and primitive way, in which he is presented to no-one else" (LI, p. 12). Commentators have made heavy weather over two issues about this: first, whether it is consistent with the constant "linguistic meaning" of a context-sensitive expression; and, secondly, whether it is consistent with Frege's doctrine that thoughts are objective.

On the first issue, some philosophers have written as if accommodating the constancy of linguistic meaning would require crediting a context-sensitive expression with a mode of presentation constant across all univocal uses of it (see McGinn, pp. 64–5). Such a mode of presentation would not be a Fregean sense, since it would not determine the appropriate sort of *Bedeutung* except in conjunction with a context. What would serve would be something on the lines of David Kaplan's notion of *character*: characters are functions from contexts to 'Russellian propositions' or their constituents.[11]

This may seem to yield independent support for Burge's picture of the relation between content and context. But that is an illusion, since constancy of linguistic meaning can be accommodated in terms of *de re* senses. Particular *de re* senses, each specific to its *res*, can be grouped into sorts. Different *de re* senses (modes of presentation) can present their different *res* in the same sort of way: for instance, by exploiting their perceptual presence. And the univocity of a context-sensitive expression can be registered by associating it with a single sort of *de re* sense.[12]

These two ways of accommodating constancy – in terms of character and in terms of sort of *de re* sense – are very different. Given a context, a suitable sub-sentential character will determine an object, or else – if no object is suitably involved in the context – nothing. Even in the latter sort of case, the character is still, according to this way of thinking, available to be expressed: a constituent of a sub-propositional conceptual content. Contrast *de re* senses. Given a context, a sort of *de re* sense may determine a *de re* sense (if one cares to put it like that), or else it too may determine nothing. And in the latter sort of case, according to this way of thinking, there can only be a gap – an absence – at, so to speak, the relevant place in the mind – the place where, given that the sort of *de re* sense in question appears to be instantiated, there appears to be a specific *de re* sense.[13]

---

[11] See Kaplan, "On the Logic of Demonstratives", in *Contemporary Perspectives in the Philosophy of Language*, ed. P. A. French, T. E. Uehling, Jr., and H. K. Wettstein (Minneapolis, 1979), 401–12; cf. the concept of *role* introduced by Perry, p. 479.

[12] See Evans, "Understanding Demonstratives", p. 298. This point removes the motivation for Michael Dummett's idea (IFP, Ch. 6) that indexical expressions force on Frege a distinction (which he fails to draw) between sense as linguistic significance and sense as mode of presentation. A corollary is that there is no need to play down Frege's interest in linguistic meaning in order to defend him: cf. Burge 2, p. 357, and, with more elaboration, Burge 3, pp. 399–407.

[13] Perhaps there is a thought symbol (a means of representation) at a place corresponding to the gap. But to accept this is not to accept that there is, at that place, an *aspect* or *ingredient* of content. What there is at that place, if this suggestion is accepted, is a putative *bearer* or *vehicle* of content.

It may seem, contrary to what I have just said, that one could capture the effect of a Fregean conception of *de re* thoughts in terms of a special kind of Russellian proposition: Russellian propositions with both *res* and characters as constituents. On this view, an ordered pair of *res* and character might represent a *de re* sense: such an item certainly depends on the *res* for its existence, and it determines, but is not determined by, a *Bedeutung* of the appropriate sort, namely the *res*.[14] However, although this suggestion does thus mimic aspects of a genuinely Fregean position, the resemblance is only superficial. This suggestion secures a *de re* nature for these "thoughts" only by violating Frege's doctrine that thoughts are senses with senses, not *Bedeutungen*, as constituents. It is another way of making the same point to say that at best this suggestion shows the possibility of grafting a version of the Fregean terminology on to a picture of the *de re* that would be quite congenial to Burge; this can raise at best a verbal question about Burge's conception of the relation between content and context.[15]

6. The second issue is about the consistency of *de re* senses, and in particular Frege's remarks about the pronoun 'I', with the doctrine that thoughts are objective.[16]

It is true that Frege sometimes connects the objectivity of thoughts with their being communicable. And it is true that he cannot see how thoughts involving the "special and primitive way" in which each person is presented to himself can figure in communication. What he suggests is that for purposes of communication a person "must use 'I' in a sense which can be grasped by others, perhaps in the sense of 'he who is speaking to you at this moment' " (LI, p. 13). In fact this is quite unsatisfactory, as becomes clear if we try to construct a parallel account of the role of 'I'-thoughts in receiving communication as opposed to issuing it. Suppose someone says to me, "You have mud on your face". If I am to understand him, I must entertain an 'I'-thought, thinking something to this effect: "I have mud on my face: that is what he is saying." Frege's strategy for keeping the special and primitive way in which I am presented to myself out of communication suggests nothing better than the

---

[14] See Peacocke, "Demonstrative Thought and Psychological Explanation", p. 197. At p. 195, Peacocke denies that what he calls "type modes of presentation" are characters, but on the doubtful ground that "character is essentially linguistic"; I cannot see that he says anything that excludes interpreting his "type modes of presentation" as functions from contexts to objects. The fact that such functions are available to be expressed even when they determine no objects makes the 'type'-'token' terminology very odd, but in a way that Peacocke seems not to mind; see his *Sense and Content* (Oxford, 1983), p. 9, n. 6.
[15] See McGinn, p. 68, n. 17. I think McGinn's point tells against Peacocke (see n. 14 above); and also against Evans's "notational variant" argument against Perry ("Understanding Demonstratives", pp. 298–300), which seems to me to be a slip on Evans's part. It does not apply to the position that I am defending.
[16] For commentators' worries about this, see especially Perry, and McGinn, Ch. 5.

following: the 'I'-sense involved here is the sense of "he who is being addressed". But this would not do. I can entertain the thought that he who is being addressed has mud on his face, as what is being said, and not understand the remark; I may not know that *I* am he who is being addressed.[17]

Frege's troubles about 'I' cannot be blamed simply on the idea of special and primitive senses; they result, rather, from the assumption – which is what denies the special and primitive senses any role in communication – that communication must involve a sharing of thoughts between communicator and audience.[18] That assumption is quite natural, and Frege seems to take it for granted. But there is no obvious reason why he could not have held, instead, that in linguistic interchange of the appropriate kind, mutual understanding – which is what successful communication achieves – requires not shared thoughts but different thoughts which, however, stand and are mutually known to stand in a suitable relation of correspondence. (Notice that the correspondence in question is not the one that Frege recognizes in this passage:

> ... with a proper name, it is a matter of the way the object so designated is presented. This may happen in different ways, and to every such way there corresponds a special sense of a sentence containing the proper name. The different thoughts thus obtained from the same sentences correspond in truth-value, of course; that is to say, if one is true then all are true, and if one is false then all are false. Nevertheless the difference must be recognized. (LI, p. 12)

Here we have thoughts related by mere co-reference in modes of presentation that they contain; whereas in view of the point about "he who is being addressed", that would not suffice for the communication-allowing correspondence that I am envisaging.[19])

When he insists that thoughts are objective, Frege's main purpose is to deny that the being of a thought is dependent on its being entertained (or grasped), as the being of an idea is dependent on its having a bearer. This purpose is in no way obstructed by countenancing *de re* senses for 'I', one for each person. This gives me (for instance) 'I'-thoughts that only I can entertain; but it does not follow that they are not available to be entertained independently of my actually entertaining them. Sustaining the idea that even special and primitive 'I'-thoughts are mind-independent in this sense would perhaps be facilitated by showing that such thoughts can figure in mutual understanding, as I have claimed that Frege could have done. Publicity in any stronger sense is not

---

[17] This point is made by Evans, p. 314.
[18] For a questioning of the assumption, see Evans, pp. 40, 315–6.
[19] This paragraph suggests the possibility of an alternative to Evans's treatment of certain phenomena of "cognitive dynamics" (a phrase of Kaplan's) in terms of "dynamic thoughts", sketched in § 3 above. I shall not pursue this here.

needed; Frege is led to suggest otherwise by his connecting communication with the sharing of thought, but the connection is not compulsory. The notion of *de re* 'I'-senses need not be in tension with anything that is essential to a Fregean conception of thought.[20]

7. I have argued that Burge's theoretical framework is not cogently supported; I shall end with two considerations that tell against it.

On a Fregean account of the *de re*, Burge's supposedly unitary distinction between *de re* and *de dicto* would divide into two distinctions, which it would be open to us to regard as largely independent: first, a distinction between *de re* and *de dicto attributions* of, say, belief, marked by whether or not designations of the relevant *res* can be replaced *salva veritate* by other designations of them or by variables bound by initial existential quantifiers; and, secondly, a distinction between *contents* that are *de re*, in the sense that they depend on the existence of the relevant *res*, and contents that are not *de re* in that sense.[21] A belief with a *de re* content may be attributed in the *de re* way, but need not. And it is not obvious that any belief that is attributable in the *de re* way has a *de re* content.[22] In any case, even if *de re* attributability does imply *de re* content, *de re* attributions do not display the logical form of states with *de re* content; on the Fregean view, a *de re* attribution – one in which the relevant *res* is mentioned outside the specification of content – is true, if it is, in virtue of the truth of an attribution involving a "complete" propositional content.[23] (If, as may happen, we cannot place ourselves in a context such as we would need to exploit in order to give "complete expression" to the content, we may retain the capacity for a *de re* attribution, true in virtue of the truth of a *de dicto* attribution whose expression is beyond us.)

---

[20] These considerations undermine the motivation for Peacocke's insistence ("Demonstrative Thought and Psychological Explanation", pp. 191-3) that we must everywhere distinguish between expressing ("exploying") modes of presentation and referring to them. Certainly a Fregean view has senses referred to by words in content-specifying 'that'-clauses; but the best construal of Fregean theory has them expressed there as well. This fits Dummett's dissolution (FPL, Ch. 9) of the supposed problem of an infinite hierarchy of oblique senses. Peacocke mentions Dummett's discussion approvingly, but makes an exception for demonstrative modes of presentation. But there is no need for the exception. (Of course not just any mention of a mode of presentation will count as expressing it.)

[21] '*De dicto*' is clearly inappropriate to mark this contrast.

[22] Uncontaminated by philosophy, we are quite casual about "exportation" in cases of the "shortest spy" sort. (For the terminology here, see W. V. Quine, "Quantifiers and Propositional Attitudes", *Journal of Philosophy*, 53 (1956), 177-87; and David Kaplan, "Quantifying In", in *Words and Objections*, ed. D. Davidson and J. Hintikka (Dordrecht, 1969), 206—42. Burge's insistence (Burge 2, p. 346) that the logical form is different in such cases (involving a complete *dictum*, unlike canonical cases of *de re* attribution) seems strained; his excellent motivation for this claim (to preserve a robust conception of *de re* propositional attitudes) can be gratified in a different way.

[23] "True in virtue of" rather than – as suggested by, e.g., Kaplan, "Quantifying In" – "analysable in terms of". I doubt whether there is much system in our practice with *de re* attributions. (See n. 22 above.)

Now consider the logical form of a *de re* attribution of, say, a belief. Roughly speaking, it is a relational expression with argument-places occupied by designations of the believer, the *res*, and a propositional fragment.[24] How does the relational expression relate the *res* to the propositional fragment?[25] In the state of affairs that the attribution represents, the propositional fragment should figure as somehow tied to the *res* by a predicational tie; can this intuitive requirement be met? If, as in the Fregean position, the *de re* attribution is conceived as true in virtue of the truth of a *de dicto* attribution, this question holds no terrors: in the underlying *de dicto* attribution, the required predicational tie will be explicitly expressed. But if, as in Burge's framework, the *de re* attribution is conceived as "barely true",[26] the belief relation has to secure the presence of the predicational tie all on its own; and it is quite unclear that it can be explained so as to carry the weight. This difficulty for any position like Burge's is due to Russell (following Wittgenstein);[27] so far as I know it has never been dealt with by adherents of this sort of position.

8. The second consideration is that Burge's framework forces us to choose between a pair of positions each of which is compellingly motivated by the deficiencies of the other.

With the framework in place, the only Fregean treatment of context-sensitive singular terms is to credit particular uses of them with senses that determine objects in such a way that the senses are expressible whether the objects exist or not. At best this generates a falsification of, for instance, demonstrative thought, akin to the falsification of perceptual experience that is induced by representative realism. Representative realism postulates items that are "before the mind" in experience whether objects are perceived or not, with the effect that even when an object is perceived, it is conceived as "present to the mind" only by proxy. Analogously, if an object thought of demonstratively is present to the mind only by way of something which could have been deployed in thought even if the object had not existed, the object is before the mind only by

---

[24] We can ignore such niceties as that the second argument should really be a sequence (so that we can vary the number of *res* without needing new relations). We can also ignore divergences over the nature and internal structure of the propositional fragment.

[25] Having fixed the logical form, we go on to look for elucidation of the semantical primitive: see Donald Davidson, "Truth and Meaning", *Synthese*, 17 (1967), 304–33.

[26] See Dummett, "What is a Theory of Meaning? (II)", in *Truth and Meaning*, ed. G. Evans and J. McDowell (Oxford, 1976), 67–137, p. 89.

[27] For Russell's exposition, see *The Philosophy of Logical Atomism*, pp. 81–3. If we understood how a Russellian proposition could be a kind of proposition, we would certainly have no problems in saying what it was for one of them to be true; but the point that Russell takes from Wittgenstein is that a precondition for so much as supposing that we are dealing with a bearer of truth-value is not satisfied. (That is not how Russell puts it.)

proxy.[28] Without some seemingly inescapable compulsion, it is hard to believe that anyone would tolerate this indirectness in an account of how demonstrative thinking relates us to objects.

The felt compulsion comes from a perception of how genuinely unattractive is the only alternative that the framework allows.[29] Consider, for instance, how strange it is to suggest that what a belief is about can be partly determined by something that is "not part of the cognitive world of the believer" (Burge 2 p. 359) – by something "external to what cognitively transpires in the mind of the thinker" (McGinn, p. 68). The resistance that this suggestion naturally elicits cannot be disarmed by introducing a use of 'mind' according to which a *de re* "content", jointly determined by aspects of a thinker's "cognitive world" and by matters external to it, can count as "in the mind".[30] Once the subject's cognitive world has been segregated from his involvement with real objects,[31] this merely terminological move cannot restore genuine sense to the idea that we can get our minds around what we believe – even when the belief is *de re*.[32] Here again, it seems implausible that anyone could fail to see how unattractive

---

[28] This description fits the theory of indexically expressible thought expounded by Searle, *Intentionality*, pp. 218–30; note Searle's insistence that such thoughts could be entertained by a brain in a vat. On Searle's account, the object of a perceptually demonstrative thought is specified in terms of a causal relation to a current perceptual experience; *qua* object of thought, the object is present to the mind only by proxy, and this virtually necessitates a construal of the "current perceptual experience" on representative lines (spoiling the insight that Searle expresses at p. 46 by saying that perceptual experiences are presentations rather than representations). Burge mentions a connection between rejection of his view of the *de re* and representative realism – Burge 2, p. 350, n. 12 – but he does not elaborate; this may be partly because he does not consider a position like Searle's at all. Certainly his objection of obscurantism (p. 353; cf. Burge 3, pp. 427–30) seems not to apply to Searle: it fits a mere postulation of Fregean senses, not the highly detailed specifications that Searle offers.

[29] This motivation is very clear in Searle, *Intentionality*.

[30] See McGinn, "The Structure of Content", in *Thought and Object* (n. 5 above), 207–58 (see especially p. 257, n. 31).

[31] It is worth noting how bizarre the segregation makes this use of 'cognitive'.

[32] There is supposed to be an argument from the nature of explanations of behaviour for separating off this supposed aspect of the mental (whatever one calls it); but this is well answered by Evans, pp. 203–4. Dissatisfaction with the terminological move is not alleviated, but if anything reinforced, when one notes how adherents of this bipartite conception of mind typically single out the supposed cognitive aspect of the mental by means of distorted forms of features that are intuitively attributable to the mental as such. I shall mention two examples: first, interiority, which in fact fits the mental as such (*de re* beliefs are internal in the appropriate sense, which is a metaphorical one), but which is literalized ("in the head") and used to characterize the supposed cognitive aspect of the mental; and, secondly, availability to introspection, which is oddly glossed in this position as requiring infallibility (see McGinn, "The Structure of Content", pp. 253–5) – whereas in the only good sense we can give to the notion of introspection, *de re* beliefs are (fallibly, of course) available to it. Simon Blackburn's phenomenological argument for a version of the position I am attacking (see *Spreading the Word* (Oxford, 1984), Ch. 9) is answerable by an application of the ideas outlined in my "Criteria, Defeasibility, and Knowledge", *Proceedings of the British Academy*, 68 (1982), 455–79; to put the point another way, it involves a misuse of the relation between appearance and reality entirely analogous to that which vitiates the Argument from Illusion.

this position is, except under a felt compulsion to suppose that this must be how things are; and a felt compulsion towards that conclusion can derive in turn from the deficiencies of the supposedly unique alternative.

This sort of oscillation, which is familiar in philosophy, should lead one to look for a suspect common assumption. Countenancing *de re* Fregean senses gratifies both the natural motivations that Burge's framework represents as incompatible: it yields thoughts which are both *de re* and part of the thinker's cognitive world. The justification for the framework is quite unconvincing, as I have pointed out. A combination of strongly held belief and uncompelling argument often betrays something philosophically deep; I believe that reflecting on the possibilities for a Fregean account of the *de re* is an excellent way to undermine pervasive and damaging prejudices in the philosophy of mind.[33]

University College, Oxford

---

[33] A useful label is 'psychologism'. In "The Basis of Reference", *Erkenntnis* 13 (1978), 171–206, Stephen Schiffer tries to rebut the charge that occupation of the first horn of this supposed dilemma is psychologistic. The attempt leaves me unconvinced; but it may somewhat allay Schiffer's sense of injustice to make it clear that I think the charge applies to occupation of the other horn too: it is psychologism, in the end, that makes the dilemma seem inescapable.

FREGE, SOMMERS, SINGULAR REFERENCE

By Gregory McCulloch

In his provocative recent book Fred Sommers sets out to formulate a traditional term logic (hereafter TFL) that is a genuine and significant alternative to the Fregean type of logic (MPL) currently accepted as standard.[1] Broadly speaking, his procedure has two components. On the one hand, he tries to develop a logical syntax, based on the TFL model, that is roughly the equal of MPL in terms of expressive and inferential power. On the other, he engages in a sustained effort to show how such a logic would be free of certain logical and semantic commitments, allegedly typical of MPL, that are, according to Sommers, implausible or otherwise unsatisfactory.

In the present paper I do not question the extent of Sommers's success in the first task; nor do I try directly to defend MPL against his strictures. My concern is with one fundamental difference between the two logical frameworks as Sommers sees them. This supposed difference concerns expressions like proper names that appear to make straightforward singular reference to particular objects. Sommers argues at length that many of the significant differences alleged to hold between the two logics can be traced to the way that they handle such expressions. This contention he links to his claim that whereas the basic propositions of MPL are *singular*, those of TFL are *general*; and this in turn he links to his view that the two logics are based upon significantly different accounts of the first-order generality expressed by words like 'all' and 'some' (Sommers, Ch. 1–5, 11–12). I try to show that these claims are greatly exaggerated.

Even if one grants that Sommers succeeds in giving a novel, TFL-style account of first-order generality, it is a mistake to think, as Sommers does, that this novelty consists in an interesting avoidance of commitment to the idea of singular reference. This is, furthermore, an entirely distinct issue from that of

---

[1] 'MPL' and 'TFL' are Sommers's own abbreviations for 'Modern Predicate Logic' and 'Traditional Formal Logic' respectively. He attempts no precise definition of what a logic must be like if it is to count as MPL-type, but seems to have in mind logics that employ quantifier/variable notations in a more or less orthodox manner. Similarly, his use of 'logic' is quite flexible, and is used to apply not merely to a given calculus but to this plus the concepts, notions, and presuppositions that a standard semantic interpretation would employ. I follow him in this, although certain dangers in this are highlighted in §§ II and III.

the semantic treatment of proper names. Sommers's claims gain a spurious plausibility because of his failure to keep these distinct questions apart. And finally, anyway, we see that one's adoption of logical framework – TFL or MPL – does not materially affect one's options when dealing with proper names: both logics can accommodate any of the usual alternatives. If I am right in all this, the appearance of deep differences over singular reference just dissolves.

Sommers's book deserves careful and extended attention. Both in the effort to reinstate TFL as a worthwhile approach, and in the claim to have succeeded, Sommers finds himself in opposition to much received 'Fregean' opinion in logic, semantics, and the philosophy of language. Illumination is to be had from a piecemeal treatment of the many issues raised here. This paper is just one restricted contribution to that enterprise.

I. SYNTAX: WILD TERMS AND INDIVIDUAL CONSTANTS

As Sommers points out,

> [e]ven the traditional logician often regiment[s] sentences for logical reckoning . . . Such regimentations put sentences into logically useful patterns by isolating their terms (p. 1).

That is, given a fragment of language used to express deductive reasoning, the logician's job is to provide "every non-canonical sentence in the logically relevant fragment [with] a canonical paraphrase" (p. 8). It is here, at the level of logical syntax, that Sommers sees the first great advantage for TFL over MPL, since the regimentations of the former, he claims, "do not significantly depart from the syntax of the sentence[s] being regimented" (p. 1).

Now as Sommers is well aware, the claim that TFL's more "natural" syntax is a philosophically relevant point in its favour rests upon some pretty weighty philosophical considerations (Sommers, Introduction). Fortunately I can skip by most of these, since the issues that concern me do not belong at this syntactic level. But it will help to bring them into focus if we start with a consideration of certain relevant canonical forms typical of MPL and Sommers's TFL. Let us than grant ourselves recognition of the logical forms 'not', 'and', 'or', '. . . is greedy' and '. . .is ugly'. Then whereas the following inferences are *not* valid:

A.1. Every man is greedy or ugly, *ergo* Every man is greedy or every man is ugly.

A.2. Some man is greedy and some man is ugly, *ergo* Some man is greedy and ugly.

A.3. Not: every man is greedy, *ergo* Every man is not greedy.

the following *are*:

B.1. Socrates is greedy or ugly, *ergo* Socrates is greedy or Socrates is ugly.
B.2. Socrates is greedy and Socrates is ugly, *ergo* Socrates is greedy and ugly.
B.3. Not: Socrates is greedy, *ergo* Socrates is not greedy.[2]

What this familiar fact means is that any worthwhile logical syntax must distinguish between expressions that go with 'Socrates', and those that go with 'every man' or 'some man', so that the rules for manipulating the expressions of the calculus, themselves couched in terms that refer to the regimentations allowed by the syntax, will license the Bs but not the As.

In MPL, this distinction is standardly represented by that between individual constants, on the one hand, and variable-binding quantifiers on the other. No such distinction is to be found in Sommers's TFL. Instead, Sommers takes up Leibniz's idea that proper names like 'Socrates' have *wild quantity*. What this means is that such expressions may be treated indifferently under regimentation as having either of the forms [every S] or [some S]. Thus a sentence like 'Socrates is greedy' is given the canonical form [some/every S is P] [$\pm S + P$] in Sommers's notation), and the understanding is that one may ignore either sign of quantity (i.e. 'some' or 'every') as required. At a stroke, according to Sommers, this captures the inferences under B, since (with wild 'Socrates') they can be treated as instances of the valid

C.1. Some S is greedy or ugly, *ergo* Some S is greedy or some S is ugly
C.2. Every S is greedy and every S is ugly, *ergo* Every S is greedy and ugly
C.3. Not: every S is greedy, *ergo* Some S is not greedy.[3]

Now there is no doubting the extreme ingenuity of this proposal for signalling, within logical syntax, the logical differences between the As and the B-s. And there is no doubting that we have here a genuine difference between TFL and standard presentations of MPL. Within the former system, 'Socrates is greedy' and 'Every man is greedy' are alike treated as being made up of both logical and non-logical particles; whereas the latter system usually sees 'Socrates is greedy' as devoid of any logical vocabulary, and therefore as differing radically from the quantified sentence. But at least three questions immediately arise, and it is with these questions that the bulk of the present paper is concerned. Firstly, we may ask what, if anything, is the deeper significance of this syntactic difference between the two approaches. As the A

---
[2] I include this example – as does Sommers in the discussion I am here summarising – even though his official view seems to be that this inference is invalid: see Ch. 14 esp. § 7.
[3] Cf. Sommers, Ch. 2, esp. § 3.

and B examples show, any logical syntax worth its salt must provide for the validity of the B-s in such a way that the A-s are excluded. Standard presentations of MPL 'discern' individual constants, TFL wild terms. But what else is signified by thus *writing* them differently? Secondly, as my mention of "standard presentations" of MPL has hinted, we may wonder about the exact target of Sommers's protracted anti-Fregean arguments. For as Quine has shown – and as Sommers acknowledges (e.g., on p. 61) – one can formulate MP-logics that regiment names as general terms, and which lack individual constants altogether (see Quine, §§26–7). Admittedly, there is still a contrast between such logics and Sommers's TFL over how sentences containing names are to be regimented, most markedly in virtue of the MPL apparatus of quantifiers and bound variables, which Sommers does not employ. But it is not clear – to say the least – either what further significance *this* difference is supposed to have, or what relation it bears, if any, to the differences with respect to singular reference that are alleged to exist between TFL and MPL. Clearly, in view of this Quinean treatment of names, one will get at no fundamental difference between the two logical frameworks merely by contrasting wild terms with individual constants. My third question concerns wildness itself. The idea is as odd-sounding as it is ingenious; and we may legitimately enquire whether a logic that employs it is satisfactory, let alone an improvement on available MPL treatments of names.

My discussion of these three questions threads through a number of issues concerning the semantic treatment of quantifiers and proper names, and the notion of singular reference itself. If things go as I intend, getting straight on the present issue between Sommers and Frege provides independently valuable enlightenment on these matters.

II REFERENCE AND GENERALITY

Sommers claims that TFL differs from MPL in being essentially *subject-predicate*. On this approach, the basic form of the proposition is [Some/every S is/isn't P] ([±S±P] for Sommers), the subject being formed out of a term and a sign of quantity, the predicate out of a term and a sign of quality. All terms can appear in subjects *and* predicates (Sommers, p. 17 ff.; Ch. 3, 9). Central to this proposal is the idea that the subject of a proposition of TFL refers or purports to refer to some or all of the things that its term applies to, and the predicate describes or purports to describe them as being thus or so. As we have already seen, a word like 'Socrates' is regimented as 'some/every Socrates', under which regimentation it is then grouped with phrases like 'some man'. And corresponding to this syntactic grouping is the semantic proposal, just mentioned, to treat expressions like [some S] or [every S] indifferently as referring subject expressions, regardless of whether S is a proper name or ordinary general term.

What is more, Sommers offers an account of the truth-conditions of sentences that express first-order generality which incorporates this referential thesis. 'Every' is defined in termrms of 'some' (Ch. 13, 14), and the truth-conditions of sentences beginning with the latter are specified as follows:

> one who says that some S is P has said what is true only if he has said of an S-that-is-P *that* it is P,

an utterance of such a sentence that fails to do that being false (pp. 52–3). Success here is said to depend upon referring with the subject [some S], and this is said to be "*primary* reference", not definable in more primitive terms (p. 61 n.9; cf. Ch. 13). This account of generality is left informal, and I do not know whether it can be made to work satisfactorily. But no matter: it suits my argument just to *allow*, for the sake of it, that it can.[4] So let us do this, and ask the question how, and with what alleged significant upshot, this TFL account of generality compares with the MP-logician's.

The divergence from standard MPL doctrine seems drastic indeed. One basic idea of Fregean orthodoxy is that quantifier phrases are to be *contrasted* with individual constants on the score of referring to objects. According to the MP-logician, the latter always, and the former never, have this function (see, for instance, Geach, Ch. 1–4; FPL Ch. 2). Sommers tries to establish that this difference between MPL and TFL points to a deep difference over the notion of singular reference (Ch. 1–6). The account on which he concentrates attention is Frege's own; and it will be useful to describe this briefly.

Frege's view is that sentences containing expressions of generality must be treated as *nested* with respect to these expressions, taken one at a time in an order that should be syntactically determined. Corresponding to the principal or outermost such expression one must isolate a functional expression which is itself incomplete in respect of containing one or more gaps into which certain other expressions may be inserted. Then the contribution of the quantifier expression, to the truth-value of the entire sentence, is given by a rule that states the conditions under which the corresponding functional expression, suitably completed, must produce truth (e.g., in every or at least one case of suitable completion) (cf. BLA, pp. 42–3). As for 'suitable completion': Frege casts his account in terms of the insertion, into the gaps of the functional expression, of Fregean Proper Names of the objects being generalised about, the notion of the truth-value of such a resulting sentence being co-ordinate with that of the named object falling under the concept referred to by the functional

---

[4] That is, I shall assume that Sommers can satisfactorily answer, for instance, the convincing-looking arguments to be found in Geach, Ch. 1 and 3.

expression (BLA, pp. 41, 37). And there is no mention or need here of the idea that the thus accounted-for quantifier expression refers to any of the quantified-over objects. By contrast, a Fregean Proper Name is understood to refer to some given object of the appropriate domain.

Sommers describes this Fregean account of generality as involving *Frege's Atomicity Thesis*: the thesis that there are *atomic propositions*, propositions that are primitive or basic with respect to general sentences, and in terms of which the logical properties of the latter can be explained. This thesis has both syntactic and semantic elements. It presupposes a regimentation that explicitly distinguishes expressions for generality from Fregean Proper Names by putting them into distinct syntactic categories. (This is the syntactic feature of standard MP-logics, discussed in §I, that distinguishes them from Sommers's TFL.) But it also incorporates a definite idea of what it is to account for the logical behaviour of expressions. Frege conceived this in terms of systematic contribution to the truth-values of embedding sentences. As far as the expressions for first-order generality are concerned, this contribution is explained by the rules, mentioned above, that refer to the truth of sentences containing Fregean Proper Names. The notion of singular reference then comes in as a supplementary theoretical notion used in specifying what is needed if these name-containing sentences themselves are to be true. I emphasise these rather obvious points because we shall soon have reason to attend closely to them.[5]

Let us call any logic that is committed, in this way, to Frege's Atomicity Thesis, a FAT logic. Then the underlying semantic significance of the syntactic difference between TFL and MPL which we described in §II is, according to Sommers, this: MPL is FAT, TFL is not. Corresponding to the former's regimentations [Φt], with t an individual constant, are the basic singular propositions, and the appeal to singular reference, posited by the Fregean account of generality. Corresponding to the latter's [$\pm$S+P] there are general propositions which are, according to Sommers's account of generality, *primitive*, both syntactically *and* semantically (cf. Sommers's account of the truth-condition of [Some S is P]). Furthermore, Sommers tends to see another, related, contrast here. If there really is this semantic difference underlying the divergent regimentations of, say, 'Socrates is greedy', then we appear to have divergent logico-semantic theories of the non-canonical proper name 'Socrates'.

---

[5] Of course, not all individual constants in a calculus need be left primitive. Some could be introduced as definitionally equivalent to quantified sentences, as in a Russellian framework. The point is that there must be *some* names that are primitive, relative to the quantifiers of that calculus, if the Fregean account of the contributions of those quantifiers is to be successfully carried through. Strictly speaking, these primitive names need not be construed as belonging to the calculus itself, but could instead be deemed to belong to a language of which that calculus is a part. But I follow Sommers here in taking a rather relaxed attitude to such niceties. One who adopts the Fregean approach is an MP-logician in that he employs the Fregean quantifier idioms, and explains these with reference to primitive names that can occupy the gaps in the same first-level predicates.

Depending upon whether it is regimented as a wild term or an individual constant, it may seem that the truth-conditions of any sentence containing it will be either irreducibly general, as on Sommers's account, or irreducibly singular, as on Frege's. Certainly this is how Sommers seems to see things (see esp. Ch. 1–3).

My thesis, to be argued for forthwith, is that *both* of these alleged contrasts between MPL and TFL are illusory. Firstly, while there *is* a sense in which MP-logics are FAT, I shall suggest that the same goes for TFL. Secondly, I shall show that this point is quite independent of the issue concerning the semantic treatment of the regimented proper names of ordinary language. This conclusion I reinforce by showing how to fit any of the standard accounts into either logical framework.

III   MPL AND TFL ARE FAT

We started with three questions that arose out of Sommers's proposal to regiment proper names as wild terms. The first – what is the further significance of doing this supposed to be – has just been addressed. The second question concerned the extent of the alleged contrast between MPL and TFL that Sommers's proposals constitute. This question arises because there are MP-logics, such as Quine's, that do not contain individual constants. Sommers claims that MPL, unlike TFL, is FAT: but how can a logic without individual constants be FAT? There is a certain obscurity here in Sommers's exposition. Of course, he is aware of logics like Quine's, and at one point *contrasts* the account of first-order generality with which they are naturally linked with the Fregean one described above (p. 21 n. 9). Here and there, too, he speaks approvingly of Quine's rejection of individual constants, and takes this to *undermine* the plausibility of orthodox Fregean views on atomicity (e.g., pp. 165–6). This is rather puzzling, since the overall, official contrast which he is at pains to make out is supposed to hold between his TFL and *any* MP-logic. And a system counts as belonging to MPL, for Sommers, if it follows the Fregean line of regimenting expressions for generality in the usual quantifier-variable notation (see e.g., p. 12 f.). But relative to this fundamental cleavage, the Quine of *Mathematical Logic* is as much an MP-logician as is Frege.

Here my argument takes a perhaps surprising turn. For I want to suggest that there *is* a sense in which MPL is FAT, even if it takes the form of Quine's and eschews individual constants. There is, in this way, good reason for the obscurity in Sommers which I have just mentioned. But here my concessions to him stop. MPL *is* FAT, in the sense that I am about to describe. But so is TFL: so there is no contrast here of the type that Sommers alleges.

If an MP-logic lacks individual constants, how is it to explain the truth-conditions of sentences containing its Fregean quantifier idioms? Frege's account, we saw, explains the role of, say, 'some', by giving a rule that states the conditions under which the relevant corresponding functional expression, *suitably completed*, gives truth. It is his account of suitable completion that makes use of the idea of the individual constant. The general trick of dispensing with this piece of apparatus is associated with Tarski (1956). Instead of using expressions belonging to a calculus, expressions which are conceived to stand for one or other of the objects being generalised about, Tarski appeals directly to the objects themselves. A suitable completion of a functional expression, on this approach, just consists in the circumstance of that expression's *applying to* some given one of the objects generalised about: and truth is produced here just if that expression *does* apply to that object.

This is familiar enough. The point that I want to emphasise, however, is that, for present purposes, this Tarskian account of generality is not materially different from Frege's. What I mean is just this. Suppose our regimented fragment to contain a generalisation of the form [ExΦx] taken to hold over some domain of objects x,y,z. . . Then on the Fregean gloss of the truth-conditions of this sentence, it will be true just if some sentence of the form [Φt] is true, where t is an individual constant that stands for one of the objects x,y,z. . . The Tarski idea, on the other hand, is that our sentence will be true just if Φ applies to at least one of x,y,z. . . Any apparent difference between these accounts disappears, as far as present purposes are concerned, upon the observation that both the Fregean '[Φt] is true', and the Tarskian 'Φ applies to x', rest upon the idea of the relevant object's being F, where F-ness is the property represented by Φ. In other words, both accounts make a fundamental appeal to the idea of a *certain given object* from the domain of quantification being thus or so (cf. FPL, pp. 16–17). What happens, in effect, is that the syntactic and the semantic aspects of FATness start to come apart. In an overall language lacking Fregean Proper Names it is perhaps not possible to isolate a syntactic feature upon which the burden of singular reference falls. But the semantic correlate of this remains. Either the idea that the concept referred to by the functional expression maps a given object on to a truth-value, or the idea that the expression itself applies or fails to apply to a given object, is appealed to in the Tarskian account of generality. In this sense, then, MP-logics – whether they contain individual constants or not – are FAT. But now – and this is a crucial question, of course – can one say *otherwise* of TFL?

Recall Sommers's account of how subjects of the form [some S] work:

'Something is Φ' is true iff some thing that is Φ is thereby said to be Φ.

Does this avoid commitment to the semantic idea of some given object from the domain of quantification being thus or so? Surely not! Surely this commitment is as present here as it is in the MPL accounts we have considered. Exactly the same conceptual resources are being utilised. In all three cases the truth of the quantified sentence is said to depend upon how it is with one or more of the relevant objects, *taken singly*. If one of them satisfies some given condition, then the original sentence is true; if not, not. This seems very obvious. And it surely does not matter whether the absence of an appropriate syntactic element makes talk of *singular reference* out of place. The key point is that object-involving *semantic atoms* — the correlates of the expressions (if any) involving singular reference – are appealed to. *This* much FATness is still present.[6]

It would be forgivable to think that things cannot be this easy. If they were, then Sommers's alleged confusion would be inexplicable. I think that two considerations are germane here. Expressions like 'basic proposition' are systematically ambiguous, sometimes referring to an element of syntax, sometimes to an element of semantics. On the first reading, the basic propositions of some calculus would be, say, the truth-valueable expressions containing only a certain number of certain specified types of expressions of the calculus. At this syntactic level, as we saw, there is a contrast between TFL and standard presentations of MPL, which may reasonably be expressed in terms of the generality or otherwise of basic propositions. Those of TFL, we saw, contain the primitive quantifier expression 'some'. And this amounts to *logical complexity* on the standard MPL account, according to which the basic propositions contain no logical vocabulary, being of the form [Φt]. But we also saw that this syntactic difference cannot point to any deep difference between MPL and TFL as Sommers normally understands them, if only because some MP-logics *lack* the individual constants. One needs to get down to the semantics in order to make his essential point, as we saw; and this involves talking about 'basic propositions' in the *semantic* sense. In this sense a proposition is an extra-linguistic entity, something invoked in order to explain the way in which the truth-values of sentences are determined. My account of FATness includes a mention of basic propositions in this sense, and in suggesting that MPL is FAT, I do suggest that its basic propositions are irreducibly singular. Any tendency to confuse the two senses of 'basic proposition', then, would result in the appearance of a deep and significant contrast between MPL and TFL of just the sort that comes out of Sommers's pages. But if – as I have just suggested – TFL is *also* FAT in the semantic sense, this appearance is illusory.

---

[6] There are further questions whether any conceivable account of first-order generality should make, or can be shown to make, an appeal to the idea of FATness: see Wallace; Kripke 1; Davies, pp. 142–8. But it seems absurd to claim that general statements *about objects* do not require an appeal to FATness for their explication; and almost as absurd to suppose that, say, 'Someone has been sitting in my chair' is not about objects. Still, I content myself in the present paper with the more restricted claim that Sommers's account of first-order generality is on all fours with Frege's and Tarski's in respect of FATness.

Furthermore, any tendency to confusion here reinforces another, closely related, confusion of which I suspect Sommers to be guilty. Consider these two claims:

(i) There are Fregean Proper Names
(ii) Proper names are (to be regimented as) Fregean Proper Names

These two claims are quite distinct.[7] But it is easy to think that they amount to the same thing, especially in the light of standard MPL regimentations of sentences containing names like 'Socrates'. Sommers is certainly prone to this way of thinking; and this again makes it look as though our two logics differ significantly over singular reference. TFL is certainly not committed to (ii), at least in Sommers's version. Moreover, MPL is FAT: and neglect of the ambiguity of 'basic proposition' would encourage one to see it thereby committed to (i). One need then only fail to distinguish (i) and (ii), and one seems to have happened upon a fundamental difference between the two logics: one seems to have found a commitment to a type of basic singular reference which is made by MPL, and not made by TFL.

MPL is in general certainly *not* committed to (i), given Quine's version of it; neither is TFL. MPL *is* (semantically) FAT; but so is TFL. So far, then, we have found no general difference between them of the sort that Sommers alleges. I shall complete my case against Sommers by showing that the two logics do not significantly differ with respect to commitment to (ii) either. In fact, I shall argue that one's treatment of the proper names of ordinary language is in no way affected by one's choice of logical syntax between MPL and TFL.

IV WILD TERMS

Our third question of §I concerned the proposal to treat names like 'Socrates' as wild terms. We asked whether the notion of a wild term makes sense, and whether this proposal is any sort of improvement on the usual MPL accounts. In answering this question, I shall have an eye to demonstrating the results just announced. But this discussion may be of some independent interest due to the ingenious novelty – to post-Fregean minds anyway – of Sommers's suggestion.

Consider the following standard equivalence:

(1) Every S is P iff not: Some S is not P.

---

[7] The quickest way to see this is to consider the Russellian ideas (a) that proper names abbreviate definite descriptions, and (b) that these descriptions are to be regimented in the style of Russell's theory of descriptions, using existential and universal quantifiers only. Such an approach is not committed to (ii) in the text. But it is clearly a further matter whether it adopts a Fregean account of its quantifiers, say by introducing *logically proper names*, thereby becoming committed to (i). These logically proper names need not be the ordinary proper names of natural language (that would be silly since it would undermine the alleged advantages of theses (a) and (b)). See Russell, p. 201.

Now suppose that S is a term which is to have wild quantity – it could be a regimentation of 'Socrates'. Then we seem to have

(2) Every S is P iff Some S is P.

So for wild S we get, from (1) and (2),

(3) Some S is P iff not: Some S is not P.

But (3), of course, is not generally valid: both

(4) (not: Some S is P) and (not: Some S is not P)

and

(5) (Some S is P) and (not: not: Some S is not P)

can be true, viz. when

(6) There is no S

and

(7) There is an S that is P, and another S that is not P,

respectively, are true.[8]

Now it is clear how the lover of wildness will proceed here. Where S is wild, it must be 'understood' both that

(8) There is an S

and

(9) There is only one S.

[8] Fregeans should peruse the following semantic tableau:

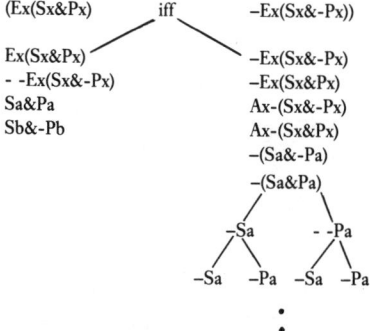

FREGE, SOMMERS, SINGULAR REFERENCE   121

In the face of these – let us call their conjunction the *Unex* condition[9] — the cases under which (3) comes out false will be ruled out for wild S, and there will be no problem about accepting (3). But how is it to be 'understood' that the wild terms of a logic satisfy the *Unex* condition?

It is quite wrong to think that this is adequately taken care of by the *syntactic* device of regimenting wild terms thus: [some/every S]. We are told that such an expression may be treated indifferently under regimentation as having particular or universal quantity – and this is what sets us off down the road from (1) to

---

[9] '*Un*' for 'uniqueness' and '*ex*' for 'existence'. The first would close the left side of the tableau in note 7 (since [a = b] would be stipulated to hold), and the second would close the right (since for some a, [Sa] would hold).

Although Sommers uses the equivalence (1) to define 'every', he does not consider it to be valid, since he considers sentences [Every S is P] to be undefined when S is vacuous (ch. 13, § 3; cf. pp. 331–3). He accordingly only tends to admit to the right-to-left conditional entailed by (2), characteristically describing wild terms as terms for which [Some S is P] entails [Every S is P]. However, it is possible to show that Sommers is committed to (8) and (9) for any wild S that appears in his calculus, without forcing (1) and (2) upon him as my argument in the text does.

(A) *Uniqueness*. Assume that we have a sentence [Φ(Socrates)] which needs to be put into TFL for 'logical reckoning'. This gives us a formula [Some S is P] with wild S. By the definition of wildness, this yields [Every S is P]. But then we certainly have [not: Some S is not P] (since this defines [Every S is P] if it is defined at all). Discharging the original assumption, then, gives [If Some S is P then not: Some S is not P], which is the left-to-right conditional entailed by (3). This conditional fails when we have

(5) (Some S is P) and (not: not: Some S is not P),

which must therefore be ruled out by stipulating (9). This is the uniqueness condition.

(B) *Existence*. This may seem more straightforward. Given [Some S is P] one might expect straight off that there would be an existential commitment that would rule out

(4) (not: Some S is P) and (not: Some S is not P).

In fact, things are rather more complicated. True, (4) would have to be ruled out for wild S to avoid contradiction (obtained by detaching its left-hand conjunct), and this we may take to be effected just in virtue of S's wildness (which results in its regimentation as [Some S]: let us waive the question of whether Sommers is committed to the invalid (3), or its right-to-left conditional, which are falsified by (4)). But there remains a reason why Sommers might resist the conclusion that his use of wild terms carries existential commitment. He denies that 'some' *generally* carries existential commitment so that, for instance, he can count as true 'a flying horse was captured by Belloperon' when the intention is to speak of the domain of fiction, which he takes to be populated by non-existent things (see p. 211ff). But there appears to be some confusion in Sommers's view here. In line with the view of fictional discourse that I have just mentioned, we find him saying that '...'some blue swans are omnivores'... is false *even though it does not assert the existence of blue swans*...' (p. 211; my emphases). Here his general idea seems to be that existential import, where it is said to be present, is derived from 'truistic' premisses like 'every omnivore exists'. But on p. 334 we find this: 'If the terms of 'some thing is P' has standard amplitude the proposition is existential...', where terms have 'standard amplitude' if they are used with the intention of speaking of the domain of existing things (cf. p. 213ff). Anyway, in his rules for manipulating wild terms, we find the following 'T-law':

$\pm A + B = \pm[+Tx + E] + [\pm[\pm x + A] + [\pm x + B]]$,

one of whose readings is glossed as

Some A is B = Some thing exists and it is A and B,

which *at least* allows one to detach a statement asserting existence when given a statement beginning with 'some' (see p. 185). So for wild terms, TFL certainly does make the existential commitment of my (8).

(6) and (7). No: it has to be built in, as part of how the system operates, that options like (6) and (7) are not available for wild S. And this involves two things. First, the rules for manipulating the syntax must be so framed that the logic of wild subjects reflects their purported satisfaction of the *Unex* condition: for instance, some theorem of TFL will correspond to (3) just when S is deemed suitable to have wild quantity ((see Sommers, pp. 123–4; 149; 173–4; 179 ff.)). Secondly, these goings-on at the level of syntax must be adequately reflected at the semantic level. Something about the interpretation must correspond to what it is to be *Unex*. Now this should be familiar.

What is familiar, of course, is that the *Unex* condition is supposed to be satisfied by the proper names of ordinary language, when the criterion of individuation involved is not typographical but semantic. Names individuated in this way refer to at most one item, and *must* refer to at least one item if sentences involving them are to be true. And since these expressions pass the test involving the forms A and B of §1, they will have to be regimented by Sommers as wild terms. Small wonder, then, that this regimentation should turn out to have to reflect the semantic factors that are built into the *Unex* condition. But more than this should catch the eye. Anyone even passingly familiar with the post-Fregean logico-philosophical literature should recognise one of its main preoccupations here: that of giving a satisfactory semantic characterisation of terms – proper names, definite descriptions – that satisfy, at least when all is as intended, the *Unex* condition. It will be instructive to list the usual alternatives:

(K) Identify a category of expressions for which the satisfaction of the *Unex* condition is reflected in a direct assignment, to each such expression, of a particular given object which is its semantic interpretation.

(R) Define each expression taken to satisfy the *Unex* condition as equivalent to another that (a) explicitly, or (b) implicitly states the relevant condition.

(E) Characterise a relation, weaker than equivalence, that is stipulated to hold between each *Unex*-satisfying expression and some other expression that either (a) explicitly or (b) implicitly states the relevant condition.

Let us, in accordance with our present interests, restrict attention to proper names. Then (K) amounts to treating them as MPL-type individual constants, standardly interpreted (see Kripke and McDowell).[10] Russell's theory of names

---

[10] Burge treats names as general terms, in the sense that they make a predicate when written after the copula. But occurrences in subject-position are regimented (in effect) thus: 'That Socrates'; and the complex phrase as a whole receives a (K)-type treatment.

as characterised in note 7 is of type (R)(a). Theories of type (R)(b) differ in that they do not define 'the' in Russell's manner, but treat it as a primitive quantifier (cf. (Davies, ch. 7)). Evans's theory of descriptive names is type (E). On this sort of account a name that is stipulated to name whatever some given definite description applies to is semantically tied to that description in (roughly) the following way: at a certain level of assessment of the truth-value of a sentence containing the name, the description is substituted for the name.[11] The (a) or (b) versions of this theory differ in the way that the (a) and (b) versions of (R) differ.

Standardly, theories of these three types are characterised in an implicitly MPL framework. But I want to show that the framework assumed could equally well be TFL's. We shall see that the choice of framework does not materially affect the character of any (K) (R) or (E) type theory that is offered. It follows from this that, relative to the theories of names displayed above, there is no significant difference between TFL and MPL over the treatment of these expressions. But if this is right, and I am right to represent (K), (R) and (E) as exhausting the possibilities, then this will establish, along with what has gone before, my main claim that TFL and MPL do not significantly differ in general over the issue of singular reference *at all*.

The issue over (K) should be clear enough. Obviously, the TFL theorist could stipulate a category of Fregean Proper Terms interpreted in the indicated way. Equally obviously, this would make MPL and TFL come out as trivial variants of one another in respect of terms like 'Socrates'. Typical problems associated with the (K) approach – possible or actual vacuousness, behaviour in contexts of propositional attitude, etc. – would bear to the same extent upon both accounts. Generally: given the availability of (R) and (E), neither logic is *committed* to (K) when dealing with proper names; and both *could* proceed in that manner.

Even an MPL logician can have Fregean Proper Terms under option (R) by treating [F(Socrates)] as [F(the Socratiser)] and then proceeding in one of the described manners with 'the' (cf. Quine, §27). Obviously TFL and MPL would not differ here, then. But such an account is pretty futile: *pace* Quine, one will still end up with an uninterpreted sentence if 'Socrates' is vacuous since the sentence will contain an uninterpreted component.

This leaves the standard Russellian method of using an otherwise interpretable predicate (e.g., 'snubby-nosed mentor of the predecessor of the last great philosopher of antiquity') to do the work of 'Socrates'. *Formulating* such a theory presents no real problem for the MP-logician. And the same goes for his TFL twin. Sommers treats [the Φ] as [some/every Φ] (see e.g. ch. 4) – that is, as involving wild quantity. As long as it is syntactically indicated that wildness

---

[11] Cf. G. Evans, "Reference and Contingency", *The Monist*, 62 (1979), and also Evans, *passim*.

requires satisfaction of the *Unex* condition, this approach is not obviously deficient. Perhaps Sommers can simply claim that uniqueness is adequately captured straight off by the wild property of being indifferently qualified by 'some' or 'every'. Typical problems associated with the (K)-type approach will be largely avoided, so long as the predicate used can be interpreted without direct invocation of the (purported) bearer of the name in question. The issue here then resolves into the different ways of treating the quantifiers adopted by MPL and TFL respectively: and we have seen that there is *no* relevant difference here (§III). So the position with respect to (R) resembles what we saw in the case of (K): MPL, TFL – it makes no difference.

This leaves (E) – the approach for which Sommers opts in fact (Ch. 11, 12). For Sommers, a proper name is a device of cross reference – an expression whose logical role is given by establishing to which antecedent expression it harks back (and by interpreting that expression). Roughly, according to this sort of treatment, one must find an 'anaphoric background' in the (perhaps tacit) linguistic context that contains a quantifier phrase of the form [There is an F. . .] or [An F. . .] or [Some F. . .] to which occurrences of the proper name in question cross refer in virtue of their relation (of the weaker-than-equivalence type mentioned in the description of type (E) theories above) to a description [the (same) F]. Now whether this approach is tenable – let alone plausible – is not to the present point. The only interesting issue, in the present context, is whether or not the view is peculiar to TFL.

It is not. In order to make such a theory work one must (i) characterise the appropriate relation that is alleged to hold between the occurrences of the name and the relevant description, and (ii) handle this description in such a way that its purported satisfaction of the *Unex* condition is assured. For a way of achieving (i) in an MPL framework, see Evans. All that needs to be added to this in order to make it into a theory of names *other* than ones that are stipulated to name whatever some given description applies to, is a method for generating a description that will interpret the name in an E-type way; and this is clearly something which is not dependent on any particular type of logical allegiance. As for (ii) – well this just takes us back to (R); and we have seen that no significant difference between TFL and MPL comes up here.

V CONCLUSION

We have seen that both MPL and TFL need to regiment proper names in a way that distinguishes them from others that can occupy the same gap in, say, '. . . is greedy' (§I). We saw that such regimentations must also, somehow, register the fact that these expressions must be taken to satisfy the *Unex* condition (§IV). And we have just seen that any account of how this is to be accomplished in detail is available to the same extent to either logic. Therefore I conclude that TFL and MPL are not significantly different relative to the treatment of proper names. Furthermore, we also saw that the two logics do not significantly differ in the extent to which their accounts of the quantifiers invoke the key semantic feature of the idea of direct singular reference (§III). In respect of these two issues, then, – *pace* Sommers – MPL and TFL do not significantly differ at all.

University of Leicester

THE SENSE AND REFERENCE OF PREDICATES: A RUNNING REPAIR TO FREGE'S DOCTRINE AND A PLEA FOR THE COPULA

By David Wiggins

1. In a letter to Husserl dated 24th May 1891, Frege included an explanatory diagram that illustrates both the extent and the limitations of the parallelism he saw between the sense-reference relation for singular terms and the sense-reference relation for predicates:[1]

Four points about this diagram deserve particular mention here. First, in showing (as other new evidence also shows) that Frege always intended predicates to have both sense and reference, the diagram vindicates the once

---

[1] See the facsimile in *WB*. Translation of the diagram:

sentence	singular-term	concept-word	
sense of the sentence (thought)	sense of the singular-term	sense of the concept word	
reference of the sentence (truth value)	reference of the singular term (object)	reference of the concept word (concept)	object falling under the concept

THE SENSE AND REFERENCE OF PREDICATES 127

nearly solitary stand taken up by Dummett against numerous scholars who have sought to deny Frege's intention to ascribe *Sinn* and *Bedeutung* to predicates.[2] Secondly, in showing that the concept is never the sense but always the reference, it explodes a myth about Frege still lurking in departments of philosophy heavily influenced by memories of Rudolf Carnap's lectures on semantics or by Alonzo Church's "Logic of sense and denotation". Thirdly it vindicates the correctness of the general insistence (M. Dummett's, M. Furth's and others') that, for Frege, the analogies between possession of sense and reference by names and possession of sense and reference by predicates are just as important as the well-advertised differences. (Indeed, it even confirms the general correctness of various attempts, antedating the publication of the letter to Husserl, to give pictorial illustration to these analogies.[3]) Fourthly and finally, it gives clear warning of how damaging it is to seek to equate the sense-reference distinction with Mill's connotation-denotation distinction (or any of the various intension-extension distinctions that still obfuscate the exposition of Frege, as well as that of Leibniz).[4]

These are all salutary reminders. But how shall we state or explain the doctrine, now that we have Frege's picture of it? And what are we to make of any claim to the effect that it describes the actual functioning of predicate expressions?

If the diagram is where we start, and if we treat it as a supplement to the doctrine of "On Sense and Reference", we may be tempted to enlarge upon the doctrine of columns 2 and 3 as follows. Just as the sense of the singular term and its contribution to truth conditions is the mode of its presentation of the object it stands for, and just as we give the term's sense by saying what it stands for, so the sense of a predicate and its contribution to truth-conditions consists in the predicate's mode of presentation of the concept it stands for, and we give the predicate's sense by saying what concept it stands for. And, just as in the case of a singular term we show *this* sense in preference to *that* sense by using or exploiting one mode of presentation rather than another to say which object this is[5] — drawing upon and expounding one body of information in preference to

---

[2] See Dummett 2.
[3] See for instance the attempt to be discovered in my (however otherwise misconceived) "Identity Statements" in *Analytical Philosophy (Second Series)*, ed. R. J. Butler (Oxford, 1965).
[4] If you doubt this try to assign definite places to connotation and denotation in the third column (with right hand annexe) while preserving some recognizable minimum of Frege's and Mill's doctrines. See here my "Frege's Problem of the Morning Star and the Evening Star", in Schirn, II pp. 222—3.
[5] This formulation draws upon several sources, notably G. E. M. Anscombe, *Introduction to Wittgenstein's Tractatus* (London, 1959), p. 42; McDowell; D. Wiggins, *opp. citt.* (notes 3 and 4 above); FPL, p. 227 ("Even when Frege is purporting to give the sense of a word or symbol what he actually *states* is what its reference is . . . In a case in which we are concerned to convey or stipulate the sense of the expression, we shall choose that means of stating what the reference is which

another body of information to amplify our identification of the object, and carefully preferring the particular body of information that sustains the particular mode of presentation of the object one is bent on conveying —, so similarly, in the case of a predicate, we show *this* sense in preference to *that* sense, e.g., the sense of 'horse' rather than the sense of (say) 'Equus caballus', by exploiting one mode of presentation rather than another to say which concept this is, drawing upon and expounding one particular suitable body of information[6] ("A horse is an animal that has a flowing mane and tail; its voice is a neigh; and in the domestic state it is used as a beast of burden and draught, and for riding upon") in preference to any other (e.g., the body of information that says what these creatures are by classifying them as perissodactyl quadrupeds, goes on (say) to locate their species among the genus *Equus* and the family *Equidae*, then dwells on other zoological features).

2. Such a view of the sense-reference distinction as it applies to predicates, whatever its eventual difficulties as interpretation or as doctrine, would make good sense of Frege's insistence in the letter itself to Husserl and elsewhere (e.g., in the fragment "Ausführungen über Sinn und Bedeutung"[7]) that the reference of the predicate cannot be any object or objects that it it true of. Just as singular terms without reference are unfitted to figure in the expression of any judgment possessed of a significance that enables us to move forward, as we must,[8] to a truth-value, and just as any name capable of figuring in the expression of any judgment that can constitute knowledge must have reference, so must any predicate that aspires to this status. But many predicates essential to the expression of good information do not have anything they are true of. Therefore their reference is not any object they are true of.[9] Thus as Frege says:

displays the sense: we might borrow here a famous pair of terms from the *Tractatus* and say that, for Frege, we *say* what the reference of the word is, and thereby *show* what its sense is"); Evans, Ch. I. For the idea of sense as contribution to truth-conditions, see *Gg*, I.32.

[6] Or as one might say *conception*, where conceptions are *of* Fregean concepts (and therefore distinct from concepts). In *Sameness and Substance* (Oxford, 1980), pp. 78–9, I have maintained that the Fregean apparatus is readily extensible for the special case (see e.g., Putnam, "Is Semantics Possible?", *Metaphilosophy* 3 (1970)) of predicates whose sense is *extension-involving* (see pp. 10–11), where (as with 'horse' in fact) the grasp of what a horse is (the reference, i.e., that the grasp of which is the grasp of sense), is *coeval* with some mastery of some part of the extension (i.e., some knowledge of which objects 'horse' is true of). A rough and ready equivalence then becomes possible between knowledge of what Putnam calls stereotype and having a *de re* conception of what a horse is or being party to a body of *de re* knowledge of horses.

[7] In citations of this work I have drawn upon PW, p. 118ff. But, here as elsewhere, either I have changed to 'reference' the rendering 'meaning' that these translators prefer for '*Bedeutung*', or I have put back the German word.

[8] Cf. *PW*, p. 122: "The step from thought to truth-value, more generally the step from *Sinn* to *Bedeutung, has* to be taken".

[9] Note that in the scheme we have attributed to Frege, *every* predicate has a sense that is concept-involving or reference-involving. That is their normal condition. The special case with whose

THE SENSE AND REFERENCE OF PREDICATES   129

With a concept word it takes one more step to reach the object than with a proper name, and this last step may be missing – i.e., the concept may be empty – without the concept-word's ceasing to be scientifically useful. I have drawn the last step from concept to object horizontally in order to indicate that it takes place on the same level, that objects and concepts have the same objectivity (see my *Foundations of Arithmetic* §47). In literary use it is sufficient if everything has a sense; in scientific use there must also be *Bedeutungen*.[10]

This and the ensuing remark about Husserl's alternative scheme depend of course for their point on our taking the singular term/predicate analogy seriously, so seriously that even failures of analogy have to be carefully noted.

3. So far then, so good. If one already had reason to want to, one might now embrace the doctrine of column 3. Consequentially upon so doing, one might then arrange for one's semantical theory to assign to a one-place predicate like 'horse' what Dummett describes as "a property defined over every object" (one for which "it is in some manner specified for each object that that object has, or lacks, that property"),[11] rather than dispense with the route through properties (e.g., by some variant of the ontologically plainer stipulation that a sequence σ satisfies "t is a horse" iff the value for σ of the term t is a horse).[12] But this leaves over the prior question: Why in the first place would one *want* to say anything like what Frege says in the letter to Husserl? Why give predicates any *Bedeutung* at all?

One answer might allude to the supposedly imperative need to see predicates as like arithmetical functors, and (perforce) as standing for functions from objects to truth values. But we may need (and surely Frege himself must have needed) more than just one motive to see predicates in that particular way – i.e., to find the analogy with functions compelling, and as more than just an analogy. In any case, this analogical consideration hardly amounts to a deductive proof, outside Frege's framework, that predicates have a reference. (Cf. §12 below.) So we need another answer as well. (It is not as if there is a comparable temptation to make something similarly substantial of reference for the case of absolutely every expression that contributes to sentence sense, e.g., the logical constants. No doubt we can arrange our semantical theory in such a way that 'and' receives the assignment of a particular function from pairs of truth-values to

---

identifying and diagnosing I credited Putnam in n. 6 was not this but the case of predicates whose sense is *extension*-involving.
[10] Letter to Husserl dated 24th May 1891, PMC.
[11] Dummett FPL, p. 89, on which see the comments of Victor Dudman, "*Bedeutung* for Predicates" in Schirn, III, p. 72.
[12] Dudman, *op. cit.*, p. 73.

truth-values. But the existence of this possibility of assignment motivates us hardly at all to speak of the substantial *reference* of 'and'. Nor are we encouraged to speak of the sense of 'and' as the mode of presentation of this truth-function.)

The most persuasive alternative answer derives from our need to find something intelligible in second level quantification. We need to quantify over what one- and two-place predicates stand for if we are to explain all sorts of things we want to explain, even to explain such fundamental facts as what it is for the concepts F and G to be equinumerate. For this purpose we need explanations like "there exists a relation ϕ which correlates one to one the objects falling under the concept F with the objects falling under the concept G" (*Gl* §72).

Such an argument has the virtue of being at once Fregean and general in its appeal. If we take it seriously, it seems we cannot simply opt out of the project of finding the reference of predicates. What is more, this reference is something distinct from the sense which it was always assumed they had. So predicates not only contribute to sentence-sense. We even have sense as "mode of presentation of the reference" and can countenance different modes of presentation of a single reference. (Or so it seemed in §1, when we considered the everyday conception and the zoologist's conception of what a horse is.)

4. Now, however, as is well known, we confront a very considerable obstruction, placed there by Frege's doctrine of the "essentially predicative" nature of the concept which has to serve as the reference of a predicate, and reinforced by the analogy Frege is always determined to insist upon between the predicate seen as essentially incomplete (needing completion by a singular term) and an arithmetical function, which is described by Frege as "in need of supplementation, because its name has to be completed with the sign of an argument if we are to obtain any *Bedeutung* that is complete in itself" (PW, p. 119). With a concept seen as a function, we have the

> special case that the value is always a truth-value. That is to say, if we complete the name of a concept with a proper name, we obtain a sentence whose sense is a thought; and this sentence has a truth value as its reference. To acknowledge this reference as that of the True (as the True) is to judge that the object which is taken as the argument falls under the concept. What in the case of a function is called unsaturatedness, we may in the case of a concept, call its predicative nature (*ibid.*).

The difficulty is now as follows. The unity of the thought being explained in this way, and every gap in any sentence being seen as essentially "cut out", as it were, either for a singular term or for a predicate but never for one or the other indifferently, and the concept being essentially unsaturated, there is now a great obstacle in the way of expressing ourselves correctly and making ourselves understood. If I want to speak of a concept, language with an almost irresistible force compels me to use an inappropriate expression which obscures – I might almost say falsifies – the thought. One would assume, on the basis of its analogy with other expressions, that if I say 'the concept *equilateral triangle*' I am designating a concept, just as I am of course naming a planet if I say 'the planet Neptune'. But this is not the case; for we do not have anything with a predicative nature. Hence the *Bedeutung* of the expression 'the concept *equilateral triangle*' (if there is one in this case) is an object. We cannot avoid words like 'the concept', but where we use them we must always bear their inappropriateness in mind. From what we have said it follows that objects and concepts are fundamentally different and cannot stand in for one another. And the same goes for the corresponding words or signs (*loc. cit.*, pp. 119–20).

Or, as Frege puts the difficulty in "On Concept and Object",

the three words 'the concept "horse"' do designate an object, but on that very account they do not designate a concept (PW, p. 94);

and later

In logical discussions one quite often needs to assert something about a concept, and to express this in the grammatical form usual for such statements, so that what is asserted becomes the content of the grammatical predicate. Consequently, one would expect the concept to be the content of the grammatical subject; but the concept as such cannot play this part, in view of its predicative nature; it must first be converted into an object, or, speaking more precisely: an object that is connected with it in accordance with a rule must be substituted for it, and it is this object we designate by an expression of the form 'the concept *x*' (Cf. p. x of my *Grundlagen*.) So the phrase 'the concept *horse*' must be regarded as a proper name which can no more be used predicatively than can, say, 'Berlin' or 'Vesuvius' (*loc. cit.*, p. 97 col. 2).

5. The difficulty is as severe as this: that it both makes sense and is true to say that the concept *horse* is not a concept. But in that case we cannot state, or whistle (or even draw a picture of) Frege's doctrine of the sense and reference of predicates. I shall look briefly at Michael Dummett's treatment of this paradox and then suggest another line of enquiry that has its own difficulties, but seems to me to deserve exploration.

Drawing upon the same fragment, "Ausführungen über Sinn and Bedeutung", as I have been quoting as a supplement to "On Concept and Object", Dummett finds a key to the problem in Frege's suggestion (PW, p.

122) that, wherever we need to, we can designate the properly predicative entity (the concept) that is the reference of the unsaturated part of the sentence 'Jesus is a man' by using the phrase 'what the concept word 'man' refers to'. For this latter phrase *can* replace the predicate in the sentence 'Jesus is a man' both grammatically and intelligibly. – Thus: 'Jesus is what the concept-word 'man' stands for'.

But, unluckily, this is not even the beginning of the end of the difficulty. One form of it is this. Is it 'man' or is it 'ξ is a man' that is essentially unsaturated? 'Man', which is Frege's choice in the fragment quoted, seems neither saturated nor unsaturated. It neither goes into a gap to make a complete sentence nor is it such that insertion of a name into its gap gives a complete sentence. It has no gap. And all we get from the attempt to treat it as if it had one is 'Jesus man'. On the other hand, 'ξ is a man', which is indeed unsaturated (and that is the reason why Dummett prefers it), doesn't seem to fit properly with Frege's example.[13] It doesn't seem to make sense to say "Jesus is what the concept-expression 'ξ is a man' stands for" – or so one will suspect if one tries attaching a 'namely . . .' clause, which it ought to be possible to attach, to the sentence, 'Jesus is what the concept-expression 'ξ is a man' stands for, namely (is?) (a) man'. The 'namely'-clause resists the properly predicative filling, though it will certainly accept Frege's preferred filling. A similar difficulty threatens all the advantages that were gained by helping out the sense-reference paradigm by allusion to second level quantification. We can understand this kind of quantification fairly well, and (so far as one can see) perfectly referentially, if we exercise the option Frege exercises and take (*a*) *man* (or (*an*) *admirer of Hegel*) as the sort of thing quantified over in such statements as '($\exists \phi$) (I am ϕ and you are not ϕ), viz. a man (or an admirer of Hegel)' – but only if we supply the copula within the open sentence which is subjected to the quantification. But then of course the items quantified over are not unsaturated or essentially predicative. If however we try to let the quantification be over the essentially incomplete things that Dummett prefers on Frege's behalf, although there is then nothing to be supplied within the open sentence, we have the other problem: what we always need in order to understand the quantification is the item that is *not* strictly unsaturated.[14]

6. Dummett's discussions of this matter are long, ingenious and intricate, and now fairly numerous. There is much more to them than can come out here. But perhaps enough has been said to make it appear less than wholly gratuitous to look for another line of solution.

---

[13] Here I am indebted to Dudman, *op. cit.*
[14] See also P. K. Sen, "Universals and Concepts" in *Jadavpur Studies in Philosophy* 4, ed. P. K. Sen, (Macmillan of India, 1982), p. 264.

Let us start by simply following the appearances, and let us hold onto the thought that second level quantification is over what it seems to be over, viz. entities like *man, horse, admirer of Hegel, wise, run, walk, sit, work, sleep.* Such entities – let us call them concepts – are not objects, and they are neither saturated nor unsaturated. They are simply the references of grammatical predicates. But let us also take the copula and the finite endings of verbs seriously. What the copula does on this alternative view is to *combine* with a concept-word or predicate to produce an unsaturated expression that will in its turn combine in the fashion Frege himself describes with a saturated expression to produce a complete sentence.

The following stipulations may convey the general idea about the sense of the copula. Suppose that we have a fragment of English rich enough to allow us to express simple subject-predicate sentences, and that we have the simple schematic rule of truth:

Where t is a term and PRED is any predicate expression of the form of VERB, or ADJECTIVE, or 'a' + SUBSTANTIVE, True [t + copula + PRED] iff PRED is true of the designation of t (or, as Frege might have preferred to say, the designation of t falls under the concept that PRED stands for).

Suppose that designations are fixed for each singular term t by axioms like:

Designation ('Socrates') = Socrates,

and that for each primitive verb, adjective or substantive we have an axiom in the following form:

'Sit' is true of x (or, in the Fregean terminology, x falls under the concept that 'sit' stands for) iff x sits;

'(a) man' is true of x (or, in the Fregean terminology, x falls under the concept that '(a) man' stands for) iff x is a man.

Then the sense of the copula is fixed jointly by the schematic rule of truth and the axiom for each primitive verb, adjective, or substantive. Note that, pending the attainment of a better understanding that will probably displace this conception, I have elected here to view the verb in any of its finite, indicative forms (as indicated by a suffix or an auxiliary preceding the verb in participial form) as a case of [copula + PRED] and am ignoring questions of tense (which might be handled by further axioms involving the copula, where this is seen as the locus for the indication of tense, mood etc.). Note also that, with Plato's and Bradley's paradoxes and regresses in mind, I have studiously refrained from doing anything to encourage the idea that the copula stands for a relation. It does not need to do so in order to contribute to the sense of the sentence.

7. It may be illuminating to redescribe this proposal within a categorial grammar. (Cf. Evans, Ch. 1) Here one might begin by adding to the primitive categories that Frege in effect recognizes, viz. *S* (Sentence) and *N* (Singular term), a new primitive category *B* (*Begriffswort* or concept-word). Then whereas for Frege a predicate is of the category

$$S/N,$$

in the new variant theory a bare predicate is of the category

$$B$$

and the copula's role is that it combines with expressions that have concepts as their semantic value to form complex expressions that have as their semantic value functions from objects to truth-values. If someone then asks what the *reference* of 'is a man' is in 'Jesus is a man' the new answer is that it *has no reference*. Proper or substantial reference has already dropped out when we reach complex expressions of this sort. But of course this does not deprive them (or the copula) of that more general thing that Dummett calls *a semantic value*. Substantial reference exists where and only where giving the sense involves giving the mode of presentation. But for expressions in the categories N, B, and (so certain dedicated Fregeans will say) S, the way to give the semantic value is to give the substantial reference. But this is a special case and predicates fall within it not automatically or by courtesy, but only in virtue of the sorts of argument advanced in §§1 and 3.

Someone may suggest that we shall still have the analogue of the problem of the concept *horse* when we come to stating the semantic assignment for 'ξ is a horse'. But we shall not in fact have this problem if we are content to take a leaf from Frege's own book (from "On Concept and Object" for instance) and let the semantic value of such an expression be an ordinary object, e.g., a function in extension. Within the new framework, when we make the distinction between semantic value and the special case of full reference, the baby is not thrown out with the bath water. The substantial reference of the predicate and everything else we need in order to understand second-level quantification is already secure, in the shape of the concept.

8. To conclude this matter we should need a full assessment of the impact of the repair I have been proposing upon Frege's semantics. Thought would have to be given to the defences of the repaired theory against the intensional version of Russell's paradox, and to other potential difficulties. But I shall conclude on this occasion by attending to two or three elementary and much less specialized points or difficulties. I must touch on concepts and properties (§§9–11), on Frege's function paradigm for the unity of the sentence (§§12–13), and on the very idea of a repair to the system of Fregean sense and reference (§14).

9. If the copula takes an expression that stands for a concept to give us a properly unsaturated predicative phrase that can be completed by a name to give a sentence, and if concepts are indistinguishable from properties, then how is it that the copula cannot combine with the property-name 'manhood' to give us an unsaturated phrase equivalent in meaning to 'ξ is a man'? Surely, it may be said, if what I have claimed so far is right, then we ought to be able to understand

Jesus + (is + manhood)

as equivalent in meaning to

Jesus is a man.

And we cannot understand it so.

The reply to this objection is that what it really shows is that 'man' and 'manhood' do not stand for the same thing. What is more, such a distinction can be made to seem plausible by appeal to linguistic evidence that is relatively independent of the point at issue and was always there to be noticed.

Consider the designation:

The city of Paris.

The city of Paris *is* Paris. One might as well say:

The city that is Paris,

or simply:

The city, Paris.

Now consider:

The property of manhood

If this sort of 'of' behaves in any uniform way, then what this designation presumably stands for is *manhood*. But what now needs to be remarked is, first, that we also have the true identity:

The property of manhood is the property of being a man;

and secondly, that the one term we cannot licitly form as a name of this property is:

The property of man.

Still less can we affirm the identity:

The property of man is the property of manhood.

What then is manhood? Or how is the expression 'manhood' meant to behave. Surely it is synonymous with, or an alternative form of, the nominalization 'being a man', which presupposes the unsaturated expression 'ξ is a man', which (in my story, at least) presupposes the Fregean concept *man*.

10. Some confirmation for this proposal may be obtained, I believe, from the role of properties in claims about explanation. If I am right in saying that properties are best understood by reference to nominalizations, then we can see very directly why it is so natural to say "The behaviour of a thing is best explained by its properties". Suppose, as seems to be the case (is this not the one completely correct insight of the nomological-deductive model of explanation?), that all explanation is essentially propositional-cum-inferential. Then what one must do in order to explain why such and such an animal (e.g.) hibernates under this or that condition is to find a suitably interesting derivation of a sentence of the form: 'Under condition C animals of the kind K hibernate', from sentences that are true and known independently. And if so, then, surely, when we say "the thing's properties explain its behaviour", the word 'properties' precisely stands in for the nominalizations of various explanatory premisses (whatever they may be) that subsume things of the relevant kind under Fregean concepts that are both explanatorily interesting and relevant to the thing's hibernating or behaving in whatever way it does behave. (Again, cf. 'Barbarelli's size explained his nickname'. What is at issue here is an explanatory premiss about how big he was, and how unusual it was to be that big.)

This is scarcely the place to enlarge indefinitely upon such a view of properties, but there may be something to be gained from an attempt to illustrate how readily the neo-Fregean theory of concepts that is emerging here will trivially correct, but then in all other points consist with, the powerful account of properties and explanation that has been developed by Elliott Sober. In an important recent article,[15] Sober argues persuasively that evolutionary theory as we now have it generalizes over properties, and that properties, as construed by the theory in its present condition, cannot be redefined in terms of physical objects or sets of material objects. He then declares:

> What we now need to ask in our discussion of evolutionary theory is this: Are the property generalizations which one finds there mere placeholders – admissions of ignorance – which will be eliminated as we learn more about evolutionary processes, or are they part of the substance of evaluationary theory, which further information may elaborate, but never leave behind? My judgment about this question is that evolutionary theory as it matures will embrace such generalizations in greater numbers. The development of the theory to

[15] "Evolutionary Theory and the Ontological Status of Properties", *Philosophical Studies* 40 (1981).

date exhibits a proliferation of property generalizations, and this encourages the view that *it is part of the point of evolution theory to codify generalizations about what kinds of properties will be selectively advantageous in what kinds of environments* (p. 169).

This reinforces in an important way what was urged in §3 – provided that Sober's properties can be somehow aligned with Fregean concepts. To see whether they can I shall now consider just one evolutionary generalization of the kind Sober considers. In his formulation it goes:

for any property P, if there is selection for greater offspring variance-in-P, and if sexual individuals are more likely to produce offspring with greater variance-in-P, then sexual individuals will be favoured by selection. (p. 168) [16]

Sober represents this as a quantification over properties, and, even for one who accepts the distinction I have been urging between concepts and properties, there will be something to be said for that way of putting it. When we say that sexual individuals have an evolutionary advantage because (for instance) they are more likely than asexual individuals to produce offspring that vary in size, what we naturally speak of is not the concept *big* but the property of size. It would, moreover, be silly to deny that in this explanation we have a perfectly clear claim, just as it stands. But how is it that we *find* it clear? And what do we take sizes to be here? Well, a thing's size is *how big it is*. But *is* there such a thing as how big a thing is? And is that really the sort of thing (among others) that we want to see our generalization as concerned with, or as quantifying over? (There is of course such a thing as how big *Barbarelli* was, in feet. But that only takes us further away from what we want. First, the generalization that Sober is considering is concerned with such properties as size *in general*. In the second place, the particular item here offered is not a property but a number. This particular size in feet is how many feet tall Barbarelli was. – Say six.)

Perhaps then the claim is clear because we can understand it perfectly effortlessly like this: Sexual creatures have an evolutionary advantage because they are more likely than asexual individuals to produce offspring that vary in respect of *how big they are*. Perhaps we can generalize the explanation by saying (truly or falsely):

---

[16] It should be said that it is one of Sober's aims to reinstate a notion of property for which it is a substantive question whether any property corresponds to a given open sentence, and that the issue he sees here is not the danger of paradox but the business of science. In this place I shall simply put my conviction on record that any distinction of this sort that Sober can effect between open sentences can be carried over *mutatis mutandis* to the concept theory. (Though making this distinction will take a different form from the denial of any Fregean concepts.) Note also that the sense of the particular generalization quoted in the text is in fact insensitive to any such refinements as Sober envisages.

Sexual individuals are favoured by selection because, for all ϕ such that there is selection in favour of parents whose offspring vary in respect of how ϕ they are, sexual individuals are more likely to produce offspring with greater variance in respect of how ϕ they are.

Here the generalization 'for all ϕ' is over concepts and, as before, the copula is present in the open sentence quantified upon. It is ready and waiting to make an unsaturated expression from the values of the variable. If there is any difficulty of expression, it only concerns our lack in English of a pronoun that can be relied upon to do for quantifier and variable in the translation of $(\forall \phi)(\ldots \phi \ldots)$, what the pronoun 'it' will do so obligingly for pronoun and quantifier in the translation of $(\forall x)(\ldots x \ldots)$.

11. Concept words then are more fundamental than property designations, and better suited to combine the two roles which so many writers after Frege have seen as so fatally diverse: (a) the role of introducing particular principles for correlating objects with truth or falsehood and sorting those that correlate with truth (satisfy a certain condition) from those that do not; and (b) the role of standing for forms or characters or traits or universals. (a) is the role that the semantical proposals of §6 tried to catch by making it possible to prove such biconditionals as

['Socrates' + copula + 'sit'] is true if and only if Socrates sits.

(b) is the role I have tried to catch by suggesting a route to such biconditionals that goes through a clause entailing that an entity such as Socrates *falls under the concept that* 'sit' *stands for* if and only if it sits.

But can any expression really play both these parts? It will be said that so long as we concentrate on (a), and so long as we abjure the route through clauses like 'x falls under the concept that 'sit' stands for if and only if x sits', we sensibly and virtuously avoid the old problem of the unity of the sentence. Names name, predicates describe, and, having these complementary functions, names and predicates are made for one another. And nothing then invites us to fear that a sentence is insufficiently distinguished from an enumeration or list. ("When verbs are mingled with nouns then the words fit together and the simplest combination of them constitutes language . . . When anyone says '[such and such a] man learns' . . . he not only names but also achieves something by connecting verb (*rhema*) with noun (*onoma*)", as Plato puts the claim.[17]) On the other hand, so soon as we are influenced by the need to make second-level quantification intelligible, or accept the idea "that something in the realm of *Bedeutung* must correspond" to the unsaturated part of a sentence (PW, p. 192) – so soon, that is, as we try to see predicates as combining role (b)

---

[17] *Sophistes*, 262C-D.

with role (a) and find ourselves with a reason to insist that each primitive predicate of the language be characterized by a clause that mentions the concept it stands for – we cannot help but reintroduce the problem of the unity of the sentence. Or so it will be said.

My claim was that the semantical stipulations of §6 show precisely how roles (a) and (b) *can* be combined. But it seems important to compute fairly exactly just how far the proposals of §6 distance me from Frege's own way of holding these roles together and from Frege's own conception of predication.

Frege had the analogy between arithmetical functional expressions and grammatical predicates well before he drew the sense/reference distinction or came to see sentences as standing for truth-values in the same way as arithmetical functors when completed with their arguments stand for numbers (see *Bs* §9). Indeed there is a temptation to declare that the analogy always worked best for him at the time when he needed it least – that is *before* there was any issue of whether predicates had a *Bedeutung*: and that what is so unfortunate is the fact that the analogy (or assimilation) between predicate and functor begins to let him down at just the point when the problem it was meant to solve suddenly grows serious and the distinction between naming and describing becomes blurred.

Perhaps the clearest statement of his later perception of the problem and his response to it is this:

> This predicative component of our sentence has *Bedeutung* too. We call it a concept-word or *nomen appellativum*, even though it is not customary to include the copula in this. Just as it itself appears unsaturated, there is also something unsaturated in the realm of *Bedeutungen* corresponding to it: we call this the concept. This unsaturatedness of one of the components is necessary, since otherwise the components do not hold together. Of course two complete wholes can stand in a relation to one another: but then this relation is a third element – and one that is doubly unsaturated (PW, p. 177).

Here the fourth sentence must encourage the protest that, even if there really exists the incomplete sort of thing which Frege wants, it is still unclear how it can help to distinguish a sentence from a list to say that a sentence is unlike a list in mentioning both a complete thing and an incomplete thing. How is it that he who mentions something complete and then something incomplete thereby gets to say something? Or, in Fregean terminology, how can a designation of something complete followed by a designation of something incomplete combine to constitute a subject matter that can be judged or asserted as a truth?

This is not the only difficulty of Frege's formulation. We have already seen (§5) that the essentially predicative items that need to be postulated if we take his approach to the problem of the unity of the sentence are badly mismatched with the items we need for the interpretation of second level quantification. But there is also a prior difficulty, which concerns the original explanatory paradigm itself. What does it mean to say that '( )³' or 'father of ( )' stand for something incomplete? In the first place, the adjective 'incomplete' is not an absolute but an attributive term. (Incomplete *what?*) Secondly, waiving that vexation, how are we to understand the idea of reference in connexion with the most *undisputed* functional expressions themselves? Frege is so preoccupied with the problem of finding ways to state the reference of 'man' in 'Jesus is a man' (cf. §5) that he pays insufficient attention to the clarity of the one case of saturated- and unsaturatedness that is meant to be paradigmatically clear. How are we to refer to that which '( )³' or 'father of ( )' stand for? Certainly Frege's 'what '. . .' stands for' device is no use – at least if we apply it in a way which respects the theses of unsaturatedness and incompleteness. For, however we cheat with brackets or spaces or concatenation, we cannot rewrite

$$8 = (2)^3$$
$$\text{David} = \text{father of (Solomon)}$$
$$12 = (7) + (5)$$

as

8 is what '( )³' stands for (2)
David = what 'father of' stands for (Solomon)
12 = (7) what '( ) + ( )' stands for (5).

These versions are unintelligible. Yet so far from showing that it is useless to pursue the analogy with functions, the difficulty is highly instructive, and it only confirms, analogically, the case I have been presenting for some reinstatement of the copula. For if we drop Frege's insistence on counting the gap as part of the function, we can easily arrive at versions that do make sense:

8 is what the cube sign (i.e., '3' written superscript) stands for *of* (2).
David is what 'father' stands for *to* (Solomon)
12 is what '+' stands for *to* (7) *and* (5).

As soon as we distinguish the functional expression itself from the frame, and we insert the would-be equivalent into the syncategorematic structure I have indicated with brackets and italics, we get something intelligible. Just as it seemed to be a mistake in the predicate case to ignore the copula (or concatenation where that is understood as a copulative device), so it seems to be a mistake in the functor case to ignore the 'of' or the brackets or other syncategorematic material signifying the *application* of the function to the argument. Quantification tells the same story. If we want to, we can say "Harold was something *of* England, viz. king". We cannot say "Harold was something England, viz. king of" (or even "king of it"). Again, there is something that 8 is *to* 2 that 27 is *to* 3, namely the cube. When we quantify over what functions stand for, what we quantify over is not something incomplete or the designation of expressions that are unsaturated. The expressions in question are neither saturated nor unsaturated. Precisely our conclusion in §5.[18]

12. But how far, I was to say, does drawing these conclusions take us from what is central to Frege's theories? Certainly it is congenial to this approach to back off from a complete assimilation of the predicate to a straightforward functor. But, as Dummett has often remarked, the refusal to assimilate them does not amount to a rejection of the *analogy*. What we have discovered by considering the sense and reference of normal functors is a point that casts real light upon predication, as well as a recapitulation of something Frege himself stumbled upon in connection with predicates when he proposed the 'what 'man' stands for' device instead of the device the doctrine of unsaturatedness really required ('what 'ξ is a man' stands for'). Of course, once we back this preference, it will not do for us to insist in exactly Frege's way that the concept is *itself* essentially predicative. But does this difference entail that we have abandoned every single Fregean insight into the unity of the sentence? No. We still see ourselves as having started our categorial analysis from the complete sentence, and if Frege were to accept the repair proposed, he could still say that he "does the opposite" of the traditional logicians and "arrives at the concept by splitting up a whole judgeable-content" (PW, p. 17), and "only allows the formation of concepts to proceed from whole judgements" (PW, p. 16). What is

---

[18] In reaching the conclusion that second-level quantification is not quantification over things that are incomplete. I do not see myself as having to deny the importance of a kind of incompleteness that Dummett sees as dramatized or highlighted by the case of complex predicates.

We might say that, in the case of simple predicates, the slots are external to them, whereas in the case of complex predicates, they are internal. (FPL, p. 30)

What I am insisting on is only that, when we seek to speak of the reference of simple or complex predicates, the expressions we seek a reference for should not be seen as absorbing the main copula or any of the concatenational framework by which this concept may be predicated of a singular term or variable. (Once we see that in lambda-abstraction the copula is expressed by concatenation, the λ-calculus can in fact illustrate both my contention and Dummett's contention simultaneously.)

I have of course left open the whole question of the identity-criteria for concepts. But I would note that for a long time Frege felt able to do the same. See *Gl* § 68. note 1. There is some freedom here so far as semantical theory is concerned, and there may be much to be said for putting even more distance than Frege put between the problem of concept identity and anything that looks like class or extension identity. I would add that the substitutivity argument Frege advances for his preferred "extensional" criterion is not, I believe, overwhelmingly persuasive. (See for instance PW, p. 118.) Unless something more is said than Frege says about what concepts are – that they are the references of predicates and that the concept F is (quasi-)identical with the concept G if and only if everything that is F is G and *vice versa* — we can scarcely *explain or justify* the intersubstitutivity of the concept-words for F and G by reference to this quasi-identity. If we know the concepts are (quasi-)identical, we must have satisfied ourselves already that we can substitute the one expression for the other expression *salva veritate*. Frege provides us with no other route to the identity.

more, so much that he actually says about predication will still appear dead right. Consider, for instance:

> In the sentence 'Two is a prime' we find a relation designated, that of subsumption . . . This creates the impression that the relation of subsumption is a third element supervenient upon the object and the concept. This isn't the case . . . the object engages immediately with the concept without need of special cement. Object and concept are fundamentally made for one another, and in subsumption we have their fundamental union. (PW, p. 178)

Surely this cannot be wrong. How is it, however, that the object engages immediately with the concept? Frege answers (in the second omission I have marked): "the unsaturatedness of the concept brings it about that the object, in effecting the saturation [so] engages". I should answer: in a sequence of words that can be taken as a sentence – contrast something understood as an enumeration – a whole syncategoramatic structure is understood, consisting of the copula within a framework that marks places for signs of various categories (singular term and predicate, *onoma* and *rhema* or whatever). It is certainly possible, under the right conditions and within an appropriate symbolism, for the copula itself to be replaced by a convention of mere concatenation, or even by some other imaginable device. But neither this nor anything else ought to suggest that we can expect syncategorematic structure to be capable of taking over arbitrarily many of the functions of the expressions to which one would normally attribute both sense and genuine reference. It is in this direction that Wittgenstein's theory in the *Tractatus* has to exaggerate. Nor should anything suggest that expressions with sense and reference can have some sense or reference that will fit them to absorb *all* the syncategorematic functions of copula and grammatical array. This is the even more unpromising impulse to which Frege yielded when he attempted to give his whole answer to the problem of the unity of the sentence by making the distinction between saturated and unsaturated expressions or senses and a corresponding distinction between complete and incomplete references. Surely to make a sentence we really need, *pace* Wittgenstein and *pace* Frege, at least two things: not only the right syncategorematic frame or schematism for a string of words that shall be such as to combine to say something, but *also*, within that schematism, expressions of various right kinds with various corresponding grammatical functions.

In the passage that I have just quoted (PW, p. 178), Frege first calls subsumption a relation, and then denies that subsumption counts as a third element. There is some strain here. But once we see how the copula can be significant without standing for any relation, we surely have the key to preferring the denial Frege issues over the less well-considered positive claim.[19] Subsumption had better not be a relation. Finally, is nothing at all left of Frege's view that the concept is something essentially predicative? One thing remains, at least. Our enrichment of the primitive categorial basis to allow expressions of the category B to be coordinate with expressions of the category N permits sentences of both the forms 'expression *e* refers to [N]' and 'expression *e* refers to [B]', but it preserves one Fregean asymmetry. At least in the semantics we have given, the copula always combines with the predicate word, not the singular term, to discharge the predicative function in the sentence.

13. There are new trends in the interpretation of Frege that induce a certain self-consciousness about what anyone could mean by proposing a "repair" to his doctrines, especially at a point where Frege's theory is very close-knit in construction and many overlapping constraints apply. I suppose I must mean this: Taking over from Frege – inheriting from Frege – a theory that serves for us (however he would describe the purpose it served for him) as the beginnings or rudiments of a theory of how language functions and how it is possible for it to be used and understood in respect of modes of combination and composition, we obviously have to be prepared to interest ourselves in almost everything he thought or said about that theory. If we do not attempt to do this, the theory we are deriving from Frege may be much less well considered than it might have been. We have *also* to speculate about how difficulties in that theory could be cleared up or resolved – by speculating if necessary about how one could alter it and thus improve the understanding that we owe here to Frege. We seek to correct it, not because we want to pervert the historical understanding of the author and his philosophical times, or to misrepresent to ourselves the choices that were open to him and his contemporaries, but because our interest in him is that we are taking his theories as a *live option*. In the particular case I have been concerned with, those who do not treat them so seem bound first to forget them and then (in the longer run) to reinvent them.

University College, Oxford

---

[19] For Frege's perception of the syncategorematic here, it is well worth noting his observation in "On Concept and Object" (TWF, p. 47) that in 'Jesus falls under the concept *man*', 'the concept *man*' is only part of this predicate, and how he seeks to conjoin this observation with the claim that the predicate 'someone falling under the concept *man*' has the very same reference as 'a man'.

FREGE'S METAPHYSICAL ARGUMENT

By GREGORY CURRIE

Why did Frege assimilate concepts to functions? Why did he believe that concepts are unsaturated? Why did he adopt a part-whole doctrine for sense and reference: that the senses and referents of the parts of a complex expression are parts of the sense and reference of the whole? These are the questions I shall answer.

These questions have, of course, been answered before. On one influential view these doctrines are to be understood as the products of Frege's linguistic construal of philosophical questions; they derive from considerations of notational perspicuity and semantic adequacy, and they give a central place to the speaker's understanding of language. According to Michael Dummett, Frege's perception of the functional character of concepts stems from his having understood "the relation between the semantic values of sentences and those of predicates". (IFP, p. 168)[1] A function is incomplete because "it can be introduced in the first place *only* as the referent of an incomplete expression". (FPL, p. 254) Similarly for concepts and relations: "they can be explained in the first place only as being the sorts of things for which predicates and relational expressions can stand". (FPL, p. 256) The part-whole doctrine for Thoughts (the senses of sentences) seems obviously linguistic, since Frege says on a number of occasions that this is what makes it possible for us to understand sentences we have never heard before.[2] The part-whole doctrine for reference is less obviously to do with language, but perhaps for that very reason it is dismissed by Dummett as a mistaken thesis which Frege held only momentarily and therefore as something not constitutive of his philosophy. (IFP, p. 168)

If one accepts this view it is hard to resist the conclusion that Frege was first and foremost a philosopher of language; in particular a philosopher deeply sensitive to questions about how language is understood and used. I want to resist this conclusion.[3] Accordingly I shall offer the following thesis: the source

---

[1] Dummett distinguishes the recognition of the functional character of concepts from the view (which he rejects) that concepts are a special case of functions. This distinction need not concern us here.
[2] See *WB*, p. 127 (PMC, p. 79); *NS*, pp. 243, 262 (PW, pp. 235, 243); *KS*, p. 378 (LI, p. 55).
[3] See e.g., Currie.

of all the doctrines so far mentioned is an argument of Frege's which is metaphysical in a quite traditional sense; it explores the relations between entities in the world, without depending essentially on theses about the language in which these relations are expressed.

I do not claim, on the other hand, that these doctrines are entailed by the metaphysical argument (as I shall call it). A good deal of confusion on Frege's part is also an essential ingredient, and it is necessary that we should explain its role.

I

We should not, however, reject the linguistic interpretation before we have seen why it is inadequate. There are a number of places in which Frege appeals to linguistic considerations in order to ground the distinction between function and object:

> A concept – as I understand the word – is predicative. On the other hand, a name of an object, a proper name, is quite incapable of being used as a grammatical predicate.

And Frege adds a footnote to the first sentence:

> It is, in fact, the reference of a grammatical predicate. (*KS*, p. 168 (TWF, p. 43)).

> I call the function itself unsaturated . . . because its name has first to be completed with the sign of an argument if we are to obtain a completed reference (*NS*, p. 129 (PW, p. 119).

> . . . the concept is predicative in character, it is in need of supplementation, just as the predicative part of a sentence always demands a grammatical subject, being manifestly incomplete without it. (*NS*, p. 246 (PW, p. 228))[4]

Unfortunately Frege never accompanies such statements as these with a clear indication of what it is that justifies us in drawing conclusions about extra-linguistic entities from premises about the characteristics of expressions. It is at this point that his interpreters step in. It is argued that our grasp of concepts, relations and functions is necessarily dependent upon our grasp of the use of predicative and functional expressions; we have no access to these things except through our grasp of incomplete expressions, and that is what constitutes their incompleteness. David Bell, for example, notes the lacuna in Frege's argument, and goes on "to offer an interpretation and, with some modifications, a defence

---

[4] See also *KS* p. 279 (TWF, p. 115) and *NS*, p. 246 (PW, p. 228).

of the Fregean doctrine of the unsaturatedness of functions". (Bell, pp. 13–14) Speaking of the special case of relations he concludes:

> There is no reason why one could not introduce a specific relation by means of entirely non-relational expressions. But of course it is possible to do this only if one already has the generic notion of a relation. And it is this latter that cannot possibly be introduced or explained by any other means than via the common properties of relational expressions. And relational expressions are themselves abstractions from sentences (Bell, p. 81).

Bell makes it clear that he is offering "a reinterpretation of the notion of unsaturatedness". But Dummett has said that his own, similar account, illustrated by the quotations at the beginning of this paper, expresses Frege's view. (IFP, pp. 539–40) Recently he has backtracked somewhat, admitting "I have been unable to find that [Frege] ever states" this thesis. He insists however, that the view is "in accord with the spirit of Frege's thought". (FPL, pp. 234–5) We may, therefore, regard Dummett's characterization of unsaturatedness as genuine exegesis.

To repeat: we are considering the view that "an entity is incomplete if it can be introduced in the first place *only* as the referent of an incomplete expression". (FPL, p. 254)

Note that this thesis does not merely provide reasons for believing that concepts are incomplete in some antecedently understood sense of that term; rather it gives a certain content to the notion of incompleteness. Concepts, relations and functions are incomplete in the sense that our grasp of them derives essentially from our use of incomplete expressions.[5] It is a difficult question, which I do not propose to address here, whether this is an intelligible notion of incompleteness. Rather, we have to ask another question. Will this notion of incompleteness make sense of the claims that Frege makes about incomplete entities? For if not, it can hardly be accepted as an elucidation of his thought. But in fact it completely fails to account for the most important characteristic of unsaturated entities: their ability to mesh with objects in a seamless, unmediated way. I shall have a great deal more to say about this in the next section, but the essential point is easily made. According to Frege, concept and object "are fundamentally made for each other; in subsumption we have their fundamental union" which takes place without the need for any binding agent. (*NS*, p. 193 (PW, p. 178))

---

[5] That this is Dummett's view is clear from this expansion of the previous quotation: "we have now to state just *what is meant* by saying that functions are incomplete. From what has been said this has become quite evident: an entity is incomplete if it can be introduced in the first place *only* as the referent of an incomplete expression".

An object, e.g. the number 2, cannot logically adhere to another object, e.g. Julius Caesar, without some means of connection. This, in turn, cannot be an object, but rather must be unsaturated. A logical connection into a whole can come about only through this, that an unsaturated part is saturated or completed by one or more parts. Something like this is the case when we complete 'the capital of' by 'Germany' or 'Sweden' . . .(*KS*, p. 270 (FG, p. 33))

This is what Frege means by the incompleteness of concepts and functions. Arguments to the effect that we can grasp these entities only as the referents of incomplete expressions do not issue in this kind of incompleteness. The fact that we must take a certain route to an understanding of concepts does nothing to answer the question whether, and if so how, concept and object are capable of bonding together. In the rush to replace ontology by philosophy of language Frege's central characterisation of incompleteness has been forgotten.

If, on the other hand, we take Frege's own statements about the connection between the incompleteness of predicates and the incompleteness of concepts at face value – if we refuse to see them as intimations of more powerful arguments which Frege for some reason never stated – then they naturally appear as heuristic devices for introducing the notion of incompleteness rather than as arguments which issue in the conclusion that concepts are incomplete. Expressions with gaps simply provide an analogy – no doubt an imperfect one – by means of which we get some grasp of what it is for a concept to be incomplete.[6] In that case we need to look elsewhere for the reason why Frege became convinced of the need for a category of incomplete entities.

Similarly, although Frege associated the part-whole doctrine for Thoughts with an argument about our creative grasp of language, this argument is not stated before 1914, whereas the part-whole doctrine appears much earlier in his work.[7] It is unlikely that Frege would have adopted the doctrine for reasons which he did not bother to state until so much later. Again, we should look elsewhere for the source of Frege's views.

II

In order to discover this source we have to look back to the early period of his work, before he drew the distinction between sense and reference. In 1882, in a letter to Anton Marty, Frege wrote:

> A concept is unsaturated in that it requires something to fall under it; hence it cannot exist on its own. That an individual falls under it is a judgeable content and here the concept appears as a predicate and is

---

[6] See e.g., *NS*, p. 246 (PW, p. 228).
[7] See e.g., *KS*, pp. 177–8 (TWF, p. 54) and *Gg*, § 32; and also Baker & Hacker.

always predicative. In this case, where the subject is an individual, the relation of subject to predicate is not a third thing added to the two, but it belongs to the content of the predicate, which is what makes the predicate unsaturated. Now I do not believe that the construction of concepts [*Bilden der Begriffe*] can precede judgement because this would presuppose the self-subsistence of concepts, but I think of a concept as having arisen by decomposition from a judgeable content. (*WB*, p. 164 (*PMC*, p. 101))[8]

I am going to call the argument of this passage 'Frege's metaphysical argument'. I shall spend the rest of this section establishing that this is a reasonable description of the argument.

Commenting on this passage Michael Dummett says "The term 'concept' is, of course, here used in the manner proper to the period before the introduction of the distinction between sense and reference, and corresponds, rather, to the *sense* of a concept-word" (*IFP*, p. 281). This is doubly misleading. First of all, if we do read the passage in the light of Frege's later distinction it certainly appears to involve a shift of meaning. It looks as if Frege begins by using 'concept' in the way that he would later use it, as the reference of a predicate; for he talks of something 'falling under' a concept. But when he says that the concept "appears as a predicate" in a judgement and insists that the relation of subject to predicate "belongs to the content of the predicate" he could equally be understood to be talking about the sense of the predicate. And in the final claim that a concept arises "by decomposition from a judgeable content" he seems clearly to be talking about the sense of a predicate.

Dummett's remark is misleading, however, not so much because it takes 'concept' to mean 'sense of a predicate' throughout, but because it assumes that the word must correspond in meaning to one or other of the later alternatives, sense or reference. No doubt this is a consequence of Dummett's avowed policy of reading earlier works in the light of the later *Gg* (*IFP*, p. 9). In fact this passage contains no ambiguity or shift of meaning, and what is meant is neither sense nor reference. For at this time Frege was working with the idea that the content of a judgement is a state of affairs (*Umstand*).[9] In the *Bs* he says that '— A' may be read 'the state of affairs that A', and the complex sign '⊢', appended to a sign for an assertible content, is explained as a predicate meaning *is a fact* (i.e. a state of affairs which obtains). (*Bs*, §3) Such states of affairs are complex

---

[8] It may be objected that a letter should not constitute the central textual evidence for an interpretation. I cite the letter to Marty because it brings together, in an illuminating way, a number of strands from Frege's thought. As will become clear, all the elements are repeated in works either published or intended for publication. (There is some doubt as to whether the letter is to Marty or to Stumpf: see *WB*, p. 162).

[9] See *Bs*, § 2. Here at least I seem to be in agreement with Dummett: see *IFP*, p. 177.

entities. The state of affairs, Napoleon being short, is constituted from the individual Napoleon and the concept (property) *is short*. (In what follows I shall simply treat 'fact' and 'state of affairs' as synonymous.)

As Frege makes clear in the letter, Napoleon's relation to the concept *being short* is a matter of intimate connection between the two. Concepts are unsaturated: they cannot exist on their own. They exist only in connection with objects, without the mediation of any third entity. As Frege hints in his letter, this promises the solution to a threatening regress; if concept and object required a relation between them to bring them together as a fact, a further relation would be required to bring together the object, concept and relation. And so on. I shall call this 'the regress of predication'. Much later he referred again to the regress and its solution:

> In the sentence 'Two is prime' we find a relation designated . . . We may also say that the object falls under the concept *prime*, but if we do so, we must not forget the imprecision of linguistic expression we have just mentioned. This also creates the impression that the relation of subsumption is a third element added to [*hinzukommen*] the object and the concept. This is not the case; the unsaturatedness of the concept brings it about that the object, in effecting the saturation, engages immediately with the concept, without need of any special cement (*NS*, p. 193 (PW, p. 178)).

We will consider some of the statements in this passage and in the previous one in order to clarify Frege's understanding of the regress and its solution. He claims that the relation of subsumption "is not a third thing added to the object and the concept"; that it "belongs to the content of the predicate". This is puzzling, but we may get some help if we look to Frege's exposition of his formal system in the *Gg*. (The view we are considering is stated twice, in remarkably similar language, once in 1882 and then in 1906. So it may be perfectly in order to use the *Gg* of 1893 as an aid to interpretation.)

In that system concepts and relations are construed as functions. The object which falls under the concept saturates the concept and the completed whole which results is the value of the function for that object as argument. Function and argument are therefore *parts* of the value. As Frege said: "The function is completed by the argument; what it becomes on completion I call the *value* of the function for the argument" (*Gg*, §1). (I shall return to this idea in the next section.)

Now a function of two arguments (a relation) may be partially saturated by an argument to give a new function of one argument: " . . . a function of one argument is obtained [from a function of two arguments] once a completion by means of one argument has been effected". (*Gg*, §4) On Frege's own account of the matter it would seem that the first function (of two arguments) is part of the second (of one argument). This idea may be applied to the case of subsumption. That is a function of two arguments, an object and a concept. When partially saturated with a concept it becomes that very concept. (Just as the identity function, when saturated by the number 2, becomes that very number.) In this way subsumption appears as a part of each concept which (partially) saturates it. And this is what Frege says: the subsumption relation "belongs to the content of the predicate".

Taking the relation of function and argument to value as the part-whole relation involves grave difficulties; for example, every object would appear as a proper part of itself, since there is a function which takes every object to itself. So a solution to the predication problem which depended upon so taking it would not be very attractive. But it is anyway unclear whether we have been offered a solution of any kind to that problem. By holding that subsumption is part of the concept Frege is not able to deny that subsumption is a genuine, existent relation, distinct from that concept. After all, on the part-whole account of functions, the number 5 has as parts the plus function and the numbers 2 and 3. But that is no reason to deny that any of these three things is a distinct existent entity.

The same thing can be said about all the other relations in the hierarchy. Consider a three-place relation, subsumption$_2$, which holds between our original subsumption relation (call it 'subsumption$_1$'), the concept and the object. When subsumption$_1$ is fitted into the first argument place of that relation we obtain a new relation of two arguments: subsumption$_1$ itself. So the concept has as a part subsumption$_1$, which has as a part subsumption$_2$, and so on. We still have an infinity of distinct relations. Calling each one a part of the next does not make any of them less real.[10]

It is also clear that on generally Fregean grounds the hierarchy of relations ought to be admitted. The subsumption$_1$ relation and every other relation in the hierarchy has a well defined extension, as long as we assume that every concept does; F and a stand in the subsumption$_1$ relation if and only if $F(a) = $ the true. And Frege admits no conditions on a relation other than that it have such an extension. (See *NS*, p. 194 (PW, p. 179)) These relations are pairwise distinct because their extensions are.

---

[10] Drawing on the considerations in *Gg*, §§ 22 and 25, we may form names for the relations in the hierarchy in the following way. '$\phi(\xi)$', where 'ϕ' and 'ξ' are respectively concept and object variables, is a name of subsumption$_1$. We may then introduce a conventional relational expression to denote that relation: $\Omega_\beta(\phi(\beta),\xi) = \phi(\xi)$. We obtain a name for subsumption$_2$ from the left hand side, viz., '$\omega_\beta(\phi(\epsilon),\xi)$'. Again by definition from the last expression we obtain '$\Theta_{\psi\gamma\epsilon}(\omega_\beta(\psi(\beta),\gamma),\phi(\epsilon),\xi)$'. In the obvious manner we can then obtain an expression denoting subsumption$_3$, and so on. I am grateful to Pavel Tichý for his help on this and other issues raised in this section.

So, does Frege have a solution to the problem of the predication regress? I shall try to show that he does. But I shall not defend the solution in detail. My aim here is to disambiguate Frege's view rather than to develop it.

Let us note first that there is nothing problematic *per se* about an infinite hierarchy of relations. Unless one is especially parsimonious in ontological matters – and Frege was not – one need not be troubled by the existence of such a hierarchy. The problem which confronts Frege is not 'How can we show that the hierarchy does not exist?' but rather 'What is the explanatory role of the hierarchy?'. For suppose we say that concept and object bond together because they stand in the subsumption$_1$ relation. Then, plainly, we would have to invoke the subsumption$_2$ relation in order to explain how concept and object stand in the subsumption$_1$ relation. No explanation of how predication is brought about can be satisfactory if it simply appeals to an equally mysterious instance of predication at a higher level, which is then explained by an equally mysterious . . . etc. The assumption to be rejected is clearly that bonding between concept and object takes place in virtue of the subsumption$_1$ relation holding between them. The attribution of unsaturatedness to concepts serves to make this rejection possible. When Frege says "the relation of subject to predicate is not a third thing added to the two, but it belongs to the content of the predicate" I think he is most charitably understood in this way: it is not the subsumption relation which does the work of bringing the concept and object together; the concept, because of its unsaturated nature, does that itself. It is in virtue of this that the subsumption$_1$ relation holds between the concept and the object.

Similarly, the doubly unsaturated nature of the subsumption$_1$ relation enables it to lock with the concept and object, and thereby generate the next highest relation. And so on. The direction of the *in virtue of* relation is therefore downwards to the base level of the hierarchy rather than upwards, and we may say, therefore, that predication is well-founded.[11] The regress of relations cannot be stopped, but it is not vicious. It does not threaten the coherence of predication. This, I think, is the best we can make of Frege's solution.[12]

On the basis of what has been said so far it may seem that Frege has, at most, an *ad hoc* solution to the regress problem. The problem is to show that predication is well founded. The problem is solved if we can show that the

---

[11] The *in virtue of* relation is non-causal. The same relation holds between the death of Socrates and the widowing of Xanthippe. The second holds in virtue of, but is not caused by, the first. See J. Kim, "Phenomenal Properties, Psycho-Physical Laws and the Identity Theory", *Monist* 56, [1972]. There is a brief discussion of the subsumption relation and its problems in FPL p. 255. If I understand him, Dummett thinks that the solution to the problem of the regress proposed here can be attributed unproblematically to Frege.
(Grossman calls it 'exemplification') exists, or did he hold that the unsaturated concept connects directly with the object? Answer: he held both. Moreover, the two views are mutually consistent. (See R. Grossmann, *Reflection on Frege's Philosophy* (Evanston, 1969).)

direction of the *in virtue of* relation is downwards. Frege's "solution" is to ascribe to concepts just such a property – unsaturatedness – as will ensure that this is so. But if the ascription of this property has no content over and above this, Frege's solution is surely a stipulation for which there is no independent evidence and which does not deepen our understanding of the nature of concepts.

In fact, however, Frege does give the notion of unsaturatedness more content than the mere ability of the part of the concept to lock immediately with the object. In the letter to Marty he says (third sentence) that unsaturatedness is this ability, but at the beginning of the passage he says that it is constituted by the fact that a concept requires something to fall under it; "it cannot exist on its own". It may be argued that these are two independent characterizations of unsaturatedness. One can hold that concepts lock immediately with objects and that they exist independently from objects. And one can hold that concepts exist only in connection with objects and still have a problem about how this connection is made.

Despite this I do think that Frege did not regard these ideas as wholly independent. Rather, I suspect that he regarded the existential dependence of concepts on objects as the explanation for the immediacy of bonding between the two. Thus, in the letter, he first introduces existential dependence and *then* turns to immediacy of bonding. The ability of the concept to connect with the object is not just a matter of *receptiveness to* objects, but of *dependence on* objects. To say that concepts are unsaturated is not merely to say that concepts, considered in themselves, exist only as incomplete entities; it is to say that they have no being at all outside their combination with objects. This is rather more explicit in another, later passage.

> It is clear that we cannot present a concept as self-subsistent, like an object; rather it can occur only in combination. One may say that it can be distinguished within but not separated from this combination (*KS*, p. 270 (FG, p. 34)).

So I suggest that Frege explained the immediacy of connection in the following way; the connection is immediate because there is no substantial connection between concept and object at all. Concept and object, while separable in thought, are not separable in reality; they form a seamless unit.

I labour these points because they will be important in the next section. This is merely a starting point for our investigations. Perhaps these ideas were not long influential with Frege. Could they survive the splitting up of 'content of a possible judgement' into Thought and truth value (sense and reference) and the consequent abandonment of the fact-based ontology?[13] In the remainder of this

---

[13] Announced in *KS*, p. 172 (TWF, p. 47).

paper I shall consider some of the ways in which the metaphysical argument did influence Frege's thought over a remarkably long period.

III

Let us look at some puzzles which arise in connection with Frege's functional account of predication. Two ideas from the previous section will be important to us here; first, that a concept "cannot exist on its own", and secondly that concept and object together form a fact.

The first of these ideas raises an immediate difficulty. Since mathematics can hardly do without negative existential results, Frege was ready to admit that uninstantiated concepts are legitimate. What, then, of the claim that they cannot exist on their own? I suggest that Frege tried to resolve the difficulty by giving a functional account of predication. When Frege first introduced this idea in the *Begriffsschrift* he was working with the idea that a state of affairs, e.g., Fred being tall, is the value of the function *is tall* for the argument Fred.[14] (Only later is it a truth value which is the value.) So a concept under which nothing falls is a function which takes each argument to a state of affairs which does not obtain. But such a concept is just as intimately connected to objects (i.e. its arguments) as an instantiated one is, and may be said to enjoy existence through this connection. The difference between instantiated and empty concepts arises at the level of values, not at the level of arguments.[15]

Because Frege was working at this time with an ontology of facts which are naturally construed as complex entities it was not sufficient for him to say that the fact is the value of a function (concept) for an argument (object). He must

---

[14] See *Bs*, § 9, penultimate paragraph.

[15] It might be objected that this account is anachronistic. The metaphysical argument is stated in 1882, while the functional account of predication is already evident in 1879. Two points can be made in answer to this. First, the idea that concepts cannot exist apart from objects appears in an article, possibly written in 1880 where he defends the system of the *Begriffsschrift*. There he likens a concept to 'an atom never to be found on its own, but only in combination with others'. (*NS*, p. 19 (PW, p. 17)). So the existential dependence of concepts is presented as implicit in the *Begriffsschrift* system. Secondly, there is evidence internal to the *Begriffsschrift* that Frege was thinking along these lines. In the Preface he says: "It is easy to see how regarding a content as a function of an argument leads to the formation of concepts". By 'the formation of concepts' Frege presumably means the idea that concepts may be arrived at by the decomposition of judgement contents (i.e. states of affairs), and not as self-subsistent elements from which such contents are built up. (Recall the letter to Marty: ". . . I do not believe that the construction of concepts can precede judgement because this would presuppose the self-subsistence of concepts, but I think of a concept as having arisen by decomposition from a judgeable content".) So Frege seems to be saying that the functional account of concepts allows us to recognize concepts as entities without granting them a status independent of objects. And this is exactly the hypothesis I am proposing: that the functional account of concepts enabled Frege to recognize concepts (even empty ones) without granting them ontological independence.

also hold that the concept and the object make up the fact. We have already seen that this is the view he adopts; the unsaturatedness of the function is precisely its ability to be completed by the argument and thereby *become* the value.

While it is metaphysically obscure how function and argument can be parts of the value, it is clear that the idea was forced upon Frege as long as he was working within the fact-ontology. Specifically, the idea derives from three views: that concepts cannot exist without objects, that there are empty concepts, and that a fact is constituted from a concept and an object. The first two impose the functional account of predication; the third demands that function and argument are parts of the value. When the distinction between sense and reference arrived and facts were abandoned in favour of truth values, the view that function and argument are parts of the value no longer served this purpose. For truth values, which were now taken to be the values of concepts, are not, intuitively, complex entities. So Frege could, with a sigh of relief, have abandoned the view that function and argument are parts of the value.

But somehow Frege could not rid himself of the model imposed by the metaphysical argument. He goes on insisting that the value is constituted out of the function argument pair. As he notoriously remarked in "On Sense and Reference": judgement is the distinction of parts within a truth value (See *KS*, p. 150 (FG, p. 65)).

Nor was this confusion a momentary error, as some would like to think. According to Dummett, Frege stated the thesis that the references of the parts of a referring expression are parts of the reference of the whole "once, never repeated [it], and in the end expressly repudiated [it] without mentioning that he had ever held it", (FPL, p. 266). The never repeated lapse is supposed to have occurred in "On Sense and Reference" of 1892. But ten years later Frege wrote:

> The analysis of the sentence corresponds to an analysis of the Thought, *and this in turn to something in the domain of reference,* and I should like to call this a primitive logical fact (*WB*, p. 224 (PMC, p. 142), my emphasis).

Presumably this means that, just as the sense of a sentence is analysable into parts corresponding to the analysis of the sentence, so its reference is similarly analysable. A year later Frege is again discussing the correspondence between the analysis of the sentence and the analysis of its referent.

> To this difference in the signs [which go to make up a sentence] *there of course corresponds an analogous one in the realm of reference*: to the proper name there corresponds the object; to the predicative part,

> something I call the concept ... the decomposition into a saturated and an unsaturated part must be considered as logically primitive (*KS*, p. 269 (FG, p. 33), my emphasis).

And three years later:

> Just as [the predicate] itself appears unsaturated, there is also something unsaturated in the realm of reference corresponding to it: we call this a concept. *This unsaturatedness of one of the components is necessary since otherwise the parts do not hold together* (*NS*, p. 192 (PW, p. 177) my emphasis).

Frege makes no explicit reference here or in the previous two quotations to truth values. But what, other than a truth value, is it that the components – the unsaturated concept and the object – could be components of? What is being "decomposed" to give the concept? There are several interpretative options open to us here. We can assume that Frege does mean that the parts hold together to give a truth value, or we can assume that he has silently readopted an ontology of facts and that it is the fact which the concept and object are components of. Or, and I think this is most likely, we can suppose that Frege was still not clear in his own mind as between these two alternatives; that he was uncomfortable with the idea of truth values divisible in infinitely many different ways, felt a nostalgic attraction to the idea that it is really facts that are constituted of referential parts, but was unable to integrate facts into his new ontology. Not knowing which alternative to adopt, he ended up saying something which avoids commitment to both. But despite this ambiguity one thing is clear; the part-whole doctrine for reference was not abandoned until at least 1906, perhaps not until round about 1919 when he explicitly rejects it on the grounds that, while e.g. Stockholm is the value of the function *capital of* for the argument Sweden, Sweden cannot be a part of Stockholm. (*NS*, p. 275 (PW, p. 255))

In abandoning it Frege finally pushed the remnants of his fact oriented ontology out of the realm of reference. It is significant that, just around this time, he tried to find a place for facts in the realm of sense. In 'The Thought' of 1918 he says, "What is a fact? A fact is a Thought that is true". (*KS* p. 359 (LI, p. 25)) Clearly the attraction of facts for Frege was strong; he could never quite do away with them. He began with a category of facts to serve as the contents of sentences. Officially this ontology was rejected around 1890 when the sense/reference distinction came in; when, as he put it, he split the content of judgement into Thought and truth value. But it continued to be influential, in the shape of the doctrine that each concept-object pair is constitutive of a truth value – if, indeed, it is truth values rather than facts which Frege has in mind as the constituted entity. We might almost say that facts have been identified with particular decompositions of truth values. (See IFP, pp. 180–1). When this view was finally abandoned facts were transferred to the realm of sense.

Dummett warns against taking seriously the view that truth values (and objects in general) have parts, claiming that it leads to "a piece of fantastic metaphysics which illuminates our understanding neither of reality nor of Frege's work". (IFP, p. 181) The idea may be a confused one, but this does not relieve us of the task of explaining how Frege came to adopt it. Nor is it right to minimise, on that account alone, the role it played in his thinking.

IV

So much for the part-whole doctrine for reference. Can the metaphysical argument shed light on Frege's adoption of the parallel claim for sense; that the senses of the parts of a sentence are parts of the sense of the whole? I believe it can.

The sense of a sentence is a Thought. In Frege's early system, at the time when the metaphysical argument was formulated, the content of a judgement was taken to be a fact. Facts are complex; they have parts. Later Thoughts come to play this role; it is Thoughts which are said to be the contents of judgements. Evidently the doctrine that the content of a judgement has parts survives the transition from facts to Thoughts. Now the transition from facts to Thoughts requires a reassessment of the notion of complexity. If Frege is going to insist that the sense of a sentence is internally structured he should offer new arguments. But no such argument is evident until 1914, when Frege seized on the complexity of Thoughts as the explanation of how we understand new sentences. By that time the complexity of Thoughts was well entrenched in his thinking.

I suggest that Frege adopted the complexity of Thoughts because he simply failed, at a crucial point, to distinguish the new doctrine – that the content of a judgement is a Thought – from the old one – that the content of a judgement is a fact.

The crucial passage occurs in "On Concept and Object" of 1892; the place at which Frege first announced the complexity of Thoughts. Throughout the essay Frege has been arguing against Kerry that concepts are unsaturated. Finally Frege considers the consequences of adopting the view that we

> ... might like Kerry, regard an object's falling under a concept as a relation, in which the same thing could occur now as object, now as concept. The words 'object' and 'concept' would then serve only to indicate the different positions in the relation (*KS*, p. 177–8 (TWF, p. 54)).

Here 'concept' has its correct meaning; the ordinary reference of a predicate. Frege then responds to the suggestion. To relativize the distinction between concept and object would leave us with a serious problem:

> For not all the parts of a Thought can be complete; at least one must be unsaturated or predicative; otherwise they would not hold together. For example, the sense of the phrase 'the number two' does not hold together with that of the expression 'the concept prime number' without a link (*ibid.*).

Apparently without noticing it, Frege has answered a proposal about the relation between concept and object by insisting that Thoughts have parts, at least one of which must be unsaturated. How can we explain this conflation of sense and reference? The argument would work, of course, if the complex constituted from the concept and object were the *same thing as* the Thought expressed by the sentence. The possibility suggests itself, therefore, that Frege was making exactly this identification at this point in the argument. Once again under the influence of the metaphysical argument, which has its roots in the fact ontology, he slips back into regarding the thing of which the concept and the object are parts and the Thought ("content of possible judgement") as one and the same; exactly the identification entailed by the fact-based ontology.

Our conclusions as they relate to sense seem to be these. Frege's view that a Thought is a complex unity began as a metaphysical thesis about facts, and was not motivated by considerations of meaning and understanding. And at the time the sense/reference distinction was made he asserted the complexity of Thoughts on grounds which indicate a failure to distinguish between facts as they were originally understood by him and the new Thoughts.

I have tried to show how the early metaphysical argument casts a shadow over certain elements of Frege's mature work. If I am right, the Frege who emerges from this study is certainly less systematic and more muddled than the master of clarity and precision with whom we are sometimes presented. But the confusions are relatively localized. They do not infect his logical system or his philosophy of mathematics to any significant degree. And these surely are his major achievements. Frege was a great philosopher, but greatness is not in everything he wrote. It is important for us to realise that.[16]

University of Otago

---

[16] I am grateful to Alan Musgrave, Graham Oddie, Pamela Tate and Pavel Tichý, whose comments on an earlier version of this paper led to a number of significant improvements.

WHAT DOES A CONCEPT SCRIPT DO?

By Cora Diamond

I

Two remarks made me wonder what a concept script does. The first was Hans Sluga's, in this summary of Frege's claims for his concept script:
(1) Meaningful statements possess an objective conceptual content.
(2) That content is only inadequately represented in ordinary language.
(3) It is possible to design a system of notation in which the conceptual content of any statement can be given an adequate and clear expression.

Implicit in this program is a threefold philosophical methodology. The task of philosophy is seen as *the determination of the objective content* of philosophically interesting statements, a *critique* of their expression in ordinary language, and their *translation* into an adequate language. It is a methodology which the analytic tradition has endeavored to carry out. It has done so by adopting the outline of Frege's program but modifying the details. (Sluga, p. 67)

Sluga then sees later analytical philosophy as the natural development of what Frege was at in his concept script. That line of development, I thought, could be contrasted with the line going to the *Tractatus*. Putting things crudely, on the *Tractatus* view there is no such thing as a translation of "philosophically interesting statements" into an adequate language; one point of developing such a language would be to enable us to see that there are no such translations, and thus to help us overcome our tendency to put together such statements. If the methodology of the analytical tradition is the natural development of Frege's philosophy, then the methodological pronouncements of the *Tractatus*, it would seem, are not. Well, which is? Or is there something the matter with that question? That then was one thing troubling me. The other remark that made me think that I had some problems about concept scripts was Peter Geach's, in his very illuminating piece on saying and showing in Frege and Wittgenstein. The first of the four theses he defends is:

Frege already held, and his philosophy of logic would oblige him to hold, that there are logical category-distinctions which will clearly show themselves in a well-constructed formalized language, but which cannot properly be asserted in language: the sentences in which we seek to convey them in the vernacular are logically improper and admit of no translation into well-formed formulas of symbolic logic. All the same, there is a test for these sentences having conveyed the intended distinctions – namely, that by their aid mastery of the formalized language is attainable.[1]

What puzzled me here was Geach's claim that we show our understanding of the logically ill-formed sentences which seek to convey these category distinctions in our mastery of a well-constructed formalised language. Is this meant to be consistent with the idea that a well-constructed formalised language can itself help us avoid the misunderstandings against which those logically improper sentences in the vernacular were addressed? That problem is closely related to the first, the one that arose in connection with Sluga's remarks. The central question from which I started was really: what is the relation between the idea a philosopher like Frege or Wittgenstein has of a concept script and his view (implicit or explicit) of what methods are appropriate in philosophy? In Wittgenstein there is a tight connection between the two. The development of a concept script is connected with the disappearance of philosophy as it has been practised. Are there any such links implicit in Frege's thought about a concept script? Geach's article, showing the roots of Wittgenstein's doctrines about saying and showing in Frege's work, suggests that the roots of Wittgenstein's view of philosophy itself may be looked for in Frege, and that was what I proposed to do.

II

The natural place to start is with Frege's own summary of the route he had taken.

> I started out from mathematics. The most pressing need, it seemed to me, was to provide this science with a better foundation . . .
>
> The logical imperfections of language stood in the way of such investigations. I tried to overcome these obstacles with my concept-script. In this way I was led from mathematics to logic.
>
> What is distinctive about my conception of logic is that I begin by giving pride of place to the content of the word 'true', and then

---

[1] P. T. Geach, "Saying and Showing in Frege and Wittgenstein", in *Essays on Wittgenstein in Honour of G. H. von Wright*, ed. Jaakko Hintikka, *Acta Philosophica Fennica*, 28 (1976), 54–70.

immediately go on to introduce a thought as that to which the question 'Is it true?' is in principle applicable. So I do not begin with concepts and put them together to form a thought or judgement; I come by the parts of a thought by analysing the thought.(PW, p. 253)

There is an awful lot in those few sentences. The important thing is the relation between Frege's notion of a concept script and his use of the word 'thought'. He recognised that people might object that he was using the word 'thought' in a sense different from the ordinary one. In fact, we should see him as laying out, in large part through the development of what he called a concept script, the notion of thought that he refers to.

A concept script is a mode of expression of thoughts so that what it is for them to be true is clear from how they are written, and, at the same time, the logical relations of different thoughts expressed in the notation are clear in the expressions of those thoughts. The difference between a concept script and ordinary language is, Frege tells us, that in the latter there is only an imperfect correspondence between the structure of the perceptible sentence and the structure of what is expressed by it. Similarity of construction in the expressions may hide total logical dissimilarity in the structure of what is expressed; the genuine logical relations of the constituents are a matter left for one to guess at (PW, pp. 12–13).

I said that a concept script is a mode of expression of thoughts, but I now want not exactly to go back on that but to qualify it: thoughts are what the concept script shows them to be. What I am denying could be put in terms of a crude picture, roughly this: we are told that thoughts are what can be true or false, and so we can then look around and find *which* among all the things that we can think of – sentences, propositions, thoughts, what not – have the property we are after, of being true or false. Having found what we are looking for, we could then investigate its nature. Lo and behold, it can be analysed, has such-and-such sorts of parts, or whatever. No. That with which logic is concerned has its nature made clear (or, if you like, its nature-as-far-as-logic-is-concerned) through a kind of writing of sentences in which everything of interest to logic is made clear. Making *that* clear is going to take some doing. But I can start by showing what it is to miss altogether what Frege is aiming at.

I have seen a criticism of Frege for having identified properties with concepts in his sense. Frege had said "I call the concepts under which an object falls its properties", and the comment of the critic was that that identification would not do. Since *having a heart* and *having a kidney* count for Frege as one and the same concept, but are not what we should count as the same property (because their having the same extension is accidental), we should not (according to the critic) accept Frege's use of his term 'concept' in explicating the idea of a property (Currie, p. 94). But when Frege says that he calls the concepts under

WHAT DOES A CONCEPT SCRIPT DO? 161

which an object falls its properties, he does not mean to be giving an explication of the idea of a property. The point is not the idea of a property but what a property-as-far-as-logic-is-concerned is. The Fregean identification may or may not actually do what Frege wants it to do, but what he wants to do is precisely ignore everything that belongs to our ordinary idea of a property *except* what is of interest to logic. And logic has very narrow interests. If you and I fall under all the same Fregean concepts, than as far as logic is concerned you and I are one and the same thing. Substitute a reference to you for a reference to me in any context, and truth value will never be affected. Why should properties be any better off than you and me? *Logic* will treat their identity as it treats ours, ignoring what is not of interest to it. In the *concept*, we can see – this is Frege's claim – exactly what interests logic in what we ordinarily think of as a property. The critic's mistake was to think that *properties* have certain characteristics and a philosophy of logic ought to do justice to those characteristics. But that is not philosophy of logic for Frege.

Given, then, the specialised interests of logic, how exactly does a concept script further them? In Frege we can see the beginnings of something which is fully developed in the *Tractatus*: what thought is is made clear not so much in sentences *about* thought but in the clear expression of thoughts in a concept script.

Before explaining that, I need to mention an important difference between Frege and Wittgenstein, so that it can be kept separate from a different difference between them. Within any sphere of scientific investigation, as Frege sees it, we can distinguish between two things, the making clear of the subject matter of that activity and the establishing of the laws governing that subject matter. In gravitational mechanics, for example, we are not concerned with the chemical properties of bodies, and a notation for mechanics in which we did distinguish between bodies according to their chemical properties would mark something totally irrelevant to the science; it would to that extent be a misleading notation. The same general point applies to logic as Frege sees it: it is for him a science with a realm, a subject matter, of its own. There is on the one hand the business of making clear what is of interest to it, the character of its subject matter, and on the other there is the establishing of the laws governing that subject matter. (See, e.g., FG, pp. 107–10.) If a concept script does what it is meant to do, it shows the character of thought by the systematic marking in the script of everything with which logic is concerned. The logical laws then contain thought about thought, and their content is something that goes beyond what is shown of the nature of thoughts in a concept script. (That is the view Frege takes most of the time. In one very late passage, he suggests that, if we had a logically perfect language, there would be nothing that logic itself, the discipline, could tell us that went beyond what was already clear to us in the way things were written in that language. But this late view would still be compatible with the idea that logical laws were themselves thoughts about thought.)

Wittgenstein rejects the analogy between logic and other sciences and the idea that there is on the one hand the making clear in a concept script of that with which logic is concerned, and on the other the establishing of the laws about the subject matter, the laws being then thoughts about thought. There is no 'on the other hand' here, and logic is no *science*. When you have, in the concept script, made clear the character of thought, nothing more remains to be said – or so he thought. That, then is one point on which Frege and Wittgenstein differ. It should be distinguished from another: can what is made clear of the character of thought in the way sentences are written in a concept script *also* be put directly, in sentences *about* the character of thought?

In discussing that, I am going to use, instead of the word 'thought', the expression for which it should be regarded as an abbreviation: 'that to which the question 'Is it true?' is in principle applicable'. A that-to-which-that-question-applies is expressed in a sentence. It gets expressed clearly, and with all the frills irrelevant to logic, irrelevant to the applicability to it of the question of truth or falsity, left off, in a concept script. When one is struggling to grasp a thought, one may come out first with half-sentences, stammerings, vague jumbles, and only in the end get to a proper sentence. While one is struggling to get straight something about the internal character of *thought*, of that-to-which-the-question-of-truth-applies, one's stammerings and gropings, one's beginnings to get what glimmers, take the form of sentences in ordinary language *about* thought, about the relation between thought and its expression, about the elements of a thought, and so on. But just as we may say that that-to-which-the-question-of-truth-applies has its expression in a *sentence*, thought about the nature of that-to-which-the-question-of-truth-applies gets put clearly in a *concept script*, a way of writing sentences. The word 'thought' which I have allowed to stand in the last sentence: can *that* be taken to mean that-to-which-the-question-of-truth-applies? Can such thought, or 'thought', also be put in sentences? These questions get unambiguous answers from Wittgenstein. Frege treats them differently; he does not hold that in general what can be shown cannot be said. (I cannot discuss in detail this difference between their views; I touch on it briefly again in §III.)

Let me give a simple example (and then a more complicated one) of how the character of thought may be made clear in a concept script. We may start thinking about the dependence of the truth or falsity of a thought on what the thought is *about*, and we may put together thousands of philosophical sentences in such gropings. Frege leads us to a better kind of groping, making use of the notions of argument, function and value, terms of not-so-ordinary language, supplemented with metaphors of completeness and incompleteness. But thinking in terms of *arguments* and so on is itself a move, the crucial move, towards a notation, his concept script, in which the character of the dependence is plain. I am suggesting that we see Frege's concept script and notations derived from it as standing to the previous attempts to put our thought about the dependence in something like the way a clearly put sentence stands to the half-formed thoughts that preceded it.

Another example worth looking at briefly is the dispute between Wittgenstein and Frege about the kind of articulation necessary to anything that can express a thought. In the *Tractatus*, Wittgenstein held that anything capable of having the sense that a sentence has must be logically articulated. He took himself to be disagreeing in this with Frege, and I am sure that he was right. What I take to be Frege's view (in his later writings) is that (a) the expression of thought, a sentence, has the same kind of articulation as there is in complex designations like 'Frege's birthplace', but (b) a complex designation has a sense of a sort which it is possible for an unarticulated proper name to have, which together imply that (c) the kind of sense a sentence has does not *require* that *whatever* has that sense be articulated. The sense that a sentence has could be the sense of an unarticulated proper name. (Since I want to treat this view purely as an example, I shall not discuss the grounds for ascribing it to Frege.) What is it then to take that dispute as an example of what I was talking about? Viewed as I suggest, to dispute about what articulation the expression of a thought must have is to dispute about the specifications for a concept script. Wittgenstein's "view about thoughts" gets its proper expression in a concept script, in the exclusion from places where sentences can occur of any logically unarticulated expressions, in the exclusion from places where simple and undefined expressions can occur of any logically complex expression or any sign defined via others, and so on. In a concept script of the sort Frege uses in the *Grundgesetze*, any argument place open to sentences is open to any simple or complex proper names, and vice versa. This openness of argument places is what it comes to to say, as he did, that sentences *are* proper names: logic does not need a kind of writing that marks a distinction between them by opening argument places to one but not the other.

Let me imagine, at this point, two sorts of comments.

(1) "You have been altogether too free with expressions like 'what logic needs', 'what logic is interested in'. Is it not time you were more forthcoming about what they are supposed to mean?"

(2) "You have not made very clear what is involved in the dispute between Frege and Wittgenstein about logical articulation – not, that is, made clear what kind of dispute it is. For, as you have explained the difference between them, it is a difference between two sets of specifications for a concept script, and any further point of view on the dispute would get expressed in yet another set of specifications for a concept script. That means that we cannot criticise a

concept script by *stepping outside* the business of the making of concept scripts, of working out how to write sentences so that relations of interest to logic are marked in a systematic and thoroughly consistent way. To step outside would be to say: What are we expressing in a concept script is *thoughts*. They have a logical structure, and once we find out what *that* is, we shall be able to see what logical structure to build into a concept script the better to reflect the structure thoughts have. We should be able to judge between Frege's and Wittgenstein's concept scripts by determining which has a logical structure corresponding to that of thoughts. But if we reject that view, what exactly *is* involved in criticising or evaluating a concept script? If it is true that thoughts are in essence what they are shown to be in a concept script, how is it *not* the case that Frege's concept script embodies one notion of thought and Wittgenstein's another, and that no question of which is a better embodiment of what *thought* is can arise? If it is not a substantial *thesis* about something, *thoughts*, that they are expressed in sentences which are logically speaking indistinguishable from proper names, how does Wittgenstein think that Frege is *wrong* in taking sentences to be proper names?"

To begin with, the second comment is confused. It is not the case, on the view I have been expounding, that what counts as *thought* is different in differently designed concept scripts; nor is it the case that the only way to criticise a concept script is to come up with another one. For help with both comments, we need to get back to the remarks of Frege's which I quoted earlier, which I said had so much in them. What they have in them is his conception of logic, in which, he said, he gave pride of place to the content of the word 'true'.

What made it possible for Frege to use the word 'true' to "indicate the essence of logic" was its peculiar character. If we attach the predicate 'is true' to a sentence, the sense of the sentence does not change, but the predicate is not on that account senseless. It is for this reason, Frege says, "that the word 'true' seems to make the impossible possible: it allows what corresponds to the assertoric force to assume the form of a contribution to the thought" (PW, pp. 251–2). We cannot, though, bring out what is peculiar to 'true' unless we can make clear the difference between it and some other expressions whose sense, in certain circumstances, similarly collapses, as it were, into the sense of what they have been attached to. What 'is true' does with *sentences*, these other expressions will do with some other groups of completed function expressions.

I can explain this in two ways, corresponding to two uses of 'true' as a predicate:

(1) 'p is true' = 'The thought-that-p is true' = 'The thought-that-p is a sense of the True'.

(2) 'p is true' = 'p is one and the same as the True' = 'The truth value p is one and the same as the True'.

In the first case, what is meant by 'true' is ascribed to a thought; in the second case, something else is meant by 'true' and *that* is ascribed to a truth value. But the thought that [the thought-that-p is a sense of the True] is the same as the thought that [the truth value p is one and the same as the True], and that thought is the same as the thought that p. The two differing uses of 'true' simply chop it up differently. I want to show what is peculiar to 'true' by contrasting it with other function expressions whose sense collapses in certain circumstances; and I can do that either by sticking with the first type of use of 'true' or by sticking with the second. I can get a class of peculiar function expressions in either case – a class of expressions whose sense collapses in the same way that of 'true' does. It would be more complicated, though in some ways more Fregean, to use the first kind of case; but if I stick to the second, anyone can make the moves to the more complicated case for himself. Sticking to the less complicated case will enable me to make clear what I need to; so that is what I shall do.

We can start with any group of functions whose value is always one or other of two objects, for example, with functions whose value is always Wismar or Frankfurt. Call these B-functions and expressions for them B-expressions. We can define a particular B-expression, say 'W( )', by specifying that the value of the function W( ) is Wismar whenever the argument is Wismar and is otherwise Frankfurt. 'W( )' acts with completed B-expressions in just the way '( ) is true' acts with sentences. Whatever the peculiarity is that suits 'true' for indicating the essence of logic, it is not *merely* the kind of collapsibility of sense it shares with 'W( )', for 'W( )' cannot be used to indicate the essence of logic.

How then are we to get at the significant difference between 'true' and such expressions as 'W( )', which we may call "collapsing" expressions? Let me put this in a slightly different way. 'W( )', as I have defined it, and '( ) is true', in so far as that is what Frege would regard as a predicate with a properly determinate sense, can each take *any* complete expression in its argument place. The characteristic collapse of sense occurs, for each, only in certain cases; that is one reason I have avoided calling them identity operators. But we may call the class of argument-expressions for which there is the collapse the "preferred" kind of expression. We cannot bring out the peculiar character of 'true' unless we can make clear the difference between it and collapsing function expressions whose preferred kind of argument is *not sentences*. It is the difference between a collapsing expression which is a *predicate* and others which are not. But the difference between a predicate and these other expressions is the difference between an expression for a function whose value is a truth value and expressions for functions whose value is not. The fundamental difference between the two types of expression is that the sense of a completed expression of the first sort (one for a function whose value is a truth value) is something *judgeable*; the sense of no other sort of completed function expression is. Other sorts of completed expression name this or that or the other depending on certain conditions, but their sense is never *that* any such condition is fulfilled. Thus 'Frege's birthplace' names Wismar if he was born there, but its sense is not that the Wismar conditions are fulfilled, or that the Frankfurt conditions are, or *that* anything at all. The peculiar character of 'true', does not lie in its being collapsible, but in that feature, combined with its preferred class's being sentences, and its being itself a predicate. Because it does not add anything to the sense of an expression of its preferred sort, what it seems to do when it has such an expression in its argument place is itself to express the 'these conditions are fulfilled', the characteristic of thought itself. A thought is something distinguished from other senses-of-complete-expressions in being *judgeable*; but the grammatical indicators of judgeable sense normally function also, or can do so, as indicators of assertoric force. That is why Frege repeatedly warns us to dissociate assertoric force from predication. 'True', in seeming to have as its sense the general form of thoughtish sense, the 'the truth-conditions are fulfilled' that all thoughts have in common, can *also* seem to express the *recognition* of the truth of a thought. This then is why it can seem that what it contributes to the thought as a predicate is actually the assertoric force.

The business of *recognising thoughts as true*, and the using of sentences uttered with assertoric force in expressing this recognition – that is the peculiar business indicated by the peculiar character of 'true'. What has it to do with *logic*? The general form of this peculiar business is: a thought is recognised to be true without being logically inferred from other thoughts recognised to be true, *or* it is logically inferred from others. Suppose, for example, I recognise the truth of a thought expressed by a sentence, and I take another sentence to be a material conditional whose consequent I take to express the same thought as the one whose truth I have recognised. I must then be able to infer the truth of the thought expressed by the conditional sentence as a whole. That rule belongs to the business of recognising thoughts to be true; it is a "law of thought", or, as Frege says it would better be put, a "law of judgment". What underlies it is nothing psychological but merely the relations of the truth conditions of the two thoughts. A thought being essentially that such-and-such truth conditions are fulfilled, its identity is inseparable from the logical relations it stands in to other thoughts; its inferential relations cannot change while the thought remains unchanged. The wholly non-psychological character of the rules governing judgment is thus inseparable from what judgment is. There is no room for essentially different sets of rules governing how the activity of judging should be carried on. There can be variants of chess, with variants of what is allowed. But there cannot in that sense be variants of the prescriptions to be followed in recognising thoughts to be true; there cannot be what used to be a valid inference (was a valid inference by the then laws of logic) but is no longer one. 'True' is suited to indicate the essence of logic by indicating the tie between its complete unarbitrariness and what judgment itself is.

Frege did allow that there might be beings capable of grasping thoughts without having to use perceptible expressions of thought. But given that we human beings do have to use language in the expression of thoughts, something of central importance follows from the peculiar character of logic. Or, rather, it does not, properly speaking, follow from the peculiar character of logic; it *is* the peculiar character of logic reflected in the character of language, considering language as capable of expressing thoughts. The principles through which the laws of logic bear on thought expressed in language must be the same for any language. Frege puts the point this way: the logical component of the grammar of every language (i.e., that part of the grammar that does not reflect the psychological capacities, interests and so on of the speakers) is the same in all languages (PW, pp. 6, 142). It cannot, for example, be the case that in one language you *cannot* predicate the same thing of a concept as of an object and in some other language you *can*. In the development of language many human instincts and dispositions, including the logical disposition, were at work (PW, p. 269). If there had been at work *only* the logical disposition, language would be far better adapted to the expression of thoughts, and we should be able to see clearly in it what is there but as it were overlaid in the grammar of our actual languages, the logical features shared with all languages. Talk which uses 'true' and takes advantage of its peculiar character is one way to get at something, "the essence of logic"; and the same thing is being got at if we talk about what in a sense corresponds to the peculiar character of 'true': the single logical-grammatical structure found in every language in so far as thoughts can be expressed in it at all. Corresponds: i.e., the logical component of grammar is what corresponds in the structure of language to the judgeability belonging to every thought in the stock of human thoughts, each of which (or at any rate its logical core) is expressible in every language, according to Frege. The impossibility of different logical-components-of-grammar in different languages corresponds to the impossibility of different prescriptions governing the peculiar activity of recognition of the truth of thoughts. I said that we have, in Frege's use of 'true' and in talk like his of the identity of logical grammar in all languages, two ways of getting at something. Both would be unnecessary if we had a logically perfect language, in which the essence of thought and hence the essence of logic lay open to view.

I have ignored a complication in Frege's view. Thoughts may be communicated in ordinary language without the speakers' actually relying on the logical articulation of the sentences they utter and hear. The hearers use cues to guess at what thought the sentence as a whole expresses. But Frege combined that idea with a view of the structure of natural language on which it is possible for the sense of a sentence to be constructed from that of its logical components, and not just guessed at as he thinks we often do. The possibility of constructing the sense in that way is essential for inference.

The grammar of English does not allow us to put together sentences like 'Five is greater than three is greater than three', in which a whole sentence has been put where only expressions of some other sorts may go. Frege came to believe that, in a correct notation, anywhere 'five' could go, 'Five is greater than three' could equally go. Now, given his view that the logical element of the grammar of all languages is the same, English and his concept script must share that universal logical grammar. So *if* his concept script is actually correct in allowing what corresponds in it to 'Five is greater than three is greater than three', the exclusion of such sentences from English is not done by universal logical grammar but by the "psychological" component of English grammar. (We can see that the Fregean claim I mentioned earlier, that any thought can be expressed in every language, is true only in a thin sense of 'can'. It can, i.e., the logical component of the grammar allows it to be expressed; but the non-logical component of the grammar may prevent its expression in any sentence that *it* will allow.) Just as the non-logical component of English grammar may exclude from English what logical grammar would not exclude, it may also allow combinations which logical grammar would exclude, like the putting of what *it* counts as a proper name where logical grammar cannot recognise a genuine proper name.

We are now in a position to get back to the dispute between Frege and Wittgenstein, about the character of a concept script. In so far as a language is capable of expressing thoughts at all, it must (here Frege and Wittgenstein agree) have as the logical component of its grammar what every language has. The point about *the* logical grammar applies not only to any natural language but also to a concept script designed with the intention that the logical characteristics of the thoughts expressed in its sentences should be shown clearly in the perceptible structure of those sentences. A concept script is unsatisfactory when it treats in the same way what is logically different (what *the* logical grammar treats as different) or treats in different ways what is logically similar. Let us stick with our example and ask what it would mean for Wittgenstein to be *right* in excluding sentences from argument places where expressions for numbers can go. If Wittgenstein is right, *and* if we assume as correct the view Frege and Wittgenstein both held about language, what follows is that there is a divergence in Frege's concept script between the logical grammar it shares with all languages and the rules fixing which combinations of expressions are well-formed sentences of the concept script. The upshot of the divergence is that, contrary to Frege's intentions and to his beliefs about what he had succeeded in doing, nonsensical combinations will be allowed. The situation is analogous to ones that arise in ordinary language, as in the example I mentioned, in which the non-logical component of grammar allows what it regards as a proper name where the logical component refuses to recognise one. If, instead, we assume Frege right and Wittgenstein wrong about the articulation of sentences, there will again be a divergence between what the rules of a concept script (one meeting Wittgenstein's specifications) allow and what its own logical grammar, *the* logical grammar, allows. In this case, the upshot of the divergence would be the exclusion from the concept script of combinations which would be allowed by the logical component of grammar; again, the situation is analogous to one which can obtain in ordinary language.

What then does all this come to as a reply to the second comment? There is, on the view I have been expounding, a right and wrong in disputes like that between Wittgenstein and Frege. When the design of a concept script goes wrong, it is not that the structure of the script fails to match something external to it, but that the concept script has structural features which diverge from its own, as it were, inevitable inner structure, which is thus not revealed clearly.

Later on, Wittgenstein came to say that, when we think that there is something queer or unique about thought, we are the victims of illusion. But at this point I am trying to make clear what it is we may thus seem to see; for it is not *all* illusion. Taking a view about the nature of thoughts is not quite like taking a view about the nature of whales, and we misread Frege and Wittgenstein both, if we forget that they themselves are concerned with the character of that difference, and thus concerned to "place" what they themselves say. I mean 'place' in the sense in which we can see Frege himself "placing" his own remarks about concepts and their incompleteness, or about 'true' and its relation to the essence of logic. In §III, I shall show the relation between this 'placing' and an understanding of what a concept script is supposed to do.

III

In §II I did not draw attention to the issue of realism. It was there, all right; and in Part III I shall be concerned with it. I shall describe a kind of realist view in order to ask what we should make of it if we took Frege seriously. Here is the view.

Among the kinds of things there are, are concepts and objects. *That* something – say, the number 4 – is an object, is why it is appropriate for a term for it to have the logical character of a proper name, i.e. what Frege calls completeness or saturatedness; *that* something is a concept is why it is appropriate for a term for it to have the logical character of a predicate, i.e. to be 'incomplete', to have one or more gaps for argument expressions of the appropriate sort, the sort that stand for things of the kind that complete the concept for which it is an expression. Our linguistic expressions thus properly have a character which matches the independently fixed logical character of the things they stand for. The logical character of those things is prior, and belongs to them on their own; and we can in the use we fix for our signs get it right or wrong.

Well, what is to be made of that, if we take Frege seriously? Wittgenstein did, and it shows, for example, in the remarks following 5.47 in the *Tractatus*, where he is discussing the relation between logic and what all sentences share simply in being sentences. Language itself, he says (at 5.4731) prevents every logical mistake. Because it does so, we cannot give a sign the wrong sense. We cannot, he means, give a sign a sense which is inappropriate to the logical character of what it stands for, cannot make a mistake about what the logical character is of the thing we want the sign to stand for, and then give the sign a kind of use appropriate to the logical character thus wrongly conceived. There is no such thing as allowing a sign to figure in a *wrong* combination with other signs, *unsuitable* given the possible combinations into which the thing meant can enter.

But why is that taking Frege seriously? I need now to show how Frege enables us to see what is wrong with the kind of realism I sketched, but not by providing as an alternative some kind of anti-realist view.

The heart of the realist view that I have sketched is that logical categories provide a kind of *classification* of things. What we can get hold of through the concept script Frege developed is a notion of 'logical category', tied directly to *kinds of argument place*. (In his explanation of the concept script, a first kind of argument place is characterised by the "completeness" of the arguments, and others by the number and kinds of argument places in the arguments that they are themselves open to. I shall spell it out in more detail later.) If we grasp that notion, the question 'Are logical categories a classification of things?' will simply not be askable; it will drop away as mere muddle.

In the kind of realism I sketched there might be some question whether one was correct in putting *Socrates* in the logical place for an object. One would have committed some kind of logical gaffe if one had got his logical character wrong in thinking that he was an object, and had got him in the wrong kind of place, given his logical character. But, for Frege, what is *in* the logical place of an object *is* an object. Take, for example, his well-known discussion, in 'On Concept and Object' about the concept *horse* (TWF, pp. 45–8). It is true that what he says there can be criticised on quite distinct grounds and was not his own last word on the matter; it is important for me at this point, though, as an illustration of his method. He argues that when we say that the concept *horse* is a concept easily attained, 'the concept *horse*' stands for an object. It is, logically speaking, the subject; what it refers to is thus in the logical place for an object and therefore is an object. He is not going on the fact that 'the concept *horse*' is a *grammatical* subject; the grammatical subject of 'A horse is what you probably were in your last incarnation' would not have been taken by Frege to be a logical subject. As Peter Geach has pointed out in discussing 'On Concept and Object', Frege had not in it "deliberately adopted an 'ontology' " with "special classes of object that were surrogates for concepts and functions in case of need!" (Geach, *op. cit.*, p. 56). There is no possibility of logical disaster in putting Socrates in the wrong place or in referring to the concept *horse* in the absence of an obliging ontological category of concept surrogates.

Here is how the realist picture works. We think that there are things in reality, including, let us suppose, since our realist is reading Frege, objects and concepts, the concepts themselves being of various sorts. And, now, *of* any of these various things, we think that we can think: it goes into this one of the logical categories or some other. What we have got in mind, though, is the *intelligible* application of the category terms themselves to items in *different* categories. We think, that is, that we can think that Socrates is an object and have got something right. But how then are we thinking of the concept we thus take him to fall under? What is absolutely essential to the realist frame of mind is that 'it is an object' *can* be falsely said of some things. Otherwise, we could not think that we could use it in classifying things in reality. The use of 'object' as a classifying term requires that there be things which are not objects. Now Frege is unlike Wittgenstein in thinking that 'object' is a respectable predicate and *object* a respectable concept. (Here I am ignoring two sorts of complication. First, Frege did, in his early "Dialogue with Pünjer", take views closer to Wittgenstein's about such concepts; I am ignoring that piece here. Secondly, I am, where I can, ignoring complications of the general 'concept *horse* is not a concept' kind, in order not to have to say repeatedly that when I call something a concept, or, e.g., ask whether such-and-such is a respectable concept, I am unfortunately using a term with the logical character of a first-order predicate when I need to speak about a second-order concept, that I am using a term as a proper name when I cannot want that, and so on.) But, although it is for Frege a respectable concept, it is not the concept the realist wants to use (and it is going to turn out that there is no such thing as what he wants). Since *() is an object* is a first order concept, what can occur as its argument *is an object*. That is, it is true, of anything that you say is an object, that it is an object. You could not have said or thought that it was and have been wrong. 'Everything is an object' and 'There is nothing that is not an object' are *true*. And so the concept *() is an object* is useless for classifying (which is why Frege had earlier denied that such concepts have content).

What about something's being a concept? Can a corresponding point be made about that? If we complete with an appropriate argument the concept that we try to refer to by '() is a concept', we do not *always* get the truth value *true*. The second order concept we want *can* be used in classifying, but only (given

Frege's views) in classifying first order functions with one argument. Concepts are not, in fact, a logical category in the sense in which I have been using that expression in discussing Frege. Concepts and first order functions are defined for the same arguments and can occur themselves as arguments of any second order functions.

What I have just said appears to clash with Frege's own statement that the concept *horse* is not a concept but an object. For I said that the only thing you could classify with the concept we try to refer to as '( ) is a concept' is first-order functions with one argument; and if that is correct, it seems that the only thing we shall be able to say is *not* a concept is such a function. Frege himself was clear enough that the predicate of the sentence 'The concept *horse* is not a concept' does not refer to the second order concept we want (any more than the five words I just used refer to it, any more than the pronoun I have just used does). Let us find a way to refer to it.

'(x) (x is a dog is a truth value)'
'(x) (x is a tree is a truth value)'
'(x) (x's birthplace is a truth value)'

The common pattern of those three sentences is an expression for the second order concept we want: a concept that all and only first order concepts fall under, or, rather, do what is for them analogous to falling under (what Frege calls "falling into"). The second order concept we try to refer to by '( ) is not a concept' we can refer to by using the same pattern with a negation at the beginning, to get a new sentence pattern. There is no such thing as completing *either* pattern with the subject of 'The concept *horse* is easily attained', which has *no* argument places. And that is how we should understand Frege's point that 'the concept *horse* is not a concept'. The sentence looks as if it says of something that it is not a concept, but if we think about what we try to say with '( ) is not a concept', we can see that there is no such thing as saying, or thinking, what the sentence looks as if it says.

Let me turn to the second order concept we try to refer to by '( ) is a first order function with one argument'. Frege gives us one expression for this concept: '$\dot{\epsilon}\phi(e)$'. So '$\dot{\epsilon}$ ($\epsilon \cdot 3 + 4$)' is a way of saying properly what we try to say by '$\xi \cdot 3 + 4$ is a function' (PMC p. 136). Frege's point is that *any* expression for the second order concept we want will have to contain an indication that its arguments are first order functions with one argument place of their own. One can make the same point by using the common pattern of the pair

'(x) (x is a dog is an object)'
'(x) (x's birthplace is an object)'

or (given a Fregean definition of the conditional for all proper names) of the pair

'(x) (x is a dog $\supset$ x is a dog)'
'(x) (x's birthplace $\supset$ x's birthplace)'.

In the case of each pair, the common pattern serves to stand for the second order concept we want. Each pattern is completed into a sentence only by expressions for first order functions with one argument.

We can now get to the central point here. *Every* thought that something is an object is true; *every* thought got by completing the concept we misrefer to as '() is a first order function with one argument' is true, and correspondingly for functions of higher orders and with different numbers of arguments. The whole idea of classifying anything using these notions breaks down, since it is impossible to think truly of anything that it does not belong to a given category. It is impossible – in a sense – to make a mistake about the logical category of anything, since what we call 'making a mistake' (e.g., thinking that the concept *horse*, of which we say that it is easily attained, is a concept) will turn out not to be the thinking of the thought we thought it was. There will be no such thing as that. A good concept script will make clear to us that we were in a muddle in thinking that we had got something in mind, that we were expressing a thought at all.

We use the English word 'category' as if logical categories were pigeonholes for a kind of classification, a logical classification, of things. As if there were some kind of class that logical categories all were, and as if *belonging in* such-and-such a category were some one thing, and some items belonged in one and others in another and others in yet others; as if, that is, to be a member of a logical category were something that went across the whole lot of categories. The language of *putting things into categories* misleads us into thinking the business is like recognising that a plant goes into this or the other genus; it is the language, grammatically, of putting *objects* into classes depending on the first order concepts they fall under. We speak of grasping that *something* belongs in such-and-such a category or that an *item* does; that is, we use what ordinary language provides as variables indicating objects, in constructions which call for precisely such variables. And now what I am saying, speaking (inevitably) in that way, is that to put something into a category is not to classify it. There is no kind of class that logical categories all are.

There is an important kind of objection that people make. The things I have been saying about logical categories, that they are no kind of class, and that that way of putting the point is itself something that does not work – these are entirely dependent on one feature of Frege's concept script (duplicated in the specifications for a concept script in the *Tractatus*). That feature is that every argument place in a predicate or other function expression takes arguments of only one logical category. If we have a concept script which meets that specification, and if the concept script allows the predication of category terms at all, we shall then be able to say only of the things that actually are in the category in question that they are. Whenever we say that something is *not* in a category we shall be wrong, because only of what is in a particular category shall we be able to say that it is not in that category, and category predicates will not have a genuine classifying use. That will be the conclusion, whether we accept Frege's view that we *can* say of an object (e.g.) that it is an object or Wittgenstein's view that that is actually nonsense. In *neither* case is there any possibility of genuine classification using category predicates. So – the objection runs – what we need to do is call into question the Fregean and Wittgensteinian commitment to having *no* argument places open to more than one category. Frege himself, the objector might point out, was willing to question the commitment when he was worrying about Russell's paradox. He toyed with the idea of allowing some argument places open to proper names of one logical kind of object, some open to another, and a third sort open to both (TWF, pp. 235–6). And, the objector might continue, even if we could not point to Frege's own willingness to consider the move, there are good reasons for it. We must allow that there are genuine questions of the sort Frege's original view rules out. Take the question we may wish to ask about 'The concept *horse* is easily attained', whether the concept *horse* that we are speaking about there is something which it is possible for Bucephalus and other things to fall under. Is there not something we are saying if we should want to say that it is *not*? Or indeed if we should want to say that it *is*? Can we not be right or wrong about this? Is there not a genuine thinking of two possible thoughts here, thoughts which contradict each other?

Let me look further at the objection. The idea of argument places open to more than one kind of thing is absolutely necessary (the objector may claim), since (he says) there are things that can be said truly of items of different logical kinds. It may even seem that Frege himself is committed to the idea that there are some things we can say of items in different categories. After all, it might be asked, does he not think that both first order concepts and first order relations are *first order*, i.e., take the same kind of argument?; that they are *incomplete*, though not in the same way?; that they have as their values only the two truth values?; that neither of them can fall under a first order concept? But the appearance of his saying the same thing of concepts and relations is itself created by what he would take to be an imprecision in ordinary language. There is no concept that both first order concepts and first order relations fall under (properly, none that they fall into), and in an adequate concept script there is nothing that even looks like an expression for such a concept.

Very well; we stop trying to get Frege himself on the side of saying that some things can be truly said of items in different categories. Is it not nevertheless true? An example that was offered me in discussion was self-identity: surely (it was said), it is correct to say both of any object and of any concept that it is identical with itself.

Suppose we look at this first in a Fregean frame of mind. How close we can get to saying of a concept that it is self-identical can be seen if we consider what it is to say of a concept picked out one way that it is the same as a concept picked out another way. Given Frege's view of what we may loosely call conceptual identity, what it is for something to be f is the same as what it is for something to be g if and only if whatever is f is g, and conversely (PW, p. 120). Applying Frege's view, then, what it is to ascribe self-identity to a concept, or, rather, the nearest we can come to doing that, is to say that whatever falls under it falls under it, '(x) (x is bald ≡ x is bald)' expresses properly what someone is trying to say if he says that *bald*, the concept, is self-identical. (Since for Frege a sentence refers to a truth value, we can also write it this way: '(x) (x is bald = x is bald)'.)

If we follow Frege, then, we shall say that ordinary language gives us a false impression that we are saying the same thing of the concept *bald* and of Socrates when we say of them that they are self-identical. If we have a notation in which we say of Socrates that he is self-identical *this* way: 'Socrates = Socrates', and if we say what we were trying to say about the concept *bald this* way: '(x) (x is bald ≡ x is bald)', it would not so much as occur to us that self-identity is something ascribable to objects and concepts both. The objection that it is possible for there to be things like self-identity ascribable both to concepts and to objects, and that we therefore *need* expressions with argument places open to expressions of different logical kinds rests (at least as it was originally stated) on simply assuming what was at issue. That is what the case of self-identity shows.

We need, though, to see more clearly where the difference between the objector's view and Frege's lies. I said that what Frege's concept script gives us is a notion of category tied to *kinds of argument place*. But what counts as a *kind of argument place* depends on the needs of logic, given the way we analyse a sentence containing such-and-such terms that can be taken as logically significant. The difference between what identity comes to for objects and what it comes to for concepts (central in our example) is a reflection of the need logic has to allow for different kinds of substitution *salva veritate*.

To analyse a sentence is to take it as containing one or more expressions for arguments (each of which may occur in more than one place) and to take the rest of the sentence as having a different sort of logical role. For *that* part of the sentence (which I shall call the leftover part) to have a determinate meaning is for the truth value of the sentence as a whole to be fixed for each meaningful argument expression that can be substituted for the argument expression in our sentence (if we are construing our sentence to have only one argument expression), for each *pair* of argument expressions (if we are construing our sentence to have two argument expressions) and so on. There is a fundamental kind of analysis, available only in the case of some sentences: we *can* construe these sentences to have, as the only argument expression they contain, a proper name. Frege uses metaphor to explain what his terms 'proper name' and 'object' mean, the metaphor of 'completeness' or 'saturation'. We can see something of what is being got at by these metaphorical expressions if we recall that all analysis reflects the interests of logic: how the truth value of the sentence as a whole may be construed in terms of function and argument. We have to look at the way logic treats the use of one expression as leftover in some contexts and as argument in others, and at the way it tells, in certain circumstances, whether we have defined one leftover expression or two.

If what we view as the leftover expression in one sentence can be taken to be an argument expression in another (or in the same one, otherwise construed) – if, that is, logic will allow such an identification – logic will insist that the expression now viewed as leftover, now viewed as argument, make the same contribution to the truth or falsity of what is said. Logic will thus insist that it carry with it in the two cases the same rules for substitution *salva veritate* in sentences. When it is a leftover expression, what can be substituted for it *salva veritate* is any other expression which fixes in the same way as ours the truth or falsity of sentences as a whole for each meaningful argument expression (or set of argument expressions) by which it can be completed. If a leftover expression is to be viewed as occurring also as an argument expression, it must carry with it in the latter use exactly the same rules for substitution *salva veritate* as it had as leftover, or it would not be making the same contribution to truth value as in its use as leftover. That is, what can be substituted for it in contexts in which we are viewing it as an argument expression can be specified only in terms of the truth or falsity for sentences as a whole determined for every meaningful argument expression (or set of argument expressions) that *our* argument expression can itself be completed by in its use as leftover. Hence we write it in a concept script *with* argument places, whether it occurs as leftover or as argument expression, since these places are essential to its identity as far as logic is concerned, its identity (that is) as an expression with such-and-such reference, making the same contribution to the reference of whole sentences in which it occurs. (It thus belongs to its identity that it can only be used predicatively.)

Let us now try supposing that we had a leftover expression with one argument place, and that the truth or falsity for sentences as a whole was fixed for it, for all argument expressions with no argument places of their own (proper names) *and* for argument expressions with one argument place of their own of some determinate sort. What logic would see is that we had defined *two* equiform leftover expressions which made entirely different kinds of contribution to the whole sentences in which they were leftovers. The expression would

WHAT DOES A CONCEPT SCRIPT DO? 177

sometimes stand for one kind of function and sometimes for another; in its two uses it would have two entirely different referents. One of Frege's criticisms of Hilbert is that he defines 'point' so that it has two meanings related to each other in that way (PMC, pp. 93–4). We do not make the issues here clear if we say that for Frege and Wittgenstein no argument place can be open to more than one kind of argument expression. If it were open to more than one, logic would note that the leftover expression was being used in different contexts to make two different kinds of contribution to truth value; logic would thus count it as *two* leftover expressions with different kinds of reference. Given an expression which makes a determinate kind of contribution to truth value wherever it occurs, *there is no such thing* as putting two different kinds of argument expression into any of its argument places. A concept script does not, therefore, rule out doing *that*, for there is no such thing. What it does rule out is the use of one sign in two logically different ways. And it can do this by a mode of writing leftover expressions so that the kind of argument expression for each argument place is clearly indicated.

For there to be logical analysis of any sentence, i.e., for there to be the construal of it as argument expressions and leftover part, logic will need rules of at least two different sorts for substitution *salva veritate* of the expressions picked out by the analysis as logically significant: one sort for the leftover part and at least one other sort for the argument expressions. (The rules for substitution characterising the argument expressions in fact fix the kind of rule characterising the leftover part.) I argued earlier that, if there is any possibility of construing what was leftover in one sentence as argument expression in another, we must use the same rules for substitution *salva veritate* in both cases. These two requirements generate a structure of kinds of rule for substitution *salva veritate* of expressions. In a concept script, the structure will be clear; and any argument expression which can occur as leftover will be written with an indication of its own argument places and of the kind of substitution rule to which the expressions in them are subject. In a concept script in which the indication of argument places is thus carried out systematically, there will be argument expressions properly written with *no* argument places. Writing them that way indicates the kind of substitutability *salva veritate* they have: that of *proper names*. The substitutability rules for proper names are what correspond on the linguistic side to *identity* in the proper limited sense. (Any other kind of substitutability *salva veritate* for expressions corresponds not to identity but to a relation analogous to it, on Frege's view.) An object, Frege says, is anything the expression for which does not contain any empty place (TWF p. 32). Such an expression can never be identifiable as the same expression as one which in some analysis of some sentence is a leftover expression. It is *impossible* for a proper name to be a predicate; there is, in the eyes of logic, no such thing as that. The very close connection between *being an object* and being capable of standing in the relation of *identity* properly speaking is extremely important for Frege. When he considered avoiding Russell's paradox by splitting the logical category of objects into proper and improper objects, he thought that he would nevertheless have to have *one* relation of identity which could take as its arguments both proper and improper objects. That course makes the mess generated by the proposed solution worse than it would otherwise be; and Frege in fact rejected that solution. What is interesting is the way his description of the proposal illustrates how he saw logical categories: one thing he thought he had to leave in place in any acceptable solution was the connection between being an object and being able to stand in the relation of identity, "a relation given to us in such a specific form that it is inconceivable that various kinds of it should occur" (TWF, p. 235). There may be relations analogous to it, but for anything which is *not* a function there is, as far as logic is concerned, only *it*.

The upshot of all this is that you cannot be referring to the same thing twice (cannot be ascribing first this and then that to it) if the expression you use to refer to it makes two entirely different kinds of contribution to the truth or falsity of the sentences in which it occurs. You can refer to the same thing twice by expressions with different senses, but not by the same expression twice over when the rules for substitution *salva veritate* that it carries with it are different in the two cases. It would then refer to two different things. What kind of thing you are referring to, talking about, thinking about, is not separable from the kind of contribution to truth or falsity made by the expression for it. If we say that Socrates falls under the concept *bald* and that the concept *bald* is self-identical, we can take ourselves to be speaking about the same thing, the concept *bald*, twice, *only if* we do not take ourselves to be saying of the concept *bald* what we say of Socrates when we say that *he* is self-identical.

I went into all this to show what is involved in the dispute between Frege and the objector. The disagreement naturally expresses itself in one way, but it goes with a much more fundamental disagreement. The relatively misleading way of putting the disagreement is: it is about whether there are concepts, like *self-identity*, under which things in different logical types can fall.

What is at the heart of the disagreement is *logical analysis*. To show what I mean by that, I need briefly to set alongside *self-identity* another candidate that philosophers come up with when they look for concepts applicable to *anything* at all: being an *object of thought*. The idea is that whatever kind of thing the concept *bald* is, we can at any rate think about it, so it and Socrates share this: they are *objects of thought*.

Against this, we have Frege's remark that I quoted earlier: "I do not begin with concepts and put them together to form a thought or judgment; I come by the parts of a thought by analysing the thought". If you take the judgment itself as primary, as Frege does, what you find is that you can indeed take *bald* — the concept – as an object of thought only by its not being an *object* of thought at all. That is, in the sense in which you think about an object by having a thought in which it figures as object (expressed in a sentence in which a proper name referring to it occurs), you think about a concept by having a thought in which it occurs as a concept, i.e. a thought expressed by a sentence containing an expression used predicatively, referring to it. There is no category-unambiguous thing, *being an object of thought*, and you only think that there is if you think you find the concept *bald* on its own, when you start looking for objects of thought on their own. The concept *bald* (if we really mean the *concept*) is something you can think about, all right – only because it is not *something* you can think about. Unless we are very careful with 'something we think about', we go wildly wrong. What thinking about something *is* belongs to *what it is*, what kind of thing, and that is shown in the use of a term in the expression of thoughts.

My objector differs from Frege fundamentally in thinking that one can separate what it is one is thinking about from the kind of use terms have in the expression of thoughts. That is why he believes that one can be thinking about one and the same thing, the concept *bald*, when one says that Socrates falls under it and that it is also what Socrates himself is, namely, self-identical.

There is a sense in which the disputants pass each other by. The objector ascribes to Frege a view of a certain kind, a substantial thesis that Frege has (the objector thinks) built into his concept script, but which can be discussed independently. The supposed Fregean thesis is that nothing can be thought of things of more than one logical kind, and the objector believes that it has been built into the concept script in the rules governing what can go into argument places. He thinks that a *better* concept script would allow Socrates and the concept *bald* into the same place in some thoughts (e.g., ascriptions of self-identity) and would allow Socrates but not the concept *bald* into a place in *other* thoughts, e.g., those ascribing baldness. One could disagree with Frege about what a good concept script would allow without disagreeing in the fundamental way our objector does. He does not so much reject a view of Frege's as not see what kind of view it is. He does not see the possibility of letting the use teach you what you are talking about, where logical analysis is what shows you how a term is being used, what kind of contribution it makes (what kind of contribution logic sees it making) to the sentences in which it occurs.

Some years ago Hidé Ishiguro said that we should give up the misunderstanding of Wittgenstein, that he went from a 'Naming' theory of meaning in the *Tractatus* to a 'use' theory of meaning in his later work.[2] She argues that in an important sense he *always* held a use theory. He never thought, as Russell

---

[2] H. Ishiguro, "Use and Reference of Names", in *Studies in the Philosophy of Wittgenstein*, ed. P. Winch (London, 1969).

did, that the meaning of a name can be settled independently of its use in propositions; in the *Tractatus* he held that the identity of the object referred to by a name is settled only by the use of the name in propositions. She traces this view back to Frege and extends it to the use of terms for things in logical categories other than that of objects. What I have been trying to make clear is that at the root of the disagreement between my objector and Frege is a disagreement about the relation between the way we use terms and what it is we are talking about. The "use" theory which Miss Ishiguro ascribes to Frege is a mode of thinking about that relation utterly alien to my objector. In his position *vis-à-vis* Frege's we can see something that recurs in later philosophy. The objector (so it seems, from Frege's side) looks resolutely in the wrong direction to tell what his own terms refer to. The metaphor is Miss Ishiguro's, from her description of the form of the disagreement between Wittgenstein (in his later works) and those who claim to know from their own awareness of their mental processes *what* they are thinking or talking about.

The dispute between Frege and the objector shows us something of what it means to speak of philosophy as a battle against the bewitchment of our intelligence (PI, §109), shows us something of what *kind* of difficulty there can be in philosophy. That battle against the bewitchment of the intelligence changed its form as the role in it of logical analysis changed. But what remains is the idea of it as a battle against something that turns us away from the direction in which what needs to be seen is open to view, and also the idea that what we need to see – if only we could see that that is what we need to see! – is how our terms themselves are used.

What it was our objector was originally objecting to may have sunk from view. I had described a kind of realism about the logical character of what there is, a realism that goes with the idea that we can do a logical classification of things, put them into the logical categories in which they belong, where logical categories are thought of as themselves some kind of class, and we can supposedly get such a classification right or wrong. I argued that if we understand what is shown in Frege's concept script, that kind of realism drops away, sentences expressing it being recognised as so much muddle. The objector claimed in the first place that there *is* room for a logical classification of things and, to back that up, he claimed also that in general there is no good reason to proscribe all ascriptions of a concept to items in different logical categories. I want now to turn back to a question about realism and what a concept script does, which I shall get to from two different directions.

First, imagine someone complaining that what I have said is all very interesting but it is not *Frege*. For Frege actually says that the difference between first and second level functions is not made arbitrarily but is founded deep in the nature of things (TWF, p. 41). He would say exactly the same about the distinctions between function and object, between relation and concept and so on. But have I not been denying that he believes in any such relation between logical structures and the nature of things? Have I not been suggesting that logic can do what it likes and pretty much ignore *the nature of things*?

Secondly, imagine someone ascribing to Frege the view that there are thoughts which cannot be expressed in language, but which are nevertheless thoughts. Thus, if we say that objects and functions are totally different from each other, that is a logically improper use of language, and there is in such a case no way of getting rid of the linguistic impropriety, and of saying what we are trying to say in logically decent language. On the view we are imagining (we are imagining it ascribed to Frege), although we cannot *say* the thing we are trying to say, what we are struggling with is nevertheless a true but inexpressible thought.

We shall come round to the first point if we start with the second. I find it difficult to be tolerant about the ascription of such nonsense to Frege (or about the same ascription in the case of Wittgenstein). When there is no way of saying properly what we are trying to say, what we come out with is in fact a kind of nonsense, and corresponds to no ineffable truth. What Frege thinks is that through an inadequacy of ordinary language, we can form sentences in it which are acceptable according to its rules but which are not the expression of any thought. It is possible to become clear about what has happened, if we are led to see how thoughts are expressed in a language more nearly adequate by the standards of logic. In grasping the significance of the distinctions embodied in that language, we do not grasp any ineffable truths. A truth is a truth about something; a true thought (that is) is about whatever logic may construe it as being about. But the distinctions embodied in the concept script are not what any thought can be about.

The reasons have already been touched on. A concept script, I said in §II, does not get something external to itself right; if it is not an adequate concept script, it is not through getting something external to itself wrong. On the other hand, it is not the case that just anything goes in constructing a concept script. As Frege himself says, the distinctions embodied in it are not arbitrary but are founded deep in the nature of things. We should not ignore that remark of Frege's; we should give it the importance he attached to such points – but we have to be particularly careful not to misunderstand it. We need to ask: *what* nature of things? For, as I have just said, the distinctions which the concept script must have in it are not fixed by anything external to it. Nothing external to it fixes its logical structure; but it is not arbitrary. *Where* then is the reality that fixes what distinctions must be embodied in it? That reality lies *in it*. There is an order, a logical order, *in* thought and *in* language. Thought's being about things, its having logical order, its being that about which the question of truth can arise, its being expressible in language – language, which itself has a single logical grammar in so far as it is capable of expressing thoughts – all these come to the same. Thought is about things, but the logical order which is part of what it is for there to be any *aboutness* is not itself one of the things thought can be about. The distinctions between functions and objects, between first and second order functions and so on – those distinctions are indeed founded deep in the nature of things. But to understand someone who says *that* is to have understood the kind of 'placing' such a sentence requires. To take it to be an 'ineffable' truth is a truly perverse misreading, an attempt to represent to oneself a state of affairs while pretending that no representing to oneself is going on. Putting the matter another way: the distinctions in question come out clearly in a language which marks them systematically, by having expressions which make plain the logical character of what they stand for. But in such a language there is no expression which refers to any of these logical distinctions. Ordinary language enables us to form apparently referring expressions, like 'the distinction between first and second order functions'. But now the hard thing is to learn, from the fact that there are no corresponding expressions in a logically adequate language, that the distinctions are not objects of any thoughts. And whatever is *correct* in saying that these distinctions are founded deep in the nature of things, its correctness will not lie in the imagery that accompanies it, of functions with their functionhood, objects with their objecthood, lying there with their distinct natures in the nature of things.

Now once more about realism. Wittgenstein's later work has a significance for questions about realism and anti-realism which can be seen only through its relation to the body of ideas I have been talking about. And what characterises that body of ideas is its style of answer to questions of the general type: *Where is the reality which must guide us here?* Where is the reality to which our mode of thought must be responsible?

I described a kind of realism in §III, a realism which depends on the idea of an external relation between the logical characteristics of things and the logical features built into our modes of expression. The kind of realist I imagined thought that the logical characteristics of things and the logical structures of our mode of expression *ought* to match but that they might not do so. It is actually part of such a view that the only alternative to it which can be conceived by someone who holds it is: in our modes of expression *anything* goes. The alternatives, that is, are conceived this way: *either* there is something external to the mode of expression (the independently fixed logical character of things) which is a measure of the logical adequacy of the mode of expression, *or* there is no measure of adequacy which is in a hard logical sense *unarbitrary*. There is also an anti-realist view characterised by the acceptance of precisely the same pair of alternatives. Both views then conceive the situation this way: *there is* a logical reality independent of and external to our modes of thought and expression, *or there is not* and the logical structures of our thought and expression are fundamentally arbitrary.

Frege, in the development of a concept script as a tool for philosophical thought, allows us to get clear of the two alternatives, to leave them behind. He allows us to think about language, *any* language in which thoughts can be expressed, as having something in it, which may or may not be *clearly* there for us to see. A language is more nearly adequate by the wholly unarbitrary standards of logic in so far as it makes systematically clear what is there in it, what it shares with all languages. The standard of logical adequacy is no external one, but that does not imply any arbitrariness in the measure. He lets us see that the reality by which the adequacy of a concept script is measured is not external to it. In that way he shows us a *general* possibility of answering questions *where the reality is* to which in doing such-and-such we are responsible. By letting us see a reality somewhere else than where we were looking, he teaches us a new way to understand such questions. The realist I imagined, and the person who takes the opposite view to his, share a conception: either there is something where we are both looking for a reality, or there is not, and we are without objective standards; that is what they both think.

Look somewhere *else*: that is what we can hear in Wittgenstein's later philosophy; look where you do not think there can be any reason for looking. That is there to be heard in the *Tractatus*, and *it* simply makes clearer a message already to be heard in Frege's work. For him, the concept script was a tool of intellectual liberation. A good concept script would lay before us clearly what we need to look at, and thus help break the domination of words over the human mind; it would help free our thought from the trammels placed upon it by language inattentive to the promptings of logic (*Bs*, pp. xii–xiii; cf. TLP, 3.325).

It is a mistake to tie Frege's use of the concept script too closely to the use, in the analytic tradition, of techniques of *translation* of philosophically interesting claims into an adequate language. One point of looking at the example 'logical categories are a kind of class' was to see the significance of the fact that there is *no* translation of it into an adequate language. We need still to get clear about what is radical in Frege's vision; we can do that only by getting clear the relation between the dropping away of some philosophical views as mere muddle and the idea of the truth of logic as not something set over against what it measures but internal to it.

University of Virginia

DISCUSSIONS

REFERENCE AND SENSE: AN EPITOME

BY DAVID BELL

Although Frege nowhere states the matter in just this way, it is, I believe, possible to define his notions of *reference* and *sense* as follows:

(*R*) The reference of an expression *E* is that in virtue of whose identity expressions can be intersubstituted for *E salva veritate* throughout any context of the appropriate kind. There are three kinds of context: direct use, direct quotation, and indirect quotation.

(*S*) The sense of an expression *E* is the condition which anything must meet in order to be the reference of *E*. (This condition may of course be such that nothing in fact meets it.)

Rather than attempt to defend these statements as an epitome of Frege's views by adducing textual evidence, I shall try to show that (*R*) and (*S*) together can be made to yield virtually all the major theses which Frege advanced concerning the reference and the sense of expressions of different kinds.[1] To this end I shall take his logical syntax – or, at least, a simplified version of it – as given, and shall consider only expressions which belong to the three fundamental syntactic categories of *proper name, predicate,* and *sentence*.

1. *The reference of proper names in contexts of direct use*

Proper names '*a*' and '*b*' can be intersubstituted *salva veritate* just in case one and the same object is the bearer of those names, i.e., just in case *a* = *b*. According to (*R*), then, the reference of a proper name is the object which possesses that name.

2. *The reference of predicates in contexts of direct use*

The application of (*R*) to predicate expressions is complicated by the following dilemma. On the one hand, Frege believes, if a predicate is to be capable of performing its unifying and predicative roles within a sentence, then it must stand for something which is capable in principle of combining with an

---

[1] I here amplify some brief observations made in "On the translation of Frege's *Bedeutung*", *Analysis*, 40 (1980) pp. 191–2.

object, its argument, so as to yield a determinate truth-value. And so, Frege believed, whatever a predicate stands for, it cannot stand for an object, because an object is incapable of performing such a role or yielding such a result. On the other hand, however, the relation of identity, in terms of which (R) is articulated, is a first-level relation which accordingly only takes objects as its arguments. So if (R) is to assign a reference to predicate expressions it must be possible to assert identity of entities to which identity cannot in principle apply. Clearly no literal application of (R) is possible in the present context.

Now two predicates '$F(\ )$' and '$G(\ )$' are interchangeable *salva veritate* as long as they have the same extension, i.e. just in case $(x)(Fx \leftrightarrow Gx)$. According to (R), then, the reference of a predicate should be its extension, the class of objects to which it applies. Frege admits the temptation to say just this: "In any sentence we can substitute *salva veritate* one concept-word for another if they have the same extension ... For this reason we might easily come to propose the extension of a concept as the reference of a concept word". (PW, pp. 118–9)[2] But he immediately adds: "to do this, however, would be to overlook the fact that extensions of concepts are objects".

That Frege does not finally abandon (R), however, in his account of predicate reference is indicated by his provision of pseudo-identity conditions for concepts, couched in terms of the (proper) identity conditions of the corresponding extensions: "If we bear all this in mind", he writes, "we shall be well able to assert 'two concept-words have the same reference if and only if the extensions of the corresponding concepts coincide', without being led astray by the improper use of the expression 'the same' ". (PW, p. 122) The reference of a predicate is thus an unsaturated entity (a concept) whose "identity" condition exactly reflects the identity condition of its extension. In other words Frege *is* able to apply (R) to predicate expressions, but only by dint of an equivocation concerning the notion of identity employed therein.

3. *The reference of sentences in contexts of direct use*

Two sentences 'P' and 'Q' are intersubstitutable *salva veritate* as long as they have the same truth-value, i.e. just in case $P \leftrightarrow Q$. It follows immediately and unproblematically from (R) that its truth-value is the reference of a sentence.

4. *The reference of expressions in contexts of direct quotation*

In direct quotation, expressions of any syntactic kind can be interchanged *salva veritate* with different tokens of the same expression type. Identity of expression type is therefore what warrants intersubstitution and so, by (R), the reference of any directly quoted expression is the type of that token.

5. *The reference of expressions in contexts of indirect quotation*

---

[2] I have altered the translation of '*Bedeutung*' from 'meaning' to 'reference'.

Intuitively it seems that expressions in *oratio obliqua* are interchangeable *salva veritate* as long as they have the same meaning. In reporting the content of a remark or thought one is justified in employing any expression which accurately captures or preserves the meaning of the original. The intuitive notions of "content" or "meaning" here correspond to Frege's notion of sense. According to (R), then, because identity of sense is necessary and sufficient to allow interchange of expressions within *oratio obliqua*, the reference of such expressions is their sense. Frege's theory thus implies that such so-called intensional contexts are in fact entirely extensional: expressions with the same reference can be interchanged *salva veritate* throughout; one must, however, be careful to identify correctly what the reference *is* in such cases.

6. *The sense of proper names in contexts of direct use*

According to (S), the sense of a proper name 'a' is the condition which something must meet if it is to be the reference of 'a', i.e. if it is to be a. Such a condition will comprise an answer to the question, "Under what circumstances is it the case, for an arbitrary object x, that $x = a$?". Quite literally, then, the sense of a proper name is given by the identity condition for the reference of that name. And this is surely what Frege had in mind when he wrote, e.g., that the sense of the name 'Aristotle' "might, for instance, be taken to be the following: the pupil of Plato and teacher of Alexander the Great". (TWF, p. 58n) It does not, however, follow from this theory (though it has seemed to many to follow from Frege's unfortunate way of expressing it) that the proper name in question is synonymous with any expression which supplies the appropriate condition. The name 'Aristotle' is not *synonymous* with the phrase 'the pupil of Plato and teacher of Alexander the Great' – yet for all that, the latter is a proper elucidation of the sense of the former.

7. *The sense of predicates in contexts of direct use*

Here again, as in §2 above, there is interference from the doctrine of the unsaturatedness of concepts. *Prima facie*, the application of (S) to a predicate '$F(\ )$' should yield the result that its sense is the condition under which something is the concept F. Unfortunately, of course, it is nonsense to assert (or deny) that an object is identical with a concept; and, conversely, if some entity is identical with the concept F it cannot be a concept but must, because 'the concept F' is a singular term, be an object.

Now one of the intuitions which a theory of meaning for predicates should capture is surely this: a predicate '$F(\ )$' signifies [3] a condition on objects such that if a given object a satisfies that condition then *that a is F* is *ipso facto* a true thought. Indeed, one of the most natural ways in which to elucidate the truth-condition of a sentence of the form '$F(a)$' is to say that it is true just in case the

---

[3] For the moment 'signifies' is intended to be indeterminate as between 'expresses' and 'refers to'.

object referred to by '*a*' satisfies the condition signified by the predicate. (Here I shall simply assume that it is legitimate to identify a Fregean concept with such a condition on objects – this is indeed the only way I can understand Frege's doctrine that concepts are functions and such that their value is always a truth-value.) The question now arises: Does a predicate express such a condition as its sense, or does it refer to it, *via* its sense? There can be no doubt that the Fregean response is to identify the condition in question with the reference of the predicate; and so, by (*S*), the sense of the predicate will be the condition which something must meet in order to be that condition. The notion of *an identity condition of a condition* is certainly a coherent one – how else could we understand a question like 'Are there really two conditions here, or merely two ways of referring to one and the same condition?'? More informally, Frege would argue that the condition to which a predicate refers must be presented in some way to the understanding, and it is this *Art des Gegebenseins* which is accordingly the sense of the predicate.

8. *The sense of sentences in contexts of direct use*

The reference of a sentence is its truth-value. A literal application of (*S*) thus yields the result that the sense expressed by a sentence comprises the conditions which must obtain in order for it to have the truth-value which it in fact has. But because there are just two truth-values which are interdefinable with the help of negation, this result can be simplified. The sense of a sentence comprises the condition under which its reference = the True, i.e. its truth-condition.

9. *The sense of expressions in contexts of direct quotation*

The sense of a quoted expression *E* comprises the condition which anything must meet to be an expression of the same type as *E*. In the case of a written language the condition is typographical identity.

10. *The sense of expressions in contexts of indirect discourse*

The sense of an expression *E* in *oratio obliqua*, according to (*S*), is the condition for something's being the (normal) sense of *E*. The sense of an expression in *oratio obliqua* – as well, of course, as its reference – is thus quite different from that which it has in ordinary contexts. In a letter to Russell, Frege went so far as to say that "to avoid ambiguity, we ought really to have special signs in indirect speech, though their connection with the corresponding signs in direct speech should be easy to recognize". (PMC, p. 153) We can develop this hint and, say, introduce the convention that expressions in Roman type have their normal sense (and reference), whereas an italicized expression is to express a different sense, one which determines its normal sense as its reference. So the proper name 'Berlin' refers to a city and expresses a sense comprising identity conditions of that city. '*Berlin*', on the other hand, as it occurs in, say, 'He thought *Berlin was the capital of Germany*', refers to the sense of 'Berlin' and expresses a sense which comprises identity conditions of the sense of that word.

* * * * *

The results reached so far capture, I believe, some of the most basic tenets of Frege's semantic theory. But only some: no mention has been made, for example, of the conditions Frege provides (*Gg*, §29, BLA, p. 84) under which an expression is referential (i.e. regardless of what the identity of its reference might be); of the determination of complex reference by component reference; of the determination of complex sense by component sense; of the determination of complex reference by complex sense; or of the continuing relevance, if any, of the *Grundlagen* principle that "a word has meaning only in the context of a sentence". These are difficult matters about which one should try to get clear – but an epitome is hardly the proper place in which to try.

University of Sheffield

FREGEAN CONNECTION:
BEDEUTUNG, VALUE AND TRUTH-VALUE

By GOTTFRIED GABRIEL

In this paper I want to show how Frege's problematic connection between truth-value and *Bedeutung* by means of the well known idea that the *Bedeutung* of a sentence is its truth-value becomes more plausible when set against the background of German language and philosophy.[4]

It has already been noticed by E. Tugendhat that the meaning of the German word '*Bedeutung*' includes the meaning of the English word 'importance'. For this reason Tugendhat has proposed to translate '*Bedeutung*', in its Fregean use, as 'significance' and has argued that the *Bedeutung* of the parts of sentences is their (significant) "contribution to the truth-value of the sentences into which they may enter" (Tugendhat, p. 180)[5], a contribution which Tugendhat calls "truth-value potential". With the help of these considerations Tugendhat tries to avoid treating reference as the paradigm case of *Bedeutung* and to get a uniform theory of *Bedeutung* which includes concept-words (predicates). I do not want to go into further details concerning Tugendhat's

---
[4] Pages and paragraphs of Frege's works refer to the original German publications. I have used (without mentioning them) English translations with some changes. '*Bedeutung*' I have left untranslated.
[5] Cf. also the *Postskript 1975* to the German version in Schirn, III pp. 65–9.

approach and its discussion by Michael Dummett and others. What I wish rather to stress is the starting point of Tugendhat's argument, his observation concerning the meaning of '*Bedeutung*'. My thesis is that the *Nebenbedeutung* of '*Bedeutung*', 'importance', is even more important for the understanding of Frege's use of '*Bedeutung*' than Tugendhat himself realised, although I do not wish to deny that Frege finally comes to use '*Bedeutung*' in the sense of 'reference'.

To speak in Tugendhat's fashion of the *Bedeutung* (significance) of expressions seems to be possible only with regard to the *parts* of sentences. Only the parts make contributions to the truth-value of sentences, not the sentences themselves. *Bedeutung* with the *Nebenbedeutung* of 'importance' is always *Bedeutung* in respect of or relative to something, *Bedeutung* in this sense is "functional" as Tugendhat himself says. The parts of sentences have *Bedeutung* relative to the truth-value of sentences. Relative to what however can the sentences be said to have *Bedeutung*?

What Tugendhat does not discuss is the truth-value potential of sentences themselves. His procedure rather (the reverse of Frege's) is to start with the truth-value of sentences and to define the *Bedeutung* (significance) of the parts of sentences as their truth-value potential. And, in fact, he does not provide any argument that we are allowed to take truth-value as the *Bedeutung* (significance) of sentences. The standard Fregean argument is not available here, for to argue that the *Bedeutung* of a sentence is its truth-value *because* it is the truth-value which does not change if we substitute a singular term by another one of the same *Bedeutung* would render Tugendhat's approach circular. Consequently Tugendhat simply states that we "start from the truth-value of sentences" and "call this their significance" (Tugendhat, p. 181), which has a rather stipulative ring to it. We may have gained a uniform conception of *Bedeutung* for proper names and predicates, but on the other hand we seem to have lost an argument for taking truth-value as the *Bedeutung* of sentences. When Tugendhat points at the non-technical meaning of 'Bedeutung' in the sense of 'significance' and says "sentences are significant (*bedeutungsvoll*) in so far as they are true or false" (Tugendhat, p. 185), one could simply ask, why? Bringing in complex sentences does not help as Tugendhat himself observes: "We cannot define the significance of the sentence as its contribution to the significance of complex sentences, since its significance is already defined, it is its truth-value". (Tugendhat, p. 186).

The question remains, whether Frege simply misused the word '*Bedeutung*' when he identified the *Bedeutung* of sentences with their truth-value. To deny this we have to find a functional understanding of *Bedeutung* in the case of truth-values.

With regard to the expression 'truth-value' we should notice that here too one can distinguish in Frege a technical and a non-technical use, a fact which seems to be overlooked, or at least not fully taken into consideration, by interpreters of Frege. Anyway, let us take a closer look at the twofold origin of Frege's use of 'truth-value'. Most logicians and philosophers of language would, I think, assume this word to be a purely technical term first coined by Frege by analogy with the term 'value of a function'. A look, for instance, into *A Dictionary of Philosophy* may confirm this. Under the entry 'truth-value' we read:

> A technical term i introduced by Frege, who saw a strong analogy between concepts or predicates and mathematical functions. Consequently he thought of sentences ... as standing for, or denoting, a value in the same way that 3^2 denotes 9, the value of the function x^2 for $x=3$.[6]

According to this line of thought there were for Frege special functions, namely concepts, whose values are the True and the False, and to get a common name for these two values he introduced the artificial term 'truth-value'. This account implies that talking about truth-values makes sense only in the context of the terminology of functions and their values, or at least that the original context is this mathematical one. An initial glance at the first occurrence of the term 'truth-value' (in *FB*) seems to confirm this interpretation. Here Frege says: "I now say: 'the value of our function is a truth-value'." (*FB*, p. 13. Cf. *Gg* §2). We may understand this sentence as a stipulative introduction of 'truth-value'. But we should notice that Frege does not really say that he *names* the value of such functions 'truth-value'. He could equally well be understood as saying that he appropriates the existing expression 'truth-value', stating (not stipulating) that the value of such functions is a truth-value. This reading presupposes that there should be a context different from the mathematical one from which Frege's talk of truth-values is derived. And indeed such a context is provided in *SB*, significantly in that passage in which Frege comes to the conclusion that the truth-value is the *Bedeutung* of sentences. Here Frege uses the expression 'value' not in the sense of the value of a function but in the sense of importance: "The thought loses value for us as soon as we recognize that the *Bedeutung* of one of its parts is missing." (*SB*, p. 33)[7] (Astonishingly enough

---

[6] *A Dictionary of Philosophy*, ed. A. Flew (London 1979), p. 332.

[7] For this significant connection of value and *Bedeutung*, cf. *NS*, p. 251 and Frege's letter to Russell 28.12.1902 (*WB*, p. 235): "Now it would be impossible to see why it was of value to us to know whether or not a word had a *Bedeutung* if the whole sentence did not have a *Bedeutung* and if this *Bedeutung* was of no value to us; for whether or not that is so does not affect the thought. Moreover, this *Bedeutung* will be something which will have value for us precisely when we are interested in whether the words are meaningful (*bedeutungsvoll*), and hence, when we inquire about truth. The *Bedeutung* of the sentence must be something which does not change when one sign is replaced by another with the same *Bedeutung* but a different sense. What does not change in the process is the truth-value".

Tugendhat leaves out in his extensive citation of the full passage just this crucial sentence!)

After talking about the value (importance) of a thought (or sentence) Frege in a *second* step makes clear what kind of value he has in mind: "Why is the thought not enough for us? Because, and to the extent that, we are concerned with its truth-value". Then distinguishing this value from what we might call aesthetic or poetic value he continues: "It is the striving after truth that drives us always to advance from the sense to the *Bedeutung*" (*SB*, p. 33). Evidently Frege's introduction of the term 'truth-value' here belongs to a context, completely different from the mathematical one, that of value-theory.

To underline this understanding it should be pointed out that it was *not* Frege who first used the term 'truth-value' but the Neo-Kantian Wilhelm Windelband,[8] the founder of the value-theoretical *Südwestdeutsche* school of Neo-Kantianism. Windelband indeed used the term in a value-theoretical way. As I have shown elsewhere[9] there are many significant parallels between Windelband and Frege, which, in my view, can be traced back to the fact that both studied with Hermann Lotze in Göttingen. It is Lotze who already speaks in his *Logic* of the "value-difference" (*Wertunterschied*) between truth and untruth (*Unwahrheit*).[10] Frege was not concerned with all values value-theory treats of – not, that is, with the values 'good' and 'beautiful'; as a logician he was concerned only with the value 'true'. Yet in comparing the predicate 'true' with the predicates 'good' and 'beautiful' Frege refers to the same traditional triad of values as Windelband: "Just as the word 'beautiful' points the way for aesthetics and 'good' for ethics, so does 'true' for logic."[11] Moreover Frege clearly uses 'true' as a value-predicate in the earliest posthumous *Logic*-fragment where he connects 'true' with 'good' in the value-theoretical way of Windelband. (*NS*, p. 4)

Given this connection between Frege's use of the term 'truth-value' and the German philosophical tradition of value theory it then becomes plausible to suppose that Frege's identification of *Bedeutung* and truth-value in the case of sentences might be influenced by the meaning of '*Bedeutung*' in the sense of 'importance', a suggestion reinforced by the fact that, in German, '*Bedeutung*' in this sense is used as an expression equivalent to '*Wert*' (value). In English there is indeed an equivalence between 'importance' and 'value' (something can have importance or value, something can be important or valuable) but neither expression is equivalent to 'meaning'. Now the use of '*Bedeutung*' and '*Wert*' as equivalents is, in fact, to be found explicitly in Frege: he sometimes substitutes

---

[8] Cf. W. Windelband, *Präludien*, 5th edition, 2 vols. (Tübingen, 1915) vol. 1, p. 32.
[9] G. Gabriel, "Frege als Neukantianer", (forthcoming) in *Kant-Studien*.
[10] H. Lotze, *Logik*, (Leipzig 1874), p. 4.
[11] This is the opening passage of *Ged*. Cf. also *NS*, p. 139.

one of both expressions for the other.[12] The most significant formulations are in
Über die wissenschaftliche Berechtigung einer Begriffsschrift, where Frege talks about the *Bedeutung* (importance) and *Wert* (value) of sensible symbols for non-sensible thought.(p.49) Discussing the difference between acoustical and optical symbols he says: "But no matter how valuable (*wertvoll*) these advantages [of acoustical symbols], may be for other purposes (*Zwecke*), they have no importance (*Bedeutung*) for the rigour of logical deductions" (*ibid.*, p. 52). Here we find in Frege the use of '*Wert*' (value) and '*Bedeutung*' as two-place predicates: symbols have value (are valuable) or have *Bedeutung* with respect to a special purpose (*Zweck*). Now, after we consider the purpose Frege had in mind, we will be prepared to draw the conclusion.

Frege is mainly interested in language in so far as its purpose is to make true assertions. In this sense he distinguishes the poetic from the scientific (logical) use of language. (*SB*, p. 33; *Ged*, p. 63f.) Whereas the poetic use is directed toward the aesthetic value of beauty, the scientific use is directed toward the value of "truth and truth alone". (*Ged*, p. 64) This means, with regard to the purpose of making true assertions, sentences (more accurately, thoughts) have value insofar they are true or false; and on the basis of the previously mentioned equivalence of 'value' and '*Bedeutung*' it makes sense to say that sentences have *Bedeutung* if and only if they are true or false. The *Bedeutung* of sentences consists in their being truth-valuable[13] (*wahrheitswertvoll*), i.e. valuable for the value truth (in the sense of value theory) which is the aim of the so called "striving after truth" (*Streben nach Wahrheit*)[14]. In this case not only true but also false sentences (thoughts) are valuable. That is the reason why two truth-values are to be acknowledged, though only the value truth is "striven after".

The question remains as to why Frege, in fact, characterizes the *Bedeutung* of a sentence not only as truth-value, a conception which should be acceptable by now, but also as an object, the problematic twist whereby the *Bedeutung* of a sentence is represented as a referent. The answer seems to be that it is Frege's theory of identity which forced him to do so. "If the sign of identity is used between sentences, then the truth-value must be recognized as the *Bedeutung* of the sentences."(*WB*, p. 235) What is problematic in this formulation is not the conclusion but the premiss, for, in addition to the explicit conclusion, it also indirectly implies that truth-values are objects. Taking material equivalence as a case of identity means treating truth-values as objects, and conversely treating

---

[12] Cf. in addition to the following quotations Frege's letter to Marty (Stumpf) 29.8.1882, in which he speaks of the *value* of discoursive thinking and the *Bedeutung* of analytical judgements (*WB*, p. 163).

[13] I take over this pertinent expression from Bell, p. 42, but use it in the primary sense of value theory. In Bell's use it means, strictly speaking, 'truth-value valuable'.

[14] *SB*, p. 33; cf. the emphatic use of this phrase in Frege's letter to H. Dingler 17.11.1918 (*WB*, p. 44).

truth-values as objects allows material equivalence to be taken as a case of identity. As Frege himself concedes: "The designation of the truth-values as objects may appear to be an arbitrary fancy or perhaps a mere play upon words, from which no profound consequences could be drawn". (*SB*, p. 34) In fact, taking truth-values as objects is not an advantage for semantics in general, but only for semantics of a special formal language like Frege's concept-script. Nevertheless it makes sense to conceive the *Bedeutung* of a sentence as its truth-value; it makes sense, that is, if we turn from the question what kind of entity the *Bedeutung* of an expression *is* to the question of what it is for an expression to *have Bedeutung*. It is evident that the answer to the second question does not constitute the whole story of Frege's use of '*Bedeutung*' but at least it seems to be an important part of this story that has been overlooked. Separating these two questions we might reject Frege's answer to the first without giving up his answer to the second.

Universität Konstanz

CRITICAL STUDIES

AN UNSUCCESSFUL DIG

By Michael Dummett

G. P. BAKER AND P. M. S. HACKER, *Frege: Logical Excavations*. Oxford, Basil Blackwell; New York, O.U.P., 1984. pp. xvii + 406. Price £29.50.

I. General Aims

Frege's work has had a notoriously bizarre fate. Neglected in his lifetime and for long afterwards by all but a very few, in recent years not only acclaimed but studied, it seemed that it had at last received its due as a classic contribution to philosophy. The appearance was premature; for, in the past few years, it has been made into a battleground for exegetes. No philosophical writer can less have deserved this fate, so great are the clarity of his style and the pains he took to be explicit; yet book succeeds article and article succeeds book, each declaring that every previous exponent has misunderstood Frege from start to finish. This book (hereafter FLE) FLE is squarely in this tradition.[1] The authors (hereafter B&H) B&H announce, in their first chapter, that Frege has been converted into a mythological figure, and that their task will be to demythologise him. Previous writers have fashioned him in their own image, that of twentieth-century analytical philosophy: B&H will tell us, for the first time, what Frege really meant.

This adversarial approach is to be deplored. It obstructs progress and provokes pointless controversy. Frege is so interesting a writer because we have got so comparatively short a way beyond the point he reached. To be more exact, we have sent out forays far ahead of that point, but have secured very little further territory. Wittgenstein, in particular, made very bold expeditions into unknown country; but we are still struggling with his work, which we have not yet mastered and cannot properly evaluate. Frege's problems are therefore still our problems; his thoughts still answer to our concerns. His work was deep, and rewards sustained reflection, which can discern new aspects and uncover new connections. Such reflection is hampered by the din of battle as exegete smites exegete; and the clash of arms is unnecessary. When Frege's work was as yet generally unfamiliar, bad mistakes were indeed made: and, just because his work was so profound, anyone writing about Frege is liable to miss important points and to misrepresent his ideas to some degree. It really is not likely, however, that, at this date, any serious commentator will have gone utterly astray. The line between exposition and comment is thin, but there is nevertheless an important difference between a contribution to philosophy and an account of the views of an individual philosopher, in that the former, if wrong, is likely to be completely – though, perhaps, fruitfully – wrong, whereas the latter, even if not wholly right, may well be nearly so. It ought to be easy for those interested in Frege's work to arrive at a consensus about his meaning, a consensus that need not be static, but may be modified by new insights as they occur, but which excludes the production of radically new interpretations backed by claims that every previous writer has totally misunderstood Frege. The rule of the game, as it is now played, demands such a new interpretation from every new player, a demand which prompts not only misplaced ingenuity but unbridled exaggeration. It is controversial whether there can be progress in philosophy, but it ought to be uncontroversial that there can be progress in the understanding of a particular philosopher; the game of Frege exegesis, under the present rules, makes such progress extremely difficult.

FLE aims to expound and criticise certain aspects of Frege's philosophy, including, in particular, the context principle: the book scrutinises the notions of conceptual content, assertoric force, sense, reference, concept, function and truth-value. Other aspects, such as the definitions of 'analytic' and 'a priori', the notion of a criterion of identity and virtually the whole of Frege's philosophy of mathematics, are passed by in silence. It differs from previous entries in the competition for new interpretations in rating Frege as of low importance, philosophically or historically. FLE advances two principal second-order theses:

(A) that Frege's philosophy has no genuine affinity, and no important links, with the work of subsequent philosophers and logicians; and

(B) that his philosophy is irretrievably confused, incoherent and self-contradictory.

"The foundations" of Frege's thought "are rotten", we are told, "the principles unsound, the supporting members flawed and cracked" (p. 365); his ideas "are supported neither by cogent argument nor by compelling insight. Any attempt to build on his writings any weighty philosophical principles is doomed to sink into a quagmire of sophisticated nonsense" (p. 260). It is impossible, even in a lengthy review, to deal with all the topics discussed by B&H; I shall omit their treatment of assertoric force and of the context principle (the least interesting sections of the book). I have selected two clusters of topics, each crucial to one of the second-order theses. If, as I shall try to show, they are wrong about the topics in the first cluster, then thesis (A) fails; likewise, if they are wrong about those in the second, so does thesis (B). Before treating of these, however, I will consider one of the main issues concerning interpretation.

Save for an introductory and a concluding chapter, FLE is divided into two parts: Part I deals with Frege's early period, up to 1886, and Part II with his later period, from 1891 to his death. Now the principal problems in the exegesis of Frege turn on the relation between his earlier and later views. These problems fall under two heads. First, there are certain theses propounded in *Gl* which make no overt appearance in the later writings: the context principle; the doctrine of criteria of identity; the definitions of analyticity and aprioricity; and the dependence of geometry on a priori intuition. The exegete needs to decide how far their disappearance reflects a genuine change in Frege's philosophical beliefs. The only one of these discussed by B&H is the context principle, in respect of which they see great continuity from the earlier to the later period.

Secondly, we must ask how far the salient addition to Frege's doctrines, the distinction between sense and reference, represented a mere clarification and how far a repudiation of earlier ideas. Frege's later comments suggest that he himself took the former view of the innovation. We are not bound by this judgement, even if it be truly Frege's: it is quite possible for someone to misinterpret his own earlier work. There is nevertheless a presumption in favour of it, and, in my opinion, it was correct. In certain respects, the ideas expressed in *Bs*, *Gl* and the other early writings had not been fully worked out; when Frege attempted to work them out, he found himself forced to draw a distinction between sense and reference, not only for 'proper names', but for expressions of all types. If this is right, it is a methodological mistake to try to extract from Frege's early writings a complete systematic theory of philosophical logic comparable to, and in competition with, that propounded by him from 1891 onwards. The assumption on which B&H proceed is the opposite. They treat Frege's early writings as embodying a fully worked out system of philosophical logic, of which many features survived the transition to the mature theory, but some were rejected and replaced by new doctrines.

If, by adopting the sense/reference distinction. Frege was replacing one fully worked out theory by another, it is quite out of order, in expounding, say, *Gl*, to appeal to that distinction in order to elucidate the theses Frege advanced in that book; that, naturally, is how B&H see it. If, on the other hand, the distinction constituted a clarification of a theory not yet fully elaborated, it will be legitimate to make such an appeal, in full awareness that Frege had not made the distinction when he wrote *Gl*. Moreover, on this hypothesis, any attempt to depict the early writings as embodying a complete systematic theory will be bound to smuggle in some of the later ideas, representing them as already present in the early period. This is in fact just what B&H do: they import into Frege's early doctrine a use of the notion of a function which is only to be found in the mature writings.

B&H regard the notion of judgeable content used by Frege in his early period as equivalent to that of a thought as used from 1891 onwards. They expressly say (p. 279) that truth and falsity were, for Frege, externally related to the judgeable content. They note that he later said that he distinguished the thought and the truth-value *within* the judgeable content, which would suggest that the truth-value of a judgeable content was integral to its identity; but, although they offer no grounds, they are confident that, if Frege meant this, he was misunderstanding his earlier thinking. They declare that Frege included judgeable contents "within the category of *objects*" (pp. 148—9) and treated sentences as "names of objects" (pp. 124-5): his assimilation of sentences to proper names was thus not a feature of his mature doctrine, but "was present in his work in *Bs*" (p. 289). An occasional note of warning is sounded, to the effect that Frege did not actually *say* these things, although it is clear that he meant them: but these notes are drowned by the repeated emphasis placed on these claims.

All this represents a massive importation into Frege's early period of ideas stemming from his subsequent writings. The mature period opened with *FB*, which enunciates all the salient theses of the logical doctrine maintained by Frege throughout the period, which he had been working out during the silent years from 1886 to 1890. The early period, on the other hand, was one of steady development. In *Gl*, Frege set his whole discussion against the background of Kant's philosophy, and used a Kantian terminology. It is probably for that reason that he employed the word "object" (*Gegenstand*), which he had not previously used in any systematic way; in earldier writings he had preferred "thing" (*Ding*) or "individual thing" (*Einzelding*). So far as I am aware, he nowhere describes a judgeable content as an object or individual thing, or raises the question whether it should be so classified: there is no presumption that he took everything to be either a concept or else a thing or object. Likewise, he did not, in his early writings, call sentences 'names'. His terminology, before *Gl*, was very loose. In *Bs* he speaks of a formula, and also of a sentence, as "expressing" (*ausdrücken*) or "meaning" (*bedeuten*) a judgement, of its "meaning" a circumstance, of its "stating" (*angeben*), "indicating" (*andeuten*), "having" or "meaning" a content (the last is by far the most frequent); sometimes he speaks of the content when he means the expression, as when he speaks of it as being preceded by the content-stroke. Plainly, we have here no systematic terminology, and no evidence of an intention to represent sentences as names. It is strong evidence against such an intention that whereas, in *Gg*, there is no distinction recognised by the formation rules between sentences (there called by Frege "names of truth-values") and singular terms (names of other objects), in *Bs* there is such a distinction, residing in the principle that the judgement-stroke may precede only an expression for judgeable content.

What makes B&H so anxious to date Frege's assimilation of sentences to names as early as *Bs* is their contention that, from that work onwards, he regarded concepts as functions. According to them, the only change, from the early to the mature period, lay in what the values of these functions were taken to be. In the mature doctrine, concepts are functions from objects to truth-values, that is, from the references of names to the references of sentences. In the early period, according to B&H, they were likewise functions from the contents of names to the contents of sentences; since the content of a name was an object, they were functions from objects to judgeable contents. In this manner, they furnish Frege's early period with a logical doctrine almost as fully articulated as that expounded after 1890.

The notion of a function is used in *Bs* to explain the process of decomposing a sentence or judgeable content to obtain a predicate or concept, a process to which Frege attached fundamental importance. The process itself is explained again in *BrL*, and referred to in *Gl*, §pe010270. Did Frege conceive of the process as being applied to judgeable contents or to sentences? B&H insist that it is applied to judgeable contents, rather than to their linguistic or symbolic expressions; but Frege surely viewed it as applying to both. Thus in his letter to Russell of July 1902, having discussed the decomposition of two sentences, he added that "to the decomposition of the sentence there corresponds a decomposition of the thought". In his early writings, he expressed himself in both ways. In *BrL*, he spoke of decomposing the judgeable content, as he also did in a single sentence in the Preface to *Bs* (p. xiii). Even in §§pe0102 9 and 10, where the process is explained in detail, he occasionally deviates into talking in terms of conceptual contents or ideas. Nevertheless, he there speaks so persistently in terms of *expressions*, and does so, in particular, in the four italicised formulations, that it is impossible to doubt this way of expressing himself to be deliberate. The first of the italicised formulations, for instance, runs:

> If in an expression, whose content need not be judgeable, a simple or complex sign occurs in one or more places, and we think of it as replaceable by another expression in all or some of these places, but always by the same one, we call the invariant part of the expression the function, and the replaceable part its argument.

It is stretching credulity to ask us to believe that he meant us to understand by this that we should think of an object as replaceable by another object in one or more of its occurrences within a conceptual content, judgeable or otherwise.

B&H deliver a rebuke to Geach (p. 172n.) for crediting Frege with "the notion . . . of a function whose arguments and values are expressions": they insist that, on the contrary, Frege intended both function and argument to be taken as unjudgeable contents of different kinds, and the value as a judgeable content; he simply exhibited the typical mathematician's carelessness about use and mention. Although, indeed, he had not yet acquired that care in this regard on which he was to be the first to insist, the foregoing quotation makes that quite implausible. Now, unfortunately for B&H, *Bs* is the only one of Frege's early writings (save for a passing reference to that work under example 19 of *BrL*) in which he uses the term 'function' in this connection: the place in which he talks of functions is therefore that in which the arguments and values, and indeed the function itself, are treated as being linguistic or symbolic expressions. B&H thus have only the flimsiest case for attributing to him an interpretation of concepts as functions whose values are judgeable contents. This of course hangs together with the assimilation of sentences to names, for whose dating to the time of *Bs* they have no better case: for a predicate literally represents a function from objects to objects only if a sentence resulting from it by inserting a name of an object in its argument-place is itself a name of an object.

In his early period, Frege undoubtedly recognised an analogy between functions and expressions for concepts (which, in *Bs*, he could hardly call "predicates" after he had declared the subject/predicate distinction irrelevant to logic). It was not part of any systematic doctrine, however; it is scarcely mentioned save in *Bs*. From the text of that work, there is no saying whether we are meant to take it as more than an analogy. It is pointless to subject the use of the word 'function' in *Bs* to close scrutiny; it is far from certain that Frege himself had at that date yet attained his later clarity about the nature of functions in general. It would have been natural if Frege had also drawn an analogy between functions and concepts themselves; but there is no actual evidence that he did so. The principle of extracting concepts from judgements is indeed a definite doctrine, and appears in *BrL* as well as in *Gl*: but in both these works it is stated without appeal to the notion of a function. B&H have simply transposed to Frege's early period certain of his mature doctrines, modulated to suit the lack of the sense/reference distinction. The result is not a representation of Frege's thought, as it was at any stage, but a construct of the authors' own minds.

II. UNDERSTANDING

One of B&H's main grounds for maintaining thesis (A) is their denial that Frege was concerned with the notion of understanding, at least until late in his life. They divide his career into two periods, before and after 1891: it would have been more natural to recognise three, allowing his recognition in 1906 of the failure of his logicist programme to count as a turning-point. In fact, they see his work from 1914 onwards as, in the present respect, different in character. He acquired at this time, they say, a new interest in the concept of understanding, and proposed "to appeal to [his notion of the] senses of expressions in order to explain the understanding of sentences" (p. 382). To see his work before that date as intended to bear upon that concept is, however, a misinterpretation, according to them: on the contrary, "he was not concerned with understanding or knowing meanings" (p. 288), but "severed the internal connection between meaning and understanding" (p. 60).

It is difficult to make clear sense of this contention, let alone to reconcile it with the view, which they ascribe to Frege in his mature period (p. 247), "that the business of logic is closely entwined with the analysis of [natural] language". What is it to analyse a sentence of natural language, if not to explain how its composition serves to determine what thought it expresses? And is not the identification of that thought a major part of understanding the sentence? Is not the notion of sense, or at least of meaning, simply correlative to that of understanding? That is, is not understanding a sentence simply knowing, or grasping, its meaning, and is not its sense, in Frege's special use of the term, a major ingredient of its meaning?

The answers to these questions are not, indeed, quite straightforward. There are two correct points to be made apropos of them, and B&H indeed make both. First, Frege "regarded the task of clarifying the nature of understanding as belonging to the province of psychology, not of logic" (p. 376): for, as he confesses in a celebrated passage in his unpublished "Logik" of 1897 (*NS*, p. 157, PW, p. 145), quoted by B&H on p. 60, he is content to leave the act of grasping a thought mysterious, on the ground that "just because it is mental in character, we do not need to trouble ourselves about it in logic". This remark does not stand unqualified in the passage quoted, however; for he also says of this act that it "cannot be completely understood from a purely psychological standpoint". This might suggest that the remark of B&H quoted above is not wholly correct. It is correct, however, when construed in a suitably restricted sense. The point is that, even if meaning is correlative to understanding, that need imply no more than that we have to explain meaning in order to explain understanding. We thereby explain what must be known or grasped if an expression is to be understood, but may leave aside the problem of accounting for the nature of that knowledge or the mental act of grasping. In the same way, what someone has to know in order to be able to play chess, namely, the rules of the game, may be stated without any enquiry into the character of his knowledge. Likewise, Frege did not propose to explain sense by explaining what constitutes an individual speaker's mastery of a language, or any aspect of it: he was concerned only with what it is that he grasps in virtue of that mastery.

B&H's observation is thus true if construed to mean that Frege concerned himself with what is *understood*, as a matter for logic, but not with *understanding*, as a matter for psychology. But it is now unclear that he changed his mind on the matter in the last twelve years of his life. When he said that we understand sentences by understanding the words of which they are composed, did he mean this as a contribution to psychology? The observation is surely not so intended; it belongs to an account of *what* it is someone must know in order to grasp what thought a sentence expresses, namely the senses of the constituent words and the manner of their combination, rather than to an explanation of the nature of that knowledge. If so, however, the present point tells not at all against Frege's having been interested in understanding before 1914 in just that way in which he was interested in it after that date: both before and after, what interested him was its content.

The second point, equally correct in itself, is that a "judgeable-content is neither identical with, nor part of . . . , the meaning of a sentence" and we must likewise "sharply differentiate the later notion of the sense of a sentence from that of sentence-meaning" (p. 132): a judgeable content or a thought is a matter, not of the meaning of a (type-) sentence in the language (as someone learning the language might encounter it in an exercise), but "of what someone meant by the utterance of a token of it" (p. 131). This phrase is itself ambiguous; but sense, for Frege, embodies only what bears on the truth or falsity of what is said, and not, for instance, on what relevance it was intended to have to what had gone before. Since a thought must always have an absolute truth-value, an indexical or demonstrative must have different senses in relevantly different contexts: none of these senses can therefore coincide with its (constant) meaning in the language. This does not show, however, that sense is not correlative to understanding, since the bifurcation of the notion of meaning, acknowledged by B&H in the passage just quoted, affects that of understanding equally: understanding a (type-) sentence – knowing what the words mean – differs in just the same way from understanding what someone said on a particular occasion. In *The Varieties of Reference*, for instance, Gareth Evans concentrates on that notion of understanding what is said according to which one does not understand unless one knows enough to identify the references of the indexicals and demonstratives; and he quotes Moore as using the word 'understand' in the same manner. It is undoubtedly to understanding as so construed that Frege's notion of sense is correlative, rather than to a bare grasp of linguistic meanings.

Understanding, so construed, does not consist in merely knowing the meanings of the words in the language; as B&H say (p. 279), "to grasp a thought . . . is not to grasp the meaning of a type-sentence (though it may presuppose that)". It does not in the least follow that it does not comprise it, as B&H themselves acknowledge in their parenthesis; it is in fact quite evident that it does. What is needed, to grasp the thought expressed by an utterance – to understand it in Moore's and Evans's sense – is to know the meanings of the words, to know the relevant constructions, and to apprehend in the appropriate way the reference of the indexicals and demonstratives; and Frege's whole use of the term 'sense' accords with this. It is certainly wrong to overlook the respects in which his notion of sense diverges from that of linguistic significance: but to exaggerate the divergence distorts Frege's thinking just as badly. When he has in mind neither indexicals nor indirect speech, he repeatedly speaks of the senses of words or of expressions quite independently of context, as a glance at, say, *SB* will confirm; indeed, the requirement on a language apt for deductive reasoning that every word should bear the same sense in all contexts suggests that the use of indexicals is an imperfection of natural language.

In any case, B&H once more face a difficulty created by their having conceded that Frege became interested in understanding in his very late period. If by 'understanding' they mean what Moore and Evans do, there is no difference between this late period and that which began in 1891. If, on the other hand, they mean that Frege acquired a new interest in the knowledge of linguistic meaning, as manifested by the understanding of a type-sentence, there is nothing to be said in favour of such a contention. He indeed always had an interest in it, as the principal and often the only ingredient in a grasp of sense: but there is no change in this regard from the mature to the late period. In only one of the passages cited by B&H on pp. 381–2 from Frege's late writings does he use the word 'understand': in the rest, he speaks, as he had always spoken, of grasping a thought. *Ged* bears witness that he had not abandoned the principle that a thought is true or false absolutely; and this entails that the thought expressed by a sentence containing an indexical or demonstrative depends on the context of utterance. It follows that he retained exactly the same conception of grasping a thought as he had had in the 1890s, a conception that corresponds to one, but not, in general, to the other, sense of 'understanding'.

The two points here discussed thus wholly fail to establish B&H's contention that Frege was uninterested in understanding before 1914: they point only to necessary glosses on the claim that he had a consistent interest in it. Those two points are not, indeed, the only ones on which they rely; but the others are exceedingly flimsy. They observe, for instance (p. 129), that sentences such as imperatives and optatives, which do not, for Frege, express thoughts, nevertheless have meanings. More to the point, it might be added, most of the words in them obviously bear the same senses as they do in assertoric sentences; but, though this is a severe difficulty for Frege's position, it is no ground for denying him an interest in meaning or understanding.

III. Semantic Theories

A major pillar of thesis (A) is B&H's claim that there are "no grounds for asserting that [Frege] advanced ... to any conception that the true business of logicians is a science of language (semantics) ... The hypothesis that he intended to lay the foundations of logical semantics is implausible" (pp. 248–9). The word "semantics" is used in several different ways, but the references to logic and logicians suggest that what they have in mind is a semantic theory for a formal language as conceived in contemporary model theory. If so, their assertion is very surprising, since Part I of *Gg* appears to contain a semantic theory for the formal language, clearly separated from the account of its formation rules, axioms and rules of inference: this theory is stated by stipulating what references the primitive symbols are to have, and laying down how the reference of a complex expression is determined from the references of its constituents. In addition, Frege gives a general framework for such a theory, namely an account of the various possible logical types of expression, of their nature and how they are formed, and of what it is to assign a reference to an expression of any one such type; this is likewise clearly separated from the specific stipulations governing the primitive symbols of the system.

One reason why B&H do not see the matter in this light is that they conflate a semantic theory with a semantic definition of logical consequence. They are quite right in saying that Frege lacked the latter notion. He lacked it because he did not operate with the conception of a range of possible interpretations of a formal language; a symptom of this is that, contrary to what B&H say (pp. 112 and 205), he did not use free variables or schematic letters in his formalism: what look like them he officially interpreted as bound by tacit initial universal quantifiers. If, however, he had formed this conception, he would have had very little more work to do to arrive at the semantic notion of validity: for the background theory stated in Part I of *Gg* would immediately have yielded a formulation of what, in general, any one such interpretation should consist in. It is precisely because of the presence of this background theory, and its close, though not complete, resemblance to the notion used by modern logicians of an interpretation of a formal language within classical two-valued semantics, that Frege's work can be fruitfully compared with that of later logicians.

IV. REFERENCE

The foregoing claim that Part I of *Gg* contains a semantic theory rests on the equation of Frege's notion of reference with that of semantic value, so that a stipulation of the references of expressions of a formal language constitutes an interpretation of it in the model-theoretic sense. A more profound reason for B&H's denial of the claim lies in their summary rejection of this conception. In their sole allusion to it, they speak (p. 106) of the need that it should "be supported by an argument showing that conceptual content can be equated with the 'semantic value' assigned to symbols in the predicate calculus, not treated as a self-evident axiom in the interpretation of Frege's logic", and give a footnote reference to my FPL. The equation proposed was between semantic value and the later notion of reference, not the earlier notion of conceptual content; it was not assumed as an axiom, but argued for at some length, both in that book and in my IFP. I am not alone in having argued for it: Ernst Tugendhat, who is not mentioned in FLE, has done so, too, in a well-known article. I have, indeed, contended that he erred by going too far in the opposite direction, ignoring the contribution, to Frege's complex notion of reference, of the name/bearer prototype. However this may be, the equation of reference with semantic value is the principal premiss for the claim that Frege propounded a semantic theory; and B&H have no business to dismiss the claim without examining that premiss. Unless it lacks all *prima facie* plausibility, no idea ought to be rejected out of hand, even if it has not been argued for; the grounds for it, even if not stated, may be evident and compelling.

The grounds for seeing Frege's notion of reference as corresponding to that of semantic value, as it figures in standard classical two-valued semantics for formal languages, are twofold. Anyone reading Frege for the first time will naturally take the notion of reference as modelled on the relation of name to bearer, since it is always as applied to proper names that it is first introduced. He will then be struck by the fact that Frege goes on to ask what constitutes the reference of a sentence and what that of a predicate or of a relational or functional expression, almost always without stopping to justify the assumption that such a thing is to be ascribed to an expression of any of these types at all. The assumption that there is anything to which a sentence or a predicate stands in a relation remotely analogous to that of a name to its bearer will seem at first sight absurd to him, and yet more puzzling Frege's apparent assurance that there is a unique correct way to draw the analogy. When Frege's work was as yet not widely known, it was, perhaps, excusable to stop at this point, condemning Frege for making a large, unjustified and implausible assumption. At the present stage in the history of Frege exegesis, it is surely inexcusable: yet this is just what B&H do. They treat the *prima facie* absurdity as a conclusive refutation, saying (p. 257) that Frege "offers no argument whatever for supposing that" a predicate "stands for or designates any entity at all" and asking, "Is not this (traditional) idea absurd?". (The parenthetical adjective imports a further error, since Frege's theory differs crucially from the doctrine of universals, which can serve both as subject and as predicate.) They go on to comment that "to describe predicates as referring to concepts" obscures the "fundamental distinction" between "the role of referring", allocated to names, and "that of predicating", allocated to predicates, and ask rhetorically how "the sophistication of what predicates are supposed to stand for" can compensate for "the gross crudity" of "thinking that their logical significance should be explained solely in terms of what they stand for". The single paragraph from which these remarks are taken forms their entire treatment of the ascription of reference to incomplete expressions. They indeed discuss the notion of a concept, and its identification as a function whose values are truth-values, at considerable length: but they say no more than has here been indicated about the thesis that a concept is the reference of a predicate. If there is crudity here, it lies in their imperceptive comments, not in Frege's theories.

Anyone not ready to dismiss Frege without further ado as in the grip of a crude Augustinian model of how language works will ask what understanding he had of the notion of reference that made it appear so obvious to him that expressions of quite different logical types all have a reference; and he will seek the answer by looking to the work Frege made the notion do. As soon as we make this enquiry, we find that it did for him the same work as that of semantic value. This results from the combination of three fundamental theses:

1 the reference of a complex depends uniquely on the references of its constituents;
2 if a part lacks reference, the whole lacks reference;
3 the reference of a sentence is its truth-value.

Now the semantic role assigned to an expression by a semantic theory is that feature of it that goes to determine any sentence in which it occurs as true or otherwise; when this is taken to consist in the association of a suitable entity to the expression, that entity constitutes its semantic value. In the light of the foregoing theses concerning reference, it is apparent that Frege's notion of reference serves exactly the same purpose: an assignment of references to the constituent parts of a sentence displays how that sentence is determined as true or false in accordance with its composition. The reference of an expression is thus its semantic value according to the semantic theory propounded by Frege; for its having that reference constitutes that feature of it which goes to determine any sentence in which it occurs as true or as false. It is also plain why the denial of reference to any part of a sentence whose removal or replacement by another expression could affect whether the sentence was true or false is not a serious possibility, unless its presence has the effect of depriving the sentence of truth-value: otherwise, it must contribute in *some* way to determining the truth or falsity of the whole.

Frege remarked that it is just as bad to draw distinctions where none are needed as to fail to draw them when they are. In the same way, it is as bad to introduce technical notions that do no work as to omit to frame ones that are required. To understand a philosophical notion, we must therefore ask what work it does; the answer to this question, when it is asked about Frege's notion of reference, is that it does precisely the work of the notion of semantic value. B&H's failure to ask this question leads them to miss the point of this whole ingredient of Frege's mature logical doctrine, and quite mistakenly to reiterate that he had no semantic theory and that the notions he used admit no fruitful comparison with those employed by modern logicians.

In what respects is the relation of name to bearer the prototype for Frege of the relation of reference? It is so, principally, in that, in introducing the notion of reference, he always begins with proper names; in doing so, he explains the reference of a name as what it designates, or as what we are thinking or talking about. If Frege had, at the outset, explained the notion of reference quite generally as semantic value, he would have had to *argue* that the reference of a proper name is its bearer; as it was, he took it for granted, because this was for him part of the very notion of reference. In fact, he did not explain reference as semantic value even at a later stage: this is what makes it natural to take him, at first reading, as generalising the name/bearer relation from proper names to expressions of other kinds. It is only by reflection on the role which the notion plays in his theory, and, in particular, on the three theses concerning it enunciated above, that we can recognise that the role is precisely that of semantic value. Having recognised this, we can then see that the assignment of references to expressions other than proper names is governed by the need for them to fulfil this role, and not at all by appeal to an analogy with the name/ bearer relation. Without an appreciation of this, it is impossible to understand Frege's theory of reference.

V. CONCEPTS

How, then, has it come about that B&H have missed the point of Frege's theory of reference so widely and taken it as a mere generalisation of the relation of name to bearer? It was said in the preceding section that the remarks embodying this misconception form their entire treatment of the ascription of reference to incomplete expressions; but this might be objected to as an illusion due to their unusual viewpoint: their treatment of it lies, it may be said, precisely in their extensive discussion of the notion of a concept. To understand this objection, a certain digression will be necessary.

What did Frege do when he introduced the sense/reference distinction into his logical theory? If we concentrate on proper names, in terms of which he first explains it, we shall give the wrong answer. In their case, he already considered the object named as the content of the expression naming it: so, concentrating on this case, we shall say that the innovation was the notion of sense, foreshadowed by the talk in *Bs* of "modes of determination" (*Bestimmungsweisen*). Frege indeed needed such a distinction for names: his explanation in *Bs* of identity-statements is lame, and it is amazing that he could speak in *Gl* of "objective ideas" as divided into objects and concepts (§27, second footnote). We should not therefore exclude these as motivations for introducing the distinction; but to regard them as primary is to miss the point. It lay to hand to make some distinction between the meaning of a proper name and the object to which it referred, as Husserl did, at least when 'proper name' is understood in Frege's extended sense. What is important about Frege's notion of reference, however, is precisely that he applied it to expressions of all logical types.

At this point we must ask: Does the important innovation lie in the kinds of thing Frege took to be the references of the various types of expression? Or does it lie in his regarding them all as terms of a single relation of reference (more exactly, of a number of analogous relations)? We speak of *the* distinction between sense and reference, but in fact there are many distinctions: that between the sense of a name and an object, that between a thought and a truth-value, that between the sense of a predicate and a concept, and so on. Our question is then this. Suppose that Frege had made all these particular distinctions, but had not tied them together by describing objects, truth-values, concepts, etc., as all being the references of expressions of different types: would he have had essentially the same theory, or would the very core of it be lost?

Plainly, the very core would be lost. It would, indeed, be an overstatement to say that all the particular distinctions already existed: that the notion of an object was no new invention; that it did not need Frege to point out the difference between the thought expressed by a sentence and its truth or falsity; and that, equally, everyone was familiar with the distinction between the extension of a concept and the concept considered intensionally. Such an overstatement would ignore important innovations by Frege: his admission of abstract (*unwirkliche*) objects, including logical ones; the difference between truth-values considered as objects and the conventional notion of the properties of being true and of being false; and the unsaturated character of concepts. Important as these innovations are, however, their importance is subordinate: for there would be no point in these refinements or eccentricities (whichever they may be) save in the presence of a general doctrine concerning reference. A name cannot bear the very *same* relation to its bearer as does a predicate to the concept for which it stands: but the point lies in the analogy between those relations, an analogy encapsulated in general principles such as those enumerated in the preceding section. What counts as an object matters only if it is crucial to an account of what determines certain sentences as true or as false, and, in consequence, to an account of their senses; the unsaturated character of concepts matters only because it plays a role in explaining the unity of sentences and of thoughts; it would lack all significance to take truth-values to be objects if that did not carry with it taking concepts to be functions whose values they were.

As for the notion of sense, the innovation does not lie in the use of such a notion, since the intuitive conception of meaning is already present. It does not even lie in the differentiation between sense and tone, since that was present in the distinction between conceptual and non-conceptual content, or in that between sense and force, since that was present also. It lies, rather, in the fact that the notion of reference yields a general account of what the sense of an expression consists in, namely in the way in which its reference is given.

Not to see reference as semantic value is merely to miss an important affinity between Frege's theories and the work of later logicians: to fail to see the notion as a theoretical one whose whole substance derives from the general theoretical principles that govern it is to misunderstand Frege altogether. If one sees it thus, one will acquiesce in Frege's admittedly eccentric terminology: his quasi-technical terms mean just what his theory entails that they mean, and nothing more. A concept, for instance, is merely a function from objects to truth-values, considered extensionally: its being called a "concept" is no more than a historical accident. Frege had used the term, in his early period, as part of the accepted terminology which divided the subject-matter of logic into concepts, judgements and inferences, itself an inheritance from Kant. In *Gl* he had advanced part of the way towards his later notions, without being aware where he was heading, and so had used the word 'concept' sometimes for what he was afterwards to call the sense of a predicate, sometimes for its reference. Presumably because he had used it in the latter way in formulating several important theses, he reserved it exclusively for that use in his mature theory, greatly as that diverged from its traditional use in philosophy, let alone its non-philosophical uses.

These last observations may seem to labour the obvious. It is not obvious to B&H, however; and this is not a minor oversight, but integral to their entire approach to Frege's theory of reference. They complain bitterly about the eccentricity of Frege's use, in his mature period, of the term 'concept', asking (p. 255) how "Frege's definition of concepts as functions [can] be accepted as an analysis of our concept of a concept", denying that it clarifies "the real nature of concepts" and objecting (p. 254) that "concepts are objects of understanding, not what we speak *about* in typical assertions; they more closely resemble the senses of concept-words rather than the references". At first sight, these are mere cavils at Frege's terminology; but B&H do not so intend them. They are convinced that Frege suffered from "philosophical schizophrenia" (p. 270). The task undertaken by one half of this split personality was precisely that of "analyzing the notion of a concept which we already possess". Since his theory is in fact "at odds ... with our conception of a concept", the other half views it as that of "replacing our defective conception of a concept with something more adequate". This, however, destroys the point of his use of the notion: "both the interest and the intelligibility of his thesis that count-statements ascribe properties to concepts presupposes that we have a prior grasp of what concepts are".

The reader may well regard these contentions as bizarre. It is true enough that we cannot understand the thesis that the content of a statement of number consists in predicating something of a concept unless we grasp what Frege means by 'concept': it does not follow that we must take him to be using the word for an object of the understanding. If he were, he would be saying that a statement of number, such as that Mars has two moons, is a conceptual observation; so preposterous an interpretation is excluded by his explanation, in §47 of *Gl*, of the factual character of many statements predicating something of a concept. Admittedly, the notion of a concept here being employed was not made wholly clear, and probably was not wholly clear to Frege, until the mature writings: that is why Frege found it necessary to introduce the notion of reference in order to clarify it, and why we need to invoke that notion in order to elucidate it.

B&H cannot take this route, however. It is agreed on all hands that, in Frege's mature theory, a concept is a function from objects to truth-values. The question at issue is the status, and thereby the substance, of this thesis. If it were a mere *definition* of the word 'concept', it would as yet have no substance; this would be a shallow interpretation, which B&H rightly reject. On the view of Frege's theory of reference as a semantic theory – one explaining the determination of the truth-values of sentences in accordance with their composition – the thesis is to the effect that, in such a theory, the semantic value of a predicate should be taken to be such a function. B&H, however, have denied that this conception provides a general rationale for the notion of reference: and they have no other general account of the notion to put in its place. They have, therefore, to explain the substance of the thesis in a different way: their unconvincing explanation is that Frege thought he could best elucidate our pre-existing notion of a concept in this manner.

The key sentence for an understanding of B&H's view is: "[Frege] saw the sense/reference distinction as an adjunct of his redefinition of concepts and relations . . . , not as the ultimate philosophical foundation of his logical system" (p. 237). They do not see the general notion of reference as having any importance: for them, the important change lay in what Frege now took concepts and relations to be. Objects were already in place; Frege's essential new idea was that concepts ought to be identified as functions from objects, not to judgeable contents, but to truth values. This went along with construing sentences as names of truth-values rather than of judgeable contents, a step made possible only by classifying truth-values as objects. These steps taken, the theory had now to be supplemented with a notion of sense, on to which could be loaded all the tasks previously assigned to conceptual content but which truth-values and concepts as now conceived could obviously not perform (p. 279).

According to this view, Frege was not conferring a new use on the word 'concept': he already knew what he meant by it, but had, rather, formed a new belief about what concepts really are. B&H have difficulty, however, in conveying in what they take his understanding of the word, constant from his early to his mature period, to consist. The suggestion that it consisted in simple fidelity to the standard use of the word is highly implausible; instead of withdrawing it, as they ought, they ascribe to Frege a schizophrenic vacillation between such fidelity and a desire to replace the standard notion by a "more adequate" one. (As so often with their criticisms of Frege, the vacillation is all on their part.) This prompts the question, 'More adequate for what purpose?'. Frege must, when this half of his personality was dominant, have had some purpose in mind: the role that he intended the notion of a concept to play must have constituted his constant understanding of the word. To this question B&H give no answer. The answer is not provided by the connection, which they emphasise (e.g., on pp. 271–2 and 283), between taking sentences as naming truth-values and taking concepts as functions whose values are truth-values. The latter follows from the former *if* concepts are functions at all: but since the former has no intrinsic plausibility, the whole doctrine is pointless unless concepts, so construed, serve the explanatory or theoretical purpose for which they are needed; and we still have not been told what that is. The same goes for B&H's suggestion (p. 268) that, to accomplish a logical construction of arithmetic, Frege needed a *logical* connection between a concept and its extension. No such connection has been forged unless what is identified with the concept is plausibly so identified: to know whether it is or not, we must, again, know what role the notion of a concept is to play.

There is no sensible answer to the question, 'What are sentences names of?', taken in isolation, unless it be 'They are not names at all'. There is, equally, no sensible answer to the question, 'What do predicates stand for?', taken in isolation, unless it be 'Only names stand for anything'. If Frege had been so foolish as to give answers to these questions, taken in isolation – and a bizarre answer to the first question, at that – he would deserve all B&H's strictures. In answering them, he was *not* taking them in isolation: he was taking them in the context of a theory according to which both questions asked after the objective feature of any expression going to determine any sentence of which it is part as true or false. Only by seeing this as the point of his notion of reference can we understand his theory: only by considering a concept as the reference of a predicate, where 'reference' is so understood, are we in a position to enquire whether his account of what a concept is is the correct one. Without this principle to guide us, we can only flounder, as B&H do; whether or not, like them, we then blame our floundering on Frege is a matter of temperament.

VI. NATURAL LANGUAGES AND FORMAL LANGUAGES

B&H are wrong to deny that Frege had a semantic theory for his formal language; was his theory intended to apply to natural language? B&H are certain that Frege was not concerned, in his early period, with the analysis of sentences, but only with that of their contents: "what is analyzed in logic", they say (p. 144; see also pp. 134—5 and 156—8), "are judgeable-contents, not type-sentences or their meanings. Whether function/argument analysis can be applied to sentences . . . is irrelevant for whether it is the proper tool for analyzing judgments". Concerning his mature period, however, they become ambivalent. They describe him (p. 247) as having come to hold "that the business of logic is closely entwined with the analysis of language", acknowledge (p. 238) that the new conception of concepts and relations "is intertwined with a doctrine about the logical analysis of atomic singular statements" and express shock (p. 239) at his saying that no one who lays down logical rules can avoid appealing to linguistic distinctions. They describe his application of the principle of logical analysis to "the grammatical structures of declarative sentences" (p. 247): whereas, according to his early doctrine, "the logical category of proper names cannot in principle be isolated by any syntactic criteria" (p. 169), in his mature period he "advanced certain syntactic criteria for distinguishing 'proper names' from other expressions" (p. 250). It is difficult to see in Frege's writings the evidence for any such abrupt volte-face; in *Gl*, syntactic criteria for identifying proper names are freely used (§§ 38 and 57 in particular). In the end, B&H want to play down Frege's interest in natural language even in his mature period. They deny that "he advanced beyond the commonplace idea of a rough correspondence between logic and grammar" (p. 248); their final verdict (p. 398) is that "his concern with natural language . . . is incidental and at best indirect".

B&H rightly emphasise the importance of Frege's logical symbolism to his philosophy as a whole. In their view, it did not serve to represent the structure of sentences of natural language (p. 72), but, rather, "revealed the *true* structures of thought" (p. 69). B&H's defence of their failure to mention Frege's formulations concerning sense and reference in Part I of *Gg* therefore comes as a surprise to the reader. It occurs in a passage denying that Frege proposed a truth-conditional account of sense: and the omission requires defence, since that part of *Gg* contains Frege's full-dress formulation of his theory of logic, a definitive statement set out with a minimum of justification but a maximum of exactitude. The defence is that, although this was indeed "Frege's sole explanation of sense in terms of 'truth-conditions' ", it "is explicitly concerned only with well-formed formulae" of his formal system (p. 375). What if it were? If the logical system represents the structure of thought, we should have a truth-conditional account, if not of linguistic meaning, then at least of thought; and this, on B&H's own account, would be central to Frege's interests.

The reader of FLE cannot take for granted that he is in accord with its authors about the aim of a system of formal logic, for it is very unclear what they take that aim to be. The aim they ascribe to Frege, of representing the structure of thoughts, is also unclear, since, although they use the phrase incessantly, they never stop to enquire after the application of this metaphor. This precludes them from enquiring, either, into the general relation between the structure of a thought and that of a formula or sentence that expresses it. Their sole observation on this point is a blatant non-sequitur. They infer (p. 66) that "there is no logical necessity that the structure of a thought be reflected in the structure of a sentence expressing it" from Frege's thesis that a thought might be grasped (though not by us) without being clothed in words or signs: this is like arguing that, since not everyone has been photographed, a portrait need not resemble the sitter.

B&H are right, as I now think, not to presume, as I did in FPL, that the analysis of language was one of Frege's prime concerns, but to go into the complex matter of his attitude to language, which they do in Ch. 3 and § 5 of Ch. 9; but because they ask none of the fundamental questions just listed, they fall into confusion in doing so, and, as so often, attribute the confusion to Frege. It requires philosophical elucidation what it is to think *in* a language, they say (p. 66); "Frege provided *none*". He left it a mystery how we apprehend the structure of thoughts (p. 75); he gave no criterion for judging when the structure of a sentence is, and when it is not, a clue to this (p. 74), a quandary which rendered him "schizophrenic" (p. 260). His later advocacy of "the doctrine that" his symbolic "formulae . . . mirror the grammatical structures of declarative sentences" (p. 261) they explain as required into order to show his formal theory to be a *logic*; but they comment that nothing within the theory "hangs on the doctrine", adding that "his demonstration of the logicist thesis" does not, "of course, . . . in any way" depend on it. What is necessary to show the theory to which Frege claimed to have reduced arithmetic to be a logical theory is surely essential to his demonstration of logicism; nevertheless, B&H are confident that they have provided "insuperable obstacles" (p. 66) to regarding Frege as having contributed to the philosophy of language.

VII. SENSE AND TRUTH-CONDITIONS

One of the root causes of this series of errors is B&H's failure to grasp Frege's theory of sense. Their argument, in §§ 1 and 2 of the last chapter, against ascribing to him a truth-conditional theory of sense is rendered farcical by their admitted failure to understand what, in general, such a theory may be. Any general explanation of the notion makes it vacuous, they claim (p. 378); their remedy is to identify such a theory with the specific theory advanced by Wittgenstein in the *Tractatus*. They then have no difficulty in pointing out differences between this theory and Frege's. In a passage containing no fewer than twenty-one footnote references to me, they might have noticed that, in FPL, I was at pains to point out, more than once, the differences between Frege's theory and Wittgenstein's. Had they done so, they might have been deterred from inferring that Frege lacked "the modern conception of a theory of meaning" based on truth-conditions (p. 377) and that "the concept of truth-conditions is altogether alien to" him (p. 354).

The notion of a truth-conditional theory of sense is not in the least vacuous. Such a theory must have two essential features. First, the theory of sense must rest upon a theory of semantic value as a base; and, secondly, the semantic value of a sentence must be taken as consisting in its being true or being false. Many semantic theories fail this second condition, employing, for instance, truth-values relativised to possible worlds or to times; Heyting's theory for intuitionistic mathematics is an extreme example, repudiating as it does the assumption that every sentence is determinately either true or not true. In Frege's system (not, of course, in Wittgenstein's) the theory of *Bedeutung* constitutes the semantic theory, and fulfils the second condition. Since sense is explained as the way the reference is given – namely, to one who understands the expression, in virtue of his understanding – it fulfils the first condition also. Although, so far as I know, *Gg*, vol. I, § 32 is the only passage in which Frege uses the word 'condition', the very same conception is expounded by him in numerous places. To grasp the thought expressed by a sentence is to have a particular way of conceiving of the references of its constituents. For those of them which are functional expressions, this will involve a grasp of how the reference of each complex within the sentence, including the sentence itself, is determined by the references of its parts; and so the grasp of the thought will consist in a particular way of conceiving that which determines it as true or as false.

This theory leaves much concerning our grasp of sense to be explained; but it is foolish to carp at this, since it gave the first plausible account in the history of philosophy of what it is to grasp a thought or to understand a sentence as expressing one. It is absurd to complain that Frege failed to elucidate the notion of thinking in a language. His account of sense does precisely this; or, at least, it does so provided that we can supplement it by an explanation of what it is to treat a sentence as being determined as true in a certain way. Here we should note a bias towards an explanation of thought by way of explaining an expression of it not acknowledged by Frege. Frege held that it is the thought that is primarily said to be true or false, the sentence being called true or false only in a derivative sense; and this means that it is the sense of the sentence that primarily has the reference, and the sentence only derivatively. Frege generalised this to all expressions: for instance, it is the sense of a proper name that primarily refers to the object.

In practice, however, he never conformed to this order of priority when expounding the sense/reference distinction. He never first introduces the notion of sense, subsequently explaining that of reference as a feature of the sense: he speaks first of the *expression* as having reference, and proceeds to argue that it also has a sense or to say in what its sense consists. This order of exposition is demanded by the conception of sense as the way the reference is given: it follows from this conception that the notion of sense cannot be explained save by appeal to that of reference, and so we must first have the latter notion. If we have the notion of reference in advance of that of sense, we cannot have it as a property of the sense, but only of the expression: the thesis that it is the sense to which reference is primarily to be ascribed is therefore incorrect. This comes out clearly in Part I of *Gg*. The stipulations that determine under what condition each formula has the value *true* lay down what the *reference* of each expression is to be. Sense has yet to be mentioned: so, if we could understand what it was for an expression to have a reference only in terms of the possession by its sense of a corresponding property, those stipulations ought to be unintelligible. On the contrary, it is by invoking those stipulations that Frege explains in what the sense of each expression consists: to grasp how its reference is to be determined is to grasp its sense.

Frege believed it possible in principle to grasp a thought otherwise than as expressed linguistically; but his account of sense does not show how that is possible; it leaves it obscure how a sense can be grasped otherwise than as the sense *of* something to which reference can be ascribed; it explains nothing to say that the reference might be ascribed directly to the sense, since we must know what it is to ascribe reference before we can recognise it as a sense. This is one instance of several in which the inner dynamic of Frege's thinking drove in a linguistic direction to a greater extent than even he was aware.

VIII. LANGUAGE AND EXPRESSION

The metaphor used in speaking of the structure of a thought relates to what is essentially involved in grasping it. This idea has an obvious intuitive force: to grasp the thought that 239 is prime requires possession of the concept of a prime number; to grasp the thought that Phobos is a satellite of Mars requires a conception of one body's being a satellite of another. Now the complexity of a sentence obviously plays a part in our identification of the thought thereby conveyed; but this is not enough to qualify it as *expressing* the thought. If I speak of the weakest additional premiss needed to make a certain inference valid, I thereby pick out a unique thought, but I do not express it, because you can understand my words without grasping the thought. Only when understanding the form of words used requires a grasp of what belongs to the structure of the thought do those words express the thought: only so do those words do more than enable the hearer to identify the thought, namely communicate the thought to him. It follows that the expression of a thought can only be by reflection of its structure. It is this which distinguishes a *language*, in the wider sense in which we speak of formal languages and programming languages as well as of natural languages, from a code.

Frege obviously took natural languages to be languages in this sense; that is why he held the structure of a sentence to correspond, by and large, to the structure of the thought it expresses. It is therefore quite wrong to say, with B&H, that there is, on Frege's view, no necessity why a sentence should reflect the structure of the thought: that is essential to its being an *expression* of the thought. This follows from the fact that, in so far as we have from Frege an explanation of what it is to grasp a thought, it is the *same* explanation as that given for recognising the thought expressed by a sentence, stripped of the reference to linguistic items: to grasp a thought is to have a particular way of conceiving what determines it as true, just as to grasp the thought expressed by a sentence is to have a particular way of conceiving what determines the sentence as true. Frege of course held that sentences of natural language serve other purposes than the expression of thoughts: certain features of their structure relate to these other purposes. It is a further mistake to suppose that Frege had no principle to guide him in distinguishing those features which reflect the structure of the thought from those that do not. Given his (truth-conditional) theory of sense, the principle is evident. We have to subject the sentence to logical analysis, that is, to arrive at a semantic account of it. Such an account will explain the manner in which the sentence is determined as true or false in accordance with its composition, and, in doing so, will respect the role played by its constituents in other sentences. Such an account, if successful, reveals which features of the sentence are essential to the expression of the thought, and thereby makes apparent the structure of the thought itself.

Not only are natural languages languages in the sense explained; Frege considered his formal language to be one in the same sense. That was why he claimed for it the status of a *lingua characterica*. It could be used as a *calculus ratiocinator*, like Boole's, to give a partial representation of the structure of the thoughts involved in some particular inference, with a different coding for each instance: but it was intended as a language in which thoughts could be fully expressed and deductive reasoning carried on. Not only that, but it was an approximation to a logically perfect language, its formulas serving no purpose but to express thoughts and judgements, their structure perspicuously displaying the structure of the thoughts and devoid of the defects which make natural languages imperfect instruments.

The opposition which B&H set up between representing the structure of thoughts and representing that of ordinary sentences is thus a false one. Because both sentences of natural language and the formulas of Frege's symbolism express thoughts, they reflect their structure; for this reason, a formula cannot but reflect, in a perspicuous manner, those features of the structure of the corresponding sentence essential to the expression of the thought. Frege was neither schizophrenic nor even in a quandary.

IX. LOGIC

It is difficult to discover from FLE that Frege made any contribution to philosophy whatever. This may seem hard to maintain for the inventor of quantificational logic; but B&H consider that "a formal calculus is of very limited philosophical significance and has limited philosophical use" (p. 392). It is very obscure what use they think it has at all. They use the phrase 'logical analysis', but manifest no awareness of what such an analysis may be. This is well illustrated by their shallow criticisms of Frege's analyses. "Would anybody infer from the fact that 'All mammals are red-blooded' is synonymous with 'If anything is a mammal, it is red-blooded' that 'mammals' in the first sentence functions grammatically as a predicate?", they ask (p. 256). Even when 'grammatically' is replaced by 'logically', no one has made that inference from the mere synonymy of the sentences: it depends on the direction of explanation. In asking their rhetorical question, they simply ignore the difficulty of treating a plural subject as functioning analogously to a singular term, namely, as standing for a compound object or aggregate. Frege's remarks, in a number of places, concerning the notion of an aggregate provide strong grounds for believing a semantic account along such lines to be impossible. He argues that we need to substitute for the notion of an aggregate that of a concept. To make this substitution just *is* to interpret the plural subject-term as functioning as a predicate, and hence to explain the first sentence as equivalent to the second, in which it overtly so figures. B&H are not offering an alternative semantic treatment: it seems, rather, that it is because they not only feel no need for one, but fail to grasp why anyone should feel that need, or perhaps what it is a need for, that they miss the point so completely.

Clinching evidence of their failure to understand the task undertaken by logicians, or to grasp semantic notions, is provided by their summation of their subject's achievement in this field. "Frege's concept-script", they say (p. 389), "is simply an alternative form of representation to natural language. It allows us to present certain inferences in a manner more readily surveyable and more mechanically checkable than their normal representation in ordinary language." It does far more, of course: its syntax is apparent from the surface form of its formulas, and, on the basis of that syntax, we can construct a semantic theory for it in a very direct manner. Natural languages lack this merit. Having paid their subdued tribute to Frege's logical symbolism, B&H go on to discuss its defects, and list six features of natural language which they claim to be logically significant but to be unrepresentable in quantificational logic. Since they forswear advocating the abandonment of that logic (p. 390), the exercise is pointless, since the need either to modify or to supplement a logical theory does not show its invention not to have been a great step forward. The list would have a point if they supposed that, while *some* inferences are best surveyed when expressed in logical symbolism, for others natural language is more suited. If they think this, they are mistaken, because they lack the right idea of what it is to "survey" inferences: I greatly doubt that there are any inferences not representable in quantificational logic but of which we can give a satisfactory semantic account when they are expressed in some fragment of natural language, B&H proclaim the need to "clarify the structures of [our] concepts" (p. 391), but do not believe that a logician's analysis of inferences involving them will contribute to such clarification; their scepticism is surely due, once more, to their not understanding what logicians aim to do. This emerges again in their attack on Davidson's theory of action sentences as "ludicrous". The inferences with which he was concerned involve no unclarity, they say, but "are transparently valid"; they therefore "set a problem *for the predicate calculus*" (*ibid.*). The problem whether those inferences are representable in quantificational logic is important, and will not be solved by sneers; but B&H's principal mistake is to think it the *only* problem. As with any inferences tackled by formal logic, we need a plausible semantic account of the sentences involved, whether by appeal to exaxisting formalism or otherwise. From such an account, the validity of the inferences must follow. B&H appear to have missed the point of this requirement, which, in ordinary cases, is to test the adequacy of the semantics, not to vindicate the inferences; in such cases, the logician is taking their "transparent validity" as a *datum*. Misunderstanding the nature of formal logic has led, in FLE, to much misunderstanding of Frege.

X. CONTINGENCY

Most of the foregoing relates to B&H's thesis (A), that Frege's work has no interesting connections with that of subsequent philosophers and logicians; I come now to thesis (B), that it is inconsistent and confused. It will be recalled that B&H see as a major motivation for introducing the sense/reference distinction that Frege wanted to guarantee the logical character of class abstraction – the step from a concept to its extension. They interpret this as meaning that "the extension of these concepts must be determined by logical considerations alone", that "the extension of the concept . . . can be calculated *a priori* from the concept" (p. 268), and contrast this with the "commonly held" view that "which objects . . . fall under the concept . . . can be determined only by observation and not by close inspection of the concept" (p. 269). Hence "the proof that arithmetic is a branch of logic requires . . . an internal, *a priori* connection between concepts and their extensions which is at odds . . . with our conception of a concept" (p. 270).

This stems, in part, from B&H's conviction, already noted, that Frege aimed to capture, by his use of the word 'concept', our ordinary conception of a concept; but more than this has gone awry. There is indeed a sense in which it is a truism that, under Frege's mature use of 'concept', "whether or not a given object falls under" a concept is "built into the identity of the concept" (p. 270).

In the same sense, "it is an intrinsic feature of a function that it takes a particular value . . . for a given argument" (p. 252); and we may read the statement that "according to his account of concepts as functions, the relation between an object and a concept under which it falls . . . is always an *internal* relation" (*ibid.*) in the same sense. For concepts and functions, on Frege's mature doctrine, are purely extensional, and hence are *constituted* by what objects fall under them and what value they take for each argument. But talk of an *a priori* connection, and opposing this to determining by observation which objects fall under a concept, are quite out of place. The means of determining whether an object falls under a concept relate to the way in which the concept, and the object, too, are *given*, and thus to the *senses* of the predicate and the proper name, not their references, viz. the concept and the object in themselves. Likewise, if we use the term '*a priori*' (which Frege did not in his mature period), we must apply it to *thoughts*: there are, for Frege, no facts in the realm of reference, and the value *true*, in itself, is neither *a priori* nor *a posteriori*. It is therefore both irrelevant and gratuitous for B&H to say that "in his view, it is unintelligible to hold that the value of a well-defined function may depend on observation or experiment" (p. 244n.) and that "it is of the essence of a *function* that it be possible to *calculate* its value for any given argument" (p. 312): irrelevant, because discovering what the value is can only be relative to some way in which the function is given, i.e., to the sense of a functional expression; and gratuitous, because there is no hint of any such doctrine in Frege. (In *Gl*, § 47, he makes it plain that a statement about a concept can have an empirical content.) The confusion is compounded by B&H's attributing a different doctrine to Frege in his early period, when his conception of a function demanded that "we admit observation and experiment as legitimate procedures, in addition to calculation, for determining the values of functions" (p. 146). In that period, according to them, a concept was on Frege's view a function from objects to judgeable contents, and truth-values were extrinsic to judgeable contents. Since it can hardly be that observation or experiment is needed to discover the content of a sentence, given the object referred to, the remark must refer to functions whose values are ordinary objects. Since the content of '3' or of 'Denmark' is an object, and that of '3!' or "the capital of Denmark" another object, on B&H's systematisation of Frege's sloppy use of 'content', there would seem to be no room for any difference between Frege's conception of such functions in the two periods; the alleged difference about observation and calculation is therefore mysterious.

These are not occasional infelicities of expression; they occur repeatedly in Part II of FLE, and represent B&H's deepest objection to Frege's mature doctrine of concepts, an objection resting on a thoroughgoing confusion between sense and reference. They appear to believe that Frege abolished contingency. On p. 252 they say that Frege's "conception of concepts conflicts

AN UNSUCCESSFUL DIG 219

with the . . . common conception [which] admits the possibility that an invariant concept might have different extensions in different possible worlds"; on p. 289 that "there is no evidence that he thought that *a posteriori* identities were contingent"; and on p. 312 they come right out and assert that "the route from sense to reference must be independent of matters of fact". No contrary interpretation has any "direct warrant in [Frege's] texts", they declare (p. 313n.). Since "the connection between sense and reference must be internal", and since "the truth-value of a sentence must be determined alone by the argument and function . . . (i.e., independently of matters of fact)", "it is futile . . . to seek to broaden his account into a viable semantic theory" (p. 338). Seldom can so spirited an attack on a great philosopher have failed so dismally through such clouded perception of his doctrines.

XI. SENSES AND FUNCTIONS

Given only the value of a function for some argument, it is not possible to recover the function or the argument. For this reason, it is inappropriate to regard either the argument or the function as a *constituent* or *part* of the value, since we naturally suppose that anything is uniquely analysable into its ultimate constituents, and that the parts of a thing may be discerned by scrutiny of it. According to Frege, the term '4!', whose reference is 24, is made up out of the "proper name" '4', whose reference is 4, and the incomplete or unsaturated functional expression 'ξ!', whose reference is the factorial function. To say that the reference of the part is part of the reference of the whole would therefore be wrong, or at best utterly misleading, in such a case. The case is, however, typical. We should, accordingly, *never* say that the reference of the part is part of the reference of the whole; and Frege, despite an initial wobble in *SB*, came expressly to deny this. The model of function and value conflicts with that of part and whole.

The expression '4!' represents 24 as the value of the factorial function for the argument 4: but we cannot explain the structure of the representation itself simply by appeal to the model of function and argument. Even if we can already identify the expression '4!', we cannot explain how it is made up out of its parts by saying that it is the value of a function that maps '4' onto '4!', for there are many such functions. To talk about expressions and their structure, we need the notions of part and whole, not those of function and value. For similar reasons, the *senses* of complex expressions cannot be explained in terms of function and value, either. Given the thought expressed by the sentence, 'The Earth spins', we cannot explain the sense of the predicate 'ξ spins' as that function which carries the sense of the name 'the Earth' into that thought, for there is no unique such function; moreover, we must already know the sense of the predicate in order to grasp the thought, whereas we must be able to identify the value of a function in advance of knowing that it is the value of that function. The relation of the senses of the constituents to the sense of the sentence must also be construed on the model of part and whole, not that of function and value. That is precisely what Frege did: he consistently held that the sense of a part is part of the sense of the whole.

I argued on these grounds in FPL that the sense of an incomplete expression is not to be understood as itself being a function. B&H are highly conscious of the point, and make it repeatedly; but they deny that Frege saw it. That is, they agree with me that Frege regarded the sense of a predicate as part of the sense of a sentence containing it; but they also agree with those I was arguing against, that the sense of the predicate is a function whose value is the sense of the sentence: what they deny that Frege saw is the incompatibility of the two models. Given their mistaken view that, in his early period, Frege regarded concepts as functions whose values are judgeable contents, they have a case in respect of the early doctrine. One would naturally think that the sense/reference distinction resolved the tension: the reference of a predicate could now be taken to be a function, and the truth-value of the sentence as its value, while its sense could be taken as a part of the thought expressed by the sentence. B&H deny this: allowing that Frege could now independently specify the value of a concept for an object as argument, namely as one of the two truth-values, they allege that "curiously enough, the same muddle is immediately reintroduced at the level of *thoughts*, conceived as the values of sense-functions" (p. 281).

Those, like Geach, who have contended that the senses of predicates should be taken as functions from the senses of names to thoughts, and that Frege's talk of them as parts of thoughts "should be charitably expounded, not imitated", have had a reason; in fact, two. The first is Frege's insistence that the senses of incomplete expressions are themselves incomplete. B&H offer the same ground: "to describe the sense of a . . . predicate as unsaturated is to classify this entity as a function" (p. 323). Frege is indeed at fault for never having explained the mode of incompleteness of senses, and perhaps for not having given his mind to it. Nothing inhibits us from saying, however, that the incompleteness of the sense of a functional expression consists, not in its being a function, but in its being a way of conceiving of a function, the way a function is given to us. With this, the whole of this allegedly unresolvable tension in Frege's mature doctrine is resolved; or, rather, it would be, but for the second reason for regarding incomplete senses as functions.

B&H contend (pp. 301–7) that the only way to understand Frege's account of sense as 'mode of presentation' is in terms of the presentation of an object or a truth-value as the value of some function: "two expressions have the same sense only if they indicate an entity as the value of the same function for the same argument" (p. 305). They charge (p. 307) that the impossibility of explaining the senses of "simple expressions, whether proper names or concept-words" in this way "is an absolute gap in Frege's discussion of sense". Indeed, "there is

AN UNSUCCESSFUL DIG 221

no such thing as a mode of presentation associated with a simple name" (p. 308). This yields another ground for holding that "a thought is literally the value of a function (one thought-constituent) for an argument (another thought-constituent)" (p. 324), i.e. that the senses of predicates and functional expressions are themselves functions. For complex expressions, the reply is as before: the sense of an incomplete expression is not a function, but a 'mode of presentation' of the function which is its reference. For *simple* predicates and functional expressions, however, B&H could not entertain this reply, since they admit no mode of presentation embodied in a simple expression: for simple expressions, sense cannot in their view be distinguished from reference (cf. p. 319). All this provides a *reductio ad absurdum*, not of Frege's theory of sense, but of B&H's interpretation of it: even if we were forced to conclude that no two expressions incapable of verbal explanation could have distinct senses but the same reference, it would be absurd to *identify* their senses with their references.

XII. ALTERNATIVE ANALYSES

We expect an analysis of something into its ultimate constituents to be unique, and Frege's use of the part/whole metaphor indeed suggests that. The possibility of alternative ways of analysing a single thought, asserted by Frege, therefore creates a difficulty both for the part/whole metaphor and for the exegesis of Frege. Geach very aptly quoted Ramsey apropos of the first difficulty, with no reference on Ramsey's part to Frege; Geach's solution was to replace the part/whole model by that of function and argument, under which there is no problem about multiple representations of a thought as the value of various functions for various arguments. B&H press these points repeatedly against Frege; according to them, the tension threatens the integrity of his formal symbolism, since it is supposed to represent the structure of thoughts. On the one hand, "the possibility of essentially independent representations of a single judgeable-content is not available in concept-script" (p. 152), because the formula must display the *whole* structure of the content; on the other, it is "in principle impossible that a sentence expressing a judgeable-content should have a unique translation into concept-script" (p. 174). The sense of a complex expression depends on how it presents its referent as the value of a function: but since we may analyse it as doing so in a variety of ways, we are forced to the "conclusion that there is no such thing as *the* sense of any complex expression" (p. 310; cf. pp. 317–18).

The difficulty can only be resolved, I believe, by distinguishing the two processes which, in IFP, I called analysis and decomposition (having referred to them in FPL merely as two sorts of analysis). The distinction was not expressly drawn by Frege, but is, in my view, implicit in his writings. B&H think it worthwhile to claim, in two separate footnotes (pp. 158 and 163) that I addressed myself to the question in response to their "harping" on it in a seminar of theirs which I attended. This is not so. In IFP I was responding principally to Geach's observations; and I was in any case only spelling out more fully a distinction already drawn in FPL, as I recall Gareth Evans pointing out to B&H in the seminar. Unfortunately, they appear not to have understood it yet: they interpret it as the distinction between a complete and an incomplete analysis, whereas, for me, analysis and decomposition are quite different processes.

The process of decomposition is that described, in rather loose language, in *Bs* and in *BrL*. Stated as applied to sentences or formulas, it consists in regarding an expression, or each of two expressions, as replaceable in all or some of its occurrences by some other expression of the same type: the incomplete expression thought of as extracted from the sentence by this process is the part of the sentence invariant under such replacements. As B&H correctly observe, this process was characterised by Frege as one of concept-*formation*: it is a way of arriving at a *new* concept. In order to engage in this process, we must therefore already grasp the judgeable content or thought being decomposed, or expressed by the sentence being decomposed. We must in fact do more: if, e.g., the expression imagined as replaceable was a proper name, we must know how to determine, from the sense of any proper name, the thought expressed by a sentence in which that proper name is inserted into the argument-place of the newly formed predicate. Just because we must grasp the judgeable content or thought before decomposing it, the concept attained by decomposition, or the sense of the new predicate, is not to be taken as intrinsic to the content or thought: that is why Frege says in *Bs* that it is a matter of how we choose to regard the judgeable content. Thus, in order to grasp the thought expressed by '$17 > 1$ & $\forall n \, (n/17 \Rightarrow n = 17 \vee n = 1)$', it is as unnecessary to conceive of it as made up out of '17' and the predicate that results from removing all three occurrences of that numeral as it is to conceive of it as made up out of '1' and the predicate formed by removing both of *its* occurrences. Since the newly attained concept – here that of primality – is not a constituent of the content, the possibility of distinct decompositions of the same content poses no problem.

The main point of decomposition lies in the fact that the newly formed predicate *is* a genuine constituent of other sentences, namely, quantified ones, as Frege also points out in *Bs*. Since it is, we must ascribe a sense to it; and there is nothing to hinder us from regarding *its* sense as a function from senses of names to thoughts, since it will never be a constituent of a thought which is one of its values; it is only the sense of a simple predicate that we cannot consistently regard as such a function. Decomposition is not a reiterable process: it can be used only to yield an incomplete expression, since complete ones – sentences and proper names – do not need to be extracted from more complex ones; and it can be applied only to a complete expression. For this reason, we never have occasion to consider expressions for functions whose values are themselves functions or concepts. A function, for Frege, must always have objects as values, a principle missed by B&H, who twice envisage functions having functions or concepts as values (p. 237, under (ii), and p. 267, under (vii)), and even ascribe recognition of such a function to Frege.

Analysis, on the other hand, takes place in stages, because the sentence, or the judgeable content or thought, is to be viewed as having been formed by successive operations. The purpose of analysing a sentence is to display that structure essential to its expressing the thought, and thus the structure of the thought expressed. The analysis of any part of the sentence displays those of its constituents a grasp of whose sense is required for a grasp of the sense of that part. The process is trivial for a logical formula, which is designed to display its essential structure on its surface. For a sentence of natural language, on the other hand, analysis in this sense is the syntactic part of logical analysis: it consists in finding a representation of the structure of the sentence that will serve as a basis for a correct semantic account.

Complex predicates can be constituents of sentences, though not of those from which they can be extracted by decomposition, if the word 'constituent' is reserved for what is encountered in the course of analysis; but it is only the senses of simple predicates and other simple incomplete expressions which cannot be characterised as functions. The complete analysis of any sentence or thought into its ultimate constituents is indeed unique; in my terminology, there are only alternative decompositions. The distinction completely resolves the difficulties laboured by B&H. Frege's doctrines can hardly be interpreted save in the light of it; in its light, all becomes clear. This is not to claim that Frege was always fully conscious of the distinction: if he had been, he would have stuck to his conception of *fruitful* definitions, as expounded in *Gl* § 88, instead of maintaining that definitions are in principle dispensable and leave the content unchanged. The thought that 17 is a prime number has the concept of primality – the sense of 'ξ is prime' – as a constituent, whereas the thought expressed by the complex sentence which is its definitional equivalent does not, though we can attain the concept by viewing the latter sentence in a particular way, that is, by effecting an appropriate decomposition of it. Here there is genuinely a tension between what Frege says in different places; but not one capable of bringing his entire system tumbling headlong in ruins, as B&H so desperately wish to believe it does.

XIII. A Straightforward and Compelling Argument

B&H present a train of reasoning they call "straightforward and compelling" (p. 174). Given "a judgeable content expressed by the formula '$\Phi(A)$' ", they argue that "nothing could prevent our introducing a concept Φ' by the ... stipulation" that Φ' is to agree with Φ save on a pair of objects B and Γ distinct from A, that $\Phi'(B) = \Phi(\Gamma)$ and that $\Phi'(\Gamma) = \Phi(B)$. B&H conclude that "the object and the judgeable content fail to determine the remaining "constituent" ..., viz. the concept"; the ideal of a unique canonical symbolic representation of any judgeable content is thereby rendered incoherent.

The consequence, if genuine, would indeed be "dramatic", as they claim; for it would overthrow the whole principle of concept-formation by decomposition. The fallacy in the argument is very simple to detect, however: it lies in the assumption that every function from objects to judgeable contents is a concept. Let us assume that decomposition is applied directly to judgeable contents, and consider how we arrived at the concept Φ, and so at the representation $\Phi(A)$, in the first place. Suppose we did so by decomposition of the judgeable content, which we may call "P". We had, then, to apprehend P, not just as a whole, but as having the object A as a part. A may in fact have been a part several times over, that is, have had several "occurrences" within P. We selected certain of these, and then imagined A as replaceable, in each of them, by any one of a range of other objects, B, Γ, and so on; we had, for this purpose, to grasp what judgeable content would result from each of these replacements. By this means, we obtained the concept Φ as a function mapping each object on to the judgeable content resulting from the replacement of A by that object. (I am not endorsing this account, but simply applying Frege's account of decomposition to B&H's systematisation of his doctrine of content.)

Given that, for each replacement, a determinate content results, this process uniquely determines the function Φ. Different decompositions would yield different representations of P; by selecting different occurrences of A within P, we should find ones of the form $\Psi(A)$. Relatively to the choice of A, and of specific occurrences of A, however, no further definition of functions can call in question the uniqueness of Φ. Φ' is indeed a well-defined function, and $\Phi'(A) = P$; that is not enough to justify the representation of P by the formula $\Phi'(A)$, since Φ' has not been shown to be a concept extractable from P by decomposition, or, indeed, a concept at all. Φ' will be a concept if there are in P some occurrences of A such that $\Phi'(x)$ will, for each object x, be the result of replacing them by x. There is no reason to suppose there are any such occurrences, and it is easy to see that there cannot be.

The same refutation could be repeated if we took decomposition as applying to sentences expressing judgeable contents, but that may be left as an exercise for the reader, who will then see, even more clearly than, it is hoped, he does already, that the straightforward and compelling argument has no force whatever, but is simply a piece of legerdemain. We may notice, by the way, that the talk of discerning, and replacing, parts within a judgeable content is highly metaphorical, and patently relies on assuming such contents to have a structure very similar to that of sentences. We saw earlier that Frege wrote to Russell that a decomposition of the thought parallels that of the sentence; but we may ask which is prior. Since Frege consistently believed that thoughts are accessible to us only through their linguistic expression, the impression conveyed by *Bs*, that the process has to be understood as applied to sentences or formulas in the first place, is almost certainly correct.

XIV. Type Ambiguities

In decomposing a sentence, we must of course have in mind its sense: otherwise we shall arrive at an incomplete expression to which we cannot attach a sense, and shall not be engaged in concept-formation. We have also to be aware of the logical types of the expressions occurring in the sentence, so as to know what replacing one expression by another consists in. B&H maintain that Frege cannot consistently distinguish a proper name from an expression for a concept of second-level: " '$\Phi(A)$' ... can with equal propriety be characterised as stating that the concept Φ falls under a second-level concept ... On this ... interpretation, Frege apparently concluded ... , the symbol 'A' must ... be viewed as the name of a second-level concept" (p. 166). This shows that "the differentiation of proper names from concept-words is ... a matter of how the sentence ... is viewed" (pp. 167–8).

This reasoning is based on a misunderstanding of the classification of expressions into types, and hence of the process of extracting expressions of higher type. An ability to discriminate "proper names" from other expressions is the foundation of the entire process. The extraction of a predicate of second level cannot be understood until it is known what a predicate of first level is, and what it is for it to occur in a sentence and to be replaced, in a given occurrence, by another predicate of first level. All this has to be explained, since a predicate is an incomplete expression: you cannot tell whether it occurs in a sentence, or what would be the result of replacing it, just by looking to see if some string of symbols or words occurs and considering the substitution of another string for it. The only case in which this procedure is adequate is the basic one, when what is to be replaced is a proper name, since that is a complete expression and occurs in a sentence, and can be replaced within it, in a straightforward sense. Not every word or string of words may be significantly considered as replaceable, however: not, for instance, the symbol '>' in 'If 5 > 3, then 5 + 2 > 3 + 2'. That is why the whole theory rests on the presumption that we can distinguish a proper name from other words or strings of words.

A predicate of second level, being incomplete, is no more a separable bit of a sentence than one of first level: it is therefore in principle incapable of being identical with a proper name. It is, rather, what is left of a sentence when (say) one or more occurrences of a predicate of first level have been removed. Thus we might remove the predicate '$\xi > 3 + 2$' from the foregoing arithmetical statement to form the second-level predicate 'If 5 > 3, then $\phi(5 + 2)$'. As an extreme case, we may remove "If 5 > ξ, then 5 + 2 > ξ + 2" to obtain

"$\phi(3)$", which stands for that concept of second level under which fall all and only those first-level concepts under which 3 falls; but it is not '3' that stands for this second-level concept, since an expression standing for a concept or function must be unsaturated and hence have argument-places. The proper name '3' is not type-ambiguous at all.

XV. Conclusion

No-one can read very far in FLE without perceiving the animus against Frege; the book is relentlessly dedicated to proving that he was virtually worthless as a philosopher. It is a very bad idea to devote a book to such an aim. Virtually no one could produce a good book in this way, avoiding the merely captious and thinking through his victim's ideas sympathetically before evaluating them. Even the authors cannot suppose that there is much philosophical profit to be gained from reading it, save to be inoculated against being "mesmerised" by Frege. It is unlikely to destroy Frege's reputation, which is evidently their aim; but it might badly retard the understanding of him, which is why I have thought it worth while to comment on it in such detail. This pair of authors might have given us an illuminating comparative study of Frege and Wittgenstein; it is regrettable that they have preferred to attempt a hatchet job on a philosopher they lack the good will to understand.

New College, Oxford

DUMMETT'S FREGE

By John Skorupski

Michael Dummett, *The Interpretation of Frege's Philosophy*. London, Duckworth, 1981, pp. xviii + 621. Price £35.00, paper £9.95.

A book of over 600 pages devoted to questions in the interpretation of Frege's philosophy may seem rather too much. There is repetition here, and chapters, such as that on the "context principle", which would have been more telling had they been drastically shortened.

But Dummett is always absorbing; in straining to follow the twists and turns of his dialectic one is drawn into thinking long and hard about why language matters to philosophy. This is the essence, in Dummett's view, of Frege's importance: it is through his work that the centrality of language for philosophy, and thus the priority of the philosophy of language over other forms of philosophical inquiry, such as epistemology or metaphysics, becomes clear; and he is for this reason to be regarded as the founding father of analytic philosophy. That is the overarching thesis which Dummett defends in this volume. It leads him into historical and interpretative questions, and also into much fascinating philosophical argument. One cannot assess the thesis without inquiring into the ways in which language *does* matter to philosophy, as well as into the historical questions of how much this in recognised in analytic philosophy, and how much anticipated in Frege's work.

Even in a critical study, it is not possible to discuss or even mention everything in this book. It contains a great deal of densely packed argument, much of it showing Dummett's philosophy at its forceful and exciting best. I propose to examine first Dummett's discussion of one range of important issues, centring on the notion of sense: proper names, indexicality, *oratio obliqua*. Indexicality and *oratio obliqua* are discussed in Ch. 6, the second longest, and perhaps the most intricately argued and powerful chapter of the book. As to proper names, FPL contained a long appendix on Kripke's view of them. In IFP, Dummett again returns to his disagreements with Kripke. The issues surface in several places: in Ch. 6 itself, which contains an interesting discussion of Kripke's paper, "A puzzle about belief",[1] in Chs. 9 and 10, and most elaborately, in another appendix. This takes its starting point from remarks made by Kripke in the preface which he added to his lectures on

---

[1] S. Kripke, "A Puzzle about Belief", in *Meaning and Use*, ed. A. Margalit (London, 1979).

"Naming and Necessity" when these were published in book form; it runs to 43 pages.

I consider these questions about sense in the next section, and turn to the general issue of Frege's place in the history of philosophy in the final section.

I

Dummett distinguishes three aspects of Frege's notion of sense. First of all, the sense of an expression is its "conventional significance": where this concept approximates to the ordinary pre-theoretical notion of meaning. It is not identical with it, because, for example, in that ordinary sense, proper names would not be said to have a meaning. But they do have conventional significance, since they make a contribution to the conventional significance of sentences in which they appear, and it is an essential feature of the Fregean conception of sense that the sense of an expression is nothing other than the contribution it makes to the sense of sentences in which it appears. Secondly, to understand the sense of an expression is to grasp a "mode of presentation" of, or "route to", the reference. Finally, Frege conceived of senses as timeless, immutable denizens of a third realm, which we somehow "grasp" in our thinking. In particular, *thoughts* — the senses of sentences – are entities possessed of changeless truth-value.

Dummett thinks that these several aspects of Frege's concept strain against each other (pp. 99–104). The strain is manifested in Frege's theory of indirect reference and in his treatment of indexicals, and it is generated by the basic Fregean principle that *reference is exclusively determined by sense*. (I shall call this principle A.)

What gives rise to this principle? The conception of senses as abstract entities does not preclude the possibility that they could have changing references; nor is there anything in the notion of conventional significance to rule out expressions with constant significance but variable reference. The real work is done by the idea of sense as mode of presentation.

That idea is the subject of a great deal of fascinating discussion in the present book. It, and its difficulties, lie at the heart of Dummett's far-reaching efforts to rethink the Fregean doctrine of sense.

The natural way to explain the idea that understanding an expression is grasping a mode of presentation of its reference is by invoking the notion of a *condition* which its referent must satisfy. To understand the sense is to grasp the condition. (I shall concentrate here on the sense of singular terms and ignore the questions which arise when one tries to marry the notion of sense as mode of presentation with Frege's doctrine that incomplete expressions and sentences refer respectively to functions and truth values.) Let us distinguish between simple and conditional specification of reference. In

'Mercury' refers to Mercury,

the reference of 'Mercury' is specified simply. In

(x) ('Mercury' refers to x iff x is a planet and any planet which is at least as close to the sun as x is identical with x),

the reference of 'Mercury' is specified conditionally. The conventional significance of a term is given by the conventionally designated specification of its reference. On the Fregean view, according to which every term has a sense – understood as a mode of presentation of its reference – that specification will always be conditional.

But when the idea of sense as mode of presentation is explained in this fashion, it is not immediately clear that it must entail principle A. Consider indexical expressions. *Prima facie*, it seems attractive to exhibit the sense of an indexical by means of a specification of its reference which is conditional, but *context-relative*. Thus:

'I' refers, on a given occasion of use, to the utterer of the utterance in which it is used [used, not mentioned].

'This' refers, on a given occasion of use, to the object demonstrated by the utterer of the utterance in which it is used.

To grasp the sense of 'I' and 'this', one might think, is just to know that.

Because this proposal infringes Principle A, we cannot take it to be in the spirit of Frege's conception of sense as mode of presentation. Given principle A, 'I', 'now', 'here' cannot have constant sense but varying reference. On the other hand, their conventional significance is surely constant. A Fregean must either deny that, and hold them to be systematically ambiguous; or he must deny that they are singular terms at all and treat them as standing for functions from circumstances to persons, times and places. (Dummett points out the latter possibility but does not follow it up.) The alternative is to give up a central feature of the Fregean conception of sense, by splitting apart mode of presentation and conventional significance. We shall have to say that the conventional significance of an indexical, together with its circumstances of use, determine an associated (and inexpressible!) mode of presentation which in turn determines, on its own, the reference.

Similar difficulties arise in connexion with Frege's theory of indirect reference. According to the view Dummett put forward in FPL, the sense of an expression in oblique contexts remains constant. This is, as he says, an emendation of Frege's own view; and in IFP he defends it most interestingly and effectively, on grounds of economy and greater intuitiveness with respect to multiply indirect contexts. On Frege's view, however, what sense an expression has – direct or indirect – is determined by its sentential context. That sense then determines the reference of the expression on its own, in accordance with principle A. Given this approach, we again have to accept that sense as mode of presentation is determined by sentential context together with a constant conventional significance – so we are forced again to split apart mode of presentation and conventional significance. To allow sentential context to interact directly with a constant sense in determining reference is incompatible with principle A. In this case, however, it seems that Dummett is implicitly prepared to give up the principle.

To sum up: in both cases (indexicals and indirect reference) we have a choice between splitting up sense as conventional significance and sense as mode of presentation, or giving up principle A. But principle A is supposed to follow from the very notion of sense as mode of presentation. If that is right then to give it up is to give up that notion. It follows that if we want to retain it, we have no choice but to accept that sense as mode of presentation cannot in all cases be equated with conventional significance. Yet what is distinctive about *Frege's* notion of sense is that it does equate the two. All of this emerges in Dummett's discussion, but I am not sure that he ever stands back and takes full stock of how much damage it does to a distinctively Fregean notion of sense. So let us examine more closely the relationship between the notion of mode of presentation and principle A.

In Ch. 6 Dummett ultimately rests the connection on two premises: that modes of presentation are thought-constituents, and that "thoughts" have an absolute truth value. As he says, the latter point does not depend on treating thoughts as inhabitants of a timeless third realm. It arises from the fact that "thoughts", in Frege's sense, are what we report in indirect speech, and that we regard what a person said, believed, and so on as capable of being said again, by a different person or at a different time without change of truth-value. We therefore make appropriate adjustments in the semantic vehicle which expresses the thought, to secure constant truth value. Thus if X says, "I am sick", Y expresses the *same* thought by sentences having a *different* conventional significance: 'You are sick', or 'He is sick'. The thought expressed the day before yesterday by the sentence 'It will be fine tomorrow' is expressed today by the sentence 'It was fine yesterday'. ('You said it would be fine yesterday. You were wrong: it was not fine yesterday.')

Dummett is right to say that thoughts in this sense have absolute truth-value. But even when that is accepted, it remains to be shown that they are constituted by "modes of presentation". This latter thesis is essential for the distinctively Fregean conception of thoughts which gives rise to principle A. It rests, in Dummett's presentation of Frege, on the doctrine that there is no "irreducibly predicative knowledge", i.e., that statements ascribing *de re* knowledge to a person can be true only and exclusively in virtue of the truth of statements ascribing *de dicto* knowledge to that person.[2]

Dummett takes this doctrine to be evident; it is I think far from being so. What makes it seem evident, perhaps, is the feeling that if I have in mind no uniquely determining condition on X, there can be nothing to make my thought *a thought about X*. But why may it not be an appropriate causal connection, and a disposition to a functionally appropriate response, that makes it a thought about X? There is no space here to go properly into this teasingly elusive question. At any rate Dummett has not yet given the doctrine the defence it needs in view of the crucial role it plays in his reworking of Fregean positions.

But suppose we accept the doctrine. We have seen that if the concept of sense as mode of presentation gives rise to principle A, mode of presentation must be distinguishable from conventional significance. But in that case, what argument remains for the claim that the conventional significance of every singular term *must* be exhibited by a conditional specification of its reference? It seems to me that Dummett has not fully faced this question. When mode of presentation is split off from conventional significance, what is its relevance to the theory of meaning? And how much of Frege's distinctive conception of sense is left?

These questions come into sharp focus when we turn to the case of proper names. Here the central issue is precisely whether the significance of a name is given simply or conditionally: that is the issue between Kripke and Dummett.

In the preface he has added to *Naming and Necessity*, Kripke says that understanding a sentence, e.g., 'Aristotle was fond of dogs', involves grasping its modal value – its truth value with respect to various possible counterfactual situations. It is for that reason that we see a difference in sense between 'Aristotle was fond of dogs' and 'The teacher of Alexander was fond of dogs': they differ in respect of the counterfactual situations which would make them true.

His comments are directed against Dummett's claim, in FPL, that the linguistic phenomena which are handled by Kripke in terms of the theory that names are rigid designators, could equally well be handled by supposing that we have a convention which requires that names should always be read as having wide scope in modal contexts. Kripke's point is that if grasping the sense of a proper name is grasping a condition associated with it, which its referent – if it has one – meets, then so long as this condition is only contingently met by the referent, there will be counterfactual situations in respect of which the truth-value of 'Aristotle was fond of dogs' will depend on whether some object

---

[2] This argument for Frege's notion of sense is also put forward in Dummett's "Frege's Distinction between Sense and Reference", in *Truth and other Enigmas*.

not identical with the actual referent of 'Aristotle' likes dogs. But this goes against our grasp of the modal value of 'Aristotle was fond of dogs'.

In IFP, Dummett undertakes to defend his original claim. His example is the name 'Deutero-Isaiah', which can plausibly be "understood as standing for the author of the prophecy embodied in chapters 40 to 55 of the book of Isaiah" (p. 562). Kripke would presumably say that this description fixes the references of 'Deutero-Isaiah' but does not give its meaning. Dummett agrees that the name is not just an "abbreviation" for the description but he nevertheless thinks that it has the same Fregean sense. Consider now the following two modal sentences:

(1) The author of the prophecy . . . might have died in infancy.
(2) Deutero-Isaiah might have died in infancy.

Suppose, with Dummett, that it is impossible for an infant to compose a prophecy. Then there will be a permissible reading in which (1) is false: namely, when the definite description is taken as occurring within the scope of the modal operator. On the other hand, if the description is understood as having large scope, (1) is true.

On this, Dummett and Kripke would agree. It is when we turn to (2) that the difference between them emerges. According to Dummett (as I understand him) although 'Deutero-Isaiah' and 'the author of the prophecy . . .' have the same Fregean sense, we are, in using the name, governed by conventions which differ in various respects from those which govern our use of the description. These differences appear in various ways; e.g., in temporal contexts, and in the different behaviour of names and descriptions after such verbs as 'become'. In particular, they appear in modal contexts: a name must always be read as appearing with wide scope relative to a modal operator. Thus no reading of (2) analogous to our first way of reading (1) is possible. Hence, even granting that 'Deutero-Isaiah' has the same sense as 'the author of the prophecy . . .', there is no ambiguity. (2) is unambiguously true.

Kripke of course agrees that (2) is unambiguously true. But he acknowledges no such scope conventions, and allows names to occur with small scope. On his view, the unambiguous truth of (2) is to be explained by the fact that the reference of 'Deutero-Isaiah' is specified simply, not conditionally. It is a rigid designator.

On both views, as Dummett rightly points out (pp. 580, 588), *contra* Kripke, 'Deutero-Isaiah might not have been Deutero-Isaiah' can have no reading which makes it true. *Is* there, then, any way of choosing between Dummett's scope convention theory and Kripke's rigid designator theory?

As Dummett recognises, the obvious reaction is to consider (as Kripke does in his preface) the modal status of simple, i.e., unmodalized, sentences, such as

(3) Deutero-Isaiah died in infancy.

Surely on the rigid designator theory, this is contingently false, and on the scope-convention theory, necessarily false. Now is it not the case that our linguistic intuitions unambiguously support the rigid designator theory?

Dummett's reply is twofold. First, in so far as we *are* inclined to say that (3) is contingently false, i.e., possibly true, that is only because we accept (2) as unambiguously true:

> We have no intuition that 'Deutero-Isaiah died in infancy' is possibly true other than our intuition that 'Deutero-Isaiah might have died in infancy' is true; as already noted, the latter intuition is supported by both analyses. (p. 582)

Secondly, we do not have an unambiguous tendency:

> it would be quite a natural thing to say that 'Deutero-Isaiah died in infancy' could not possibly be true. Kripke would account for this by conceding that, though possibly true, the sentence is false *a priori*; but he can scarcely hope to ground so subtle a distinction on untutored intuition. (*ibid.*)

Dummett's first point is part of a more general claim – that our intuitions about the modal value of simple sentences issue exclusively from intuitions about the truth value of corresponding modalized sentences. This seems to me to put the cart before the horse. Kripke's point, that to grasp the significance of a sentence *is* to grasp its truth value with respect to counterfactual situations is surely a truism, which must be recognised on any view. Consider

(4) Deutero-Isaiah was the author of the prophecy.

On Dummett's view this should be analytic and *therefore* necessary. In grasping the Fregean sense of the term, i.e., the condition its referent must meet, we grasp the analytic status of (4). We do not recognise it as analytic because we recognise that *another* sentence – the necessitation of (4) – is true: it is exactly the other way about.

Dummett's second reply turns on rejecting Kripke's distinction between fixing a reference and giving a meaning – at least in the form in which Kripke envisaged it, i.e., as entailing that (4) is *a priori* but contingent.

Now although the terms 'epistemic possibility' and 'metaphysical possibility' are technical the underlying distinction *is* intuitive. For example if I say 'Cyril might (or 'may') have been in the club last week' I shall, in many contexts, naturally be understood as expressing an epistemic possibility. In that case, if I add, '... but I know for a fact that he was not', my audience will be baffled.

Applying this to the case of Deutero-Isaiah, it is clear that, simply in virtue of my knowledge of how the reference of the term is conventionally fixed, I am justified in denying that 'Deutero-Isaiah did not compose the prophecy' is true. So I will not agree with anyone who says 'Deutero-Isaiah might not have composed the prophecy', when that proposes an epistemic possibility which is in fact ruled out. But I am still not inclined to say that (4) expresses a necessary truth, while I agree that 'The author of the prophecy is the author of the prophecy' does (subject to an existential assumption). It is just these facts which are catered for by Kripke's distinction between fixing a reference and giving a meaning.

Dummett thinks it a distinction without a difference (p. 184). But he is in no position to say that. For first, on his own view that intuitions about modal value rest on judgements of truth value, any inclination to say that (3) is necessarily false could only be explained by appeal to a sense in which (2) is false. As we have seen, however, given the scope convention theory, there *is* no such sense. How then can he explain why it is "quite a natural thing to say that 'Deutero-Isaiah died in infancy' could not possibly be true", except by appeal to the notion of epistemic possibility?

Secondly, *why* should names always take wide scope? This question is left unanswered by Dummett, and is, it seems to me, unanswerable. In contrast, there are good reasons of utility for having terms in the language whose reference is specified simply rather than conditionally.

If, on the other hand, Dummett gave up the claim that we have no direct modal intuitions, he could argue that it is because we recognise that (4) is analytic, and know that infants cannot compose prophecies, that we recognise (3) as necessarily false. There would then be a direct confrontation between Kripke's and Dummett's assessment of the modal status of (3) and (4). Here, however, my intuitions at least are with Kripke and not with Dummett.

Altogether, Dummett's attempt to preserve the view that names have conditional sense against Kripke's arguments do not convince me. Trivially, of course, if sense is simply identified with conventional significance, and that in turn with truth condition contribution, names have sense. But that "sense" could be determined by their reference, so that co-referential names would have the same "sense". In fact this might be thought to follow, if one accepts that the reference of a term is to be specified simply, rather than conditionally.

In his paper "On the Sense and Reference of a Proper Name", John McDowell has denied that it follows. He argues that it is possible to accept the classic Fregean position that co-referential names may differ in sense, while accepting that their sense is given by a simple rather than a conditional specification of reference. Dummett considers this idea but rejects it – essentially, however, on the general ground that no term can have its reference specified simply. He does not examine whether McDowell's position is internally coherent, or whether instead, if we accept that the sense of names is given simply, we are forced to what Kripke has called the "Millian" view,[3] according to which co-referential names have the same conventional significance.

Yet even if one accepts Dummett's thesis that there can be no irreducibly predicative knowledge, once mode of presentation is split off from conventional significance, it will not follow from that thesis that there can be no purely referential terms. Dummett seems to recognise this at one point: "That there can be no irreducibly predicative thought does not imply that there can be no purely referential terms." (p. 592) But a paragraph later he says:

> It remains that an employment of a name as literally purely referential is an unintelligible fantasy. If speakers are to be able to employ a name with the same reference, they must not only intend to do so, but be able to discover whether they are doing so; since there is no irreducibly predicative knowledge, this means that the use of the name in the common language must rest on more than common reference. (p. 593)

However, even if we accept that it must rest on a common mode of presentation, we are no longer forced to identify that mode of presentation with the *conventional significance* of the name. But in any case, it is not even true that there must be some such shared mode of presentation to secure objectivity of sense. All that is true is that we must agree on what kind of evidence is decisive in determining the reference of a name, simply inasmuch as we share an understanding of what it is for a term to function as a *proper name*. This agreement will therefore be *a priori*. But a theory which brings out that implicit understanding need not be a theory which spells out, in general form, what kind of conditional specification of reference must be grasped by anyone who understands a name. The conventional significance of a name may still be exhibited by a simple specification of its reference.

That then leaves McDowell's view and the "Millian" view. Curiously enough, if one accepts that there is no irreducibly predicative knowledge, then it is by no means obvious either that McDowell's view can be defended as coherent, or that the "Millian" view cannot be. The problem for the latter reduces to the behaviour of names in epistemic contexts. 'Smith believes that Eric Blair was a novelist' may be false; 'Smith believes that George Orwell was a novelist' may be true. Must not 'Eric Blair' and 'George Orwell' therefore have different significance, since the two sentences apparently do? Once mode

---

[3] In "A Puzzle About Belief". Kripke does not claim that Mill himself asserted this view. If McDowell's position is tenable, it would be compatible with Mill's actual opinion, that names have denotation but no connotation, just as the "Millian" view is.

of presentation is distinguished from conventional significance, I am not convinced that the two sentences cannot be said to have the same significance, in so far as they have a clearcut significance at all. Neither strictly reports a Fregean thought, yet they might still, by pragmatic but easily intelligible conventions, be used to ascribe to Smith, with some indeterminacy, non-overlapping ranges of Fregean thoughts. But the matter cannot be pursued here.

II

Let us turn to Dummett's general conception of Frege's historical importance. In Dummett's view, Frege's work brought about a "shift of perspective" – "an altered conception of the starting point of philosophy and of the relations of dependence between the different parts of the subject." (p. 56) The new conception took the philosophy of language to be fundamental to philosophy as a whole. In effecting this shift Frege established the distinctive standpoint of "analytic philosophy".

There is something importantly right in Dummett's view of how analytic philosophy should be distinguished from what came before. It may be easy to criticise in detail, but that is true of any attempt to characterise the general historical shape of an intellectual movement. What is less convincing is his treatment of Frege's relationship to this shift. He does not take enough care to give an accurate picture of Frege's predecessors where that is required to establish what is really new in Frege. And he tends to over-interpret what Frege said, reading more into Frege's statements than a soberly historical interpretation could allow. The effect is to make Frege stand out unhistorically as a prophetic ancestor of analytic philosophy, in whose texts all its insights are already germinally contained.

To be sure, even those aspects of Frege's work which are not in dispute are quite sufficient to establish his importance in the development of analytic philosophy. *Bs*, with its syntax and semantics for propositional and predicate calculus, is indisputably seminal. The logicist programme (despite, or rather in part because of, the catastrophe of Russell's paradox) has an importance for analytic philosophy which is at least as great, though harder to pin down. At the very least, Frege's method of defining the concept of number in *Gl*, and the accompanying discussion, provided philosophy with a paradigm of analysis going well beyond its immediate relevance to the philosophy of mathematics.

But Dummett's claims for Frege are still greater than this. It is impossible to examine every aspect of his detailed and richly argued case. I must restrict myself to a few main themes – relating to Frege's conception of sense, and to two famous aspects of *Gl*: the rejection of "psychologism" and the "context principle".

Perhaps, then, it is Frege's treatment of the notion of sense that first gave language the characteristic centrality which it has acquired in analytic philosophy. That impression is powerfully conveyed by Dummett's reworking of Frege's philosophy. But how much here belongs to Frege – and how much to Dummett, or to the influence of Wittgenstein, rather than Frege, on Dummett's thought? Dummett proposes "the philosophy of thought" as

> a neutral designation for that branch of philosophy which Frege called simply "logic" ... which, as he would have been the first to insist, is to be sharply distinguished from a philosophical account of *thinking*.

He then suggests that

> the basic tenet of analytic philosophy, common to such disparate philosophers as Schlick, early and late Wittgenstein, Carnap, Ryle, Ayer, Austin, Quine and Davidson, may be expressed as being that the philosophy of thought is to be equated with the philosophy of language: more exactly, (i) an account of language does not presuppose an account of thought, (ii) an account of language yields an account of thought, and (iii) there is no other adequate means by which an account of thought may be given. (p. 39)

True; but only if 'thought' is understood in its ordinary, and not in Frege's distinctive sense. Fregean "thoughts" inhabit a "third realm". They are given to us, or at least we can discuss them, only in the distorting medium of language; but we can try to build a linguistic medium which is less distorting than our actual one: "a formalized language of Pure Thought", to quote the subtitle of *Bs*. Only in this sense could Frege be said to equate the philosophy of *thought* with the philosophy of language.

The doctrine which can be described, not implausibly, as "the basic tenet of analytical philosophy" is something altogether distinct from this. Its leading idea is that thinking, of any developed kind, is *nothing more than the exercise of an ability to use a language* — and connected with it is a pattern of notably unFregean themes.

Understanding and meaning are manifested in use. This, it is important to note, is no mere attack on mentalism. On this view, understanding is no more a process of "grasping" a Fregean thought than it is a process of associating words with mental episodes. *Both* "processes" become irrelevant.[4] Moreover, two other characterising, and connected, themes of analytic philosophy have historically grown from this kernel idea – though their true relations to it, and to each other, are matter for controversy: the view of philosophical questions as

---

[4] "Meaning is not a process which accompanies a word. For no *process* could have the consequences of meaning". (PI, II.xi).

pseudo-problems to be dissolved by careful analysis of language, and a verificationist conception of meaning together with conventionalism about necessity.

Now it is evident that these themes can in no way be attributed to Frege. One might also have thought it evident that even the kernel idea, from which they arguably grow, is quite alien to his thought. In a sense, Dummett agrees – but with curious half-heartedness:

> An explicit adherence to the fundamental tenet of analytical philosophy ... cannot be claimed for Frege; but what can be claimed is that his philosophy of thought and language leads almost inexorably in that direction;

and again:

> How close is the conception of sense as contributing to truth-conditions to the idea of meaning as exhibited by observable use? To obtain the latter from the former, we should have to say that what a speaker takes the truth-condition of a sentence to be is manifested by the use he makes of that sentence and of others containing words occurring in it. No statement of this thesis is to be found in Frege; but it is difficult to frame a consistent interpretation of him which conflicts with it. (p. 54)

This, it seems to me, is one of the points at which Dummett most clearly tries to get Wittgensteinian quarts into Fregean pint-pots. He regularly plays down the importance of the conception of senses as abstract entities in Frege's thought. The conception is indeed irrelevant to the purpose for which Frege insisted on it: safeguarding the objectivity of thought. But of course *Frege* would hardly have agreed. It may well also be true that no ultimately satisfactory account of the objectivity and communicability of thought – which Frege was so unquestionably concerned to stress – can be given, unless one clearly recognises that meaning is exhaustively manifested in use. But that gives no reason for associating the point in any way with Frege.

In a number of passages, Dummett claims that with Frege "the conception of realism came into sharp focus for the first time in the history of philosophy" (p. 443): this "absolutely sharp picture" (p. 472) of realism is provided by Frege's account of the sense of a sentence as given by its truth conditions. The claim is just: yet Dummett himself has made us acutely conscious of the connexion between the conception of meaning as use, and the *rejection* of "realism" in just this sense, in favour of an account of meaning in terms of assertibility conditions.

It would not in fact be wildly off the mark to say that the essential problematic of analytic philosophy is precisely not Fregean: in that, within this tradition, the programme which has time and again imposed itself as fundamental is that of sustaining the objectivity and communicability of thought against mentalism on the one hand, *and* against the Fregean blend of "realism" and Platonism about sense on the other. So far from stemming from Frege, the emphasis on understanding and meaning as manifestable, empirical processes should be traced back to the naturalistic empiricism which he sharply opposed. To study the ways in which a rigorously naturalistic philosophy of mind eventually leads to a rejection of the "realist" view of what it is to understand a language, one must turn to the development of American pragmatism, or to the relationship between Vienna Circle positivism and 19th century philosopher-scientists like Mach.

There is a different way in which Frege's philosophy might be seen as setting a new direction. A central debate in 19th century philosophy was that between naturalism and various forms of post-Kantian idealism. The essential point on which post-Kantian critics of naturalism were agreed, was that no purely naturalistic account of cognitive processes – of understanding, belief or inference – could explain how any kind of knowledge was possible; the nature of these processes thus became a crux in the argument. Could one perhaps say that Frege's distinctive contribution was to go beyond this conflict – by rejecting its underlying assumptions – and thus to pave the way for the distinctively 20th Century concerns of analytic philosophy? He certainly rejected them: the whole discussion of *Gl* is cast in the form of attacks on both parties. And it is presumably also true that his influence on Cambridge philosophy in the early years of this century was at least in part connected with this fact.

Yet what is significant for the development of analytic philosophy as a whole is not the success of this attempt to go beyond the 19th Century argument, but its failure. I do not have in mind the "technical" failings of logicism. Consider rather Frege's criticism of Kant's notion of analyticity as too narrow (*Gl*, § 88). In making this criticism, Frege shows himself insensitive to an essential epistemological point. The narrow notion of analyticity (or a tidied up version of it) has the crucial feature that statements which are "analytic" in the narrow sense are indisputably unproblematic epistemologically: as even the most radical empiricist ought to agree (as, for example, Mill did). The broader notion – definitional reducibility to logic – does not. It may be, as Frege suggests, that Kant was not clearly conscious of the difference between the two; but there is nevertheless clear philosophical point in his preoccupation with the narrow notion.

Kant saw a problem about the synthetic *a priori* which Frege seems simply not to feel at all. On the basis of Frege's lifelong view of geometry as synthetic *a priori*, Sluga has argued that Frege should be seen as a transcendental idealist. That interpretation is criticised at length, and in my view successfully, by Dummett in the present book. Frege saw no need to *explain* how a synthetic *a priori* is possible; he was content with what he took to be an obvious datum – that it must and does exist. Again Dummett argues, against Currie, that Frege was not primarily interested in epistemology. Quite so: he was not, in a sense in which both Kant and Mill in their very different ways were. Their epistemological interests sprang from a source – the thought that no *a priori* proposition can say anything about a mind-independent world – which never touched Frege at all. In this specific respect Frege is comparable to Moore: both Platonise dogmatically, one in the tradition of rationalism, the other in the tradition of common sense, and both, in doing so, take themselves to be going beyond a dispute which they imagine to be misguided.

When we turn to the rejection of "psychologism", and the "context principle", we encounter essentially similar points.

"Psychologism" may be the view that laws of logic are, or hold in virtue of, the laws which govern our mental processes, or again it may be the view that "meanings" are mental entities. Frege was clearly opposed to both and thought they were bound up with idealism; but then Mill too was opposed to both, and he also thought them to be bound up with idealism.[5] However there is an important difference. Mill's opposition to psychologism in the above two senses is, or should be, clear enough, but his case for what he takes to be ultimate principles of reasoning (induction) or ultimate ends (happiness) nevertheless rests on a naturalistic appeal to what we in fact agree on "in theory and practice". He will not accept that we must, at this point at least, recognise ourselves as having *a priori* knowledge of necessary relationships between Platonic entities. What marks Frege's philosophy as belonging to a new phase of the subject is not that he rejected psychologism in the senses just defined. It is that for him, separating sharply between psychological and logical questions meant something more: it meant rejecting the naturalistic attitude as such. Or rather, as with Moore, it was the *combination* of that with an equally sharp opposition to any kind of idealism that was new. But neither Frege nor Moore could offer – or saw the need to offer – any creative way of transcending these alternatives. That could only be done by extracting or dissolving their common roots.

Frege states the context principle on p. x of *Gl*, ("never to ask for the meaning of a word in isolation, but only in the context of a proposition").

---

[5] Mill has often mistakenly been accused of psychologism, in one or another of these senses – the accusation can perhaps be traced back to Husserl. The mistake is not made by Frege, who argues separately, on the one hand against psychologistic views, and on the other, against Mill's position, that the laws of arithmetic (and of logic) are known inductively, and that number terms connote attributes of physical aggregates.

Dummett distinguishes two versions of it, corresponding to the distinction between sense and reference. Now this distinction had not been made by Frege at the time he wrote *Gl*; but it remains possible, as Dummett rightly says, that both aspects of the context principle are put to use in the argument of that book.

> As a principle concerning sense, the context principle singles out sentences as having a unique role in any account of the senses of expressions ... We have ... to inquire whether the accounts of the senses of expressions of all logical types provide us, when taken together, with a plausible explanation of how the truth-conditions of sentences are determined, and provide us with nothing more than is needed for this. An account of sense in terms of the associated mental imagery, for example, is shown by the principle to be both inadequate and superfluous: inadequate in that it does not yield a workable account of the resulting truth-conditions of sentences; and superfluous in that it invokes features irrelevant to such an account. (p. 369–70)

That the context principle appears, in precisely this role, in *Gl* there can be no doubt, even though Frege could not then of course state the matter in terms of his later notion of sense.

But in its "reference version" it is I think very dubious whether it can be attributed to Frege at all. In this version, the context principle is seen by Dummett as vindicating Platonism about numbers – the view that they are, in Frege's words, "self-subsistent objects" – against a very natural objection: that we do not know, and could have no possible means of knowing, anything of such objects. Against this objection, the reference version asserts that once the sense of sentences in which a singular term occurs has been fixed, so that we know in principle at least how to set about determining their truth value, then no further *philosophical* questions remain about whether that term has reference.

If this is indeed the point of the context principle, then we can appeal to it only if we have a way of fixing the senses of sentences containing number terms which does make it clear how our knowledge of their truth value is genuinely unproblematic. The way to do that is by contextual definition of the number terms. Now, however, a difficulty arises. Once the terms have been contextually defined, i.e., a way has been found to transform, without change of sense, sentences in which they appear into sentences in which they do not, no reason seems to remain for claiming that the original sentences involved reference to abstract objects. It is strange to regard the contextual definition as demonstrating that the existence of abstract objects raises no philosophical questions, when what it shows is that our actual means of determining the truth value of such sentences can be exhibited without assuming that we enter into epistemic relations with any abstract objects. A Platonism of this kind seems but a rhetorical variation on nominalism.

At the very end of his chapter on "The Context Principle" (pp. 424—7) Dummett considers this difficulty. He comes to the conclusion that a realism about abstract objects which is defended in this way

> appears to reduce to little more than a form of words. It is for this reason that I said on p. 500 of FPL that there is a certain tension between the realism which informs Frege's whole philosophy and the context principle taken as a thesis containing [*sic*: read 'concerning'] reference, that is, as a justification for ascribing reference to abstract terms ... (p. 426)

Since the context principle, in Dummett's "reference version", does not seem to me to provide any genuine rehabilitation of Platonism, I agree that there would be a tension in Frege's thought if it could be ascribed to him.[6] But it is far from obvious that it can be. Frege deploys the context principle to fend off subjectivist accounts of the meaning of number terms. He is simply uninterested in the problem (how can we have knowledge of abstract objects?) which the "reference version" is supposed to defuse. What is more, the reference version depends on an underlying anti-realism about sense. (If we "fix the sense" of sentences containing numerical terms, we *thereby* render them epistemologically unproblematic.) Such anti-realism is what cannot be found in Frege. Once again it seems to me that Dummett is here reading into Frege themes from the later Wittgenstein which Frege never dreamt of. (This is not of course to say that the later Wittgenstein was himself sympathetic to Platonism – only that Dummett's approach to Platonism is Wittgensteinian rather than Fregean in its tenor.)

Frege's pathbreaking contributions to logic were vital to the analytic tradition, as were his logicist programme and its subsequent fortunes. But it was not Frege who made the question of the nature of language central for analytic philosophy: as it undoubtedly – in a confusing variety of ways – has been. The processes that led to that were complicated, and they stemmed from a variety of sources; one of which – but only one – was Frege's *Bs* and his semantic essays. There is as yet no comprehensive and realistic historical study of this whole development.

---

[6] Crispin Wright has recently given a carefully argued account of this approach to mathematical Platonism (Wright). Whether or not such a defence of Platonism is sound, however, there remains the question of whether it can be attributed to Frege.

Frege's general philosophical position does indeed represent a new phase in the subject—an attempt, rather like G. E. Moore's, to cut loose from the entrenched debates of the 19th Century. But this new phase was doomed to be shortlived, because it did not plumb the real depth of the epistemological issues which were at stake. It may well be that to go beyond the conflict between naturalism and idealism, at least in its 19th Century form, one must reject an assumption which was shared by both sides. That assumption, it may again be argued, is *realism*: in the distinctive sense which Dummett himself has given to the term. Finally, it is plausible to see the rejection of realism, in this sense, as an increasingly powerful *motif* in analytic philosophy. Yet it is realism of just this kind which constitutes the unquestioned *Grundgedanke* of Frege's thought. To trace the critique of realism back to its sources one must look elsewhere.

University of Glasgow

BIBLIOGRAPHY

A. *Works by Frege*
"Anwendungen der Begriffsschrift", *Jenaische Zeitschrift für Naturwissenschaft*, 13 (1879) II, 29–33.
Begriffsschrift, eine der arithmetischen nachgebildete Formelsprache des reinen Denkens (Halle, 1879).
"Booles rechnende Logik und die Begriffsschrift", *NS*, 9–52.
"Funktion und Begriff", an address given to the *Jenaische Gesellschaft für Medicin und Naturwissenschaft*, January 9, 1881.
"Der Gedanke: Eine logische Untersuchung", *Beiträge zur Philosophie des deutschen Idealismus*, 1 (1918).
Grundgesetze der Arithmetik, Begriffsschriftlich abgeleitet, Bd. I (Jena, 1893).
Die Grundlagen der Arithmetik, ein logisch-mathematische Untersuchung über den Begriff der Zahl (Breslau, 1884).
Kleine Schriften, ed. Ignacio Angelelli (Hildesheim, 1967).
Nachgelassene Schriften, ed. H. Hermes, F. Kambartel, F. Kaulbach (Hamburg, 1969).
"Uber Sinn und Bedeutung", *Zeitschrift fur Philosophie und philosophische Kritik*, 100 (1982).
Wissenschaftlicher Briefwechsel (Hamburg, 1976).
The Basic Laws of Arithmetic, tr. and ed. with an introduction by Montgomery Furth (Berkeley and Los Angeles, 1964).
G. Frege, Conceptual Notation and related articles, tr. and ed. with a biography and introduction by Terrell Ward Bynum (Oxford, 1972).
The Foundations of Arithmetic, a logico-mathematical enquiry into the concept of number, tr. J. L. Austin, (Oxford, 1959[2]).
Gottlob Frege: On the Foundations of Geometry and Formal Theories of Arithmetic, tr. with an introduction by Eike-Henner W. Kluge (New Haven and London, 1971).
Logical Investigations, tr. P. T. Geach and R. H. Stoothoff (Oxford, 1977).
Philosophical and Mathematical Correspondence, ed. G. Gabriel, H. Hermes, F. Kambartel, C. Thiel, A. Veraart, abridged for the English edition by B. McGuinness, tr. H. Kaal (Oxford, 1980).
Posthumous Writings, ed. H. Hermes, F. Kambartel, F. Kaulbach, tr. P. Long, R. White (Oxford, 1979).
Translations from the Philosophical Writings of Gottlob Frege, ed. P. T. Geach and M. Black (Oxford, 1960).

B. *Other Works*
G. P. Baker & P. M. S. Hacker, "Dummett's Purge: Frege without Functions", *The Philosophical Quarterly*, 33 (1983), 115–32.
D. Bell, *Frege's Theory of Judgement* (Oxford, 1979).
P. Benacerraf, "Frege: The Last Logicist", in *Midwest Studies in Philosophy* VI, ed. P. French et al. (Minneapolis, 1981).
T. Burge, 1. "Reference and Proper Names", *The Journal of Philosophy*, 70 (1973), 425–39.
——— 2. "Belief *De Re*", *The Journal of Philosophy*, 74 (1977), 338–62.
——— 3. "Sinning against Frege", *The Philosophical Review*, 88 (1979), 398–432.
G. Currie, *Frege: An Introduction to his Philosophy* (Brighton, 1982).
M. Davies, *Meaning, Quantification, Necessity* (London, 1981).
M. A. E. Dummett, *Frege: The Philosophy of Language* (London, 1973[1], 1981[2]).
——— *The Interpretation of Frege's Philosophy* (London, 1982).
——— 1. "The Justification of Deduction", *Proceedings of the British Academy*, 59 (1973), repr. in *Truth and Other Enigmas* (London, 1978), 290–318.
——— 2. "Frege on Functions: A reply", *Philosophical Review*, 64 (1955), repr. in *Truth and Other Enigmas*, 74–86.

G. Evans, *The Varieties of Reference*, ed. J. H. McDowell (Oxford, 1982).
P. Geach, *Reference and Generality* (Ithaca, New York, 1962).
S. Kripke, 1. *Naming and Necessity*, (Oxford, 1980).
———— 2. *Wittgenstein on Rules and Private Language* (Oxford, 1982).
J. McDowell, "On the sense and reference of a proper name" *Mind*, 86 (1977), 159–85.
C. McGinn, *The Subjective View* (Oxford, 1983).
J. Perry, "Frege on Demonstratives", *The Philosophical Review*, 86 (1977), 474–97.
W. V. Quine, *Mathematical Logic* (Cambridge, Mass., 1940).
M. Resnik, *Frege and the Philosophy of Mathematics* (Ithaca, New York, 1980).
B. Russell, "The philosophy of logical atomism", in *Logic and Knowledge*, ed. R. C. Marsh (London, 1956).
Matthias Schirn (ed.), *Studien zu Frege*, 3 vols. (Stuttgart-Bad Canstatt, 1976).
H. Sluga, *Gottlob Frege* (London, 1980).
F. Sommers, *The Logic of Natural Language* (Oxford, 1982).
P. Strawson, *Introduction to Logical Theory* (London, 1952).
A. Tarski, "The concept of truth in formalised languages" in *Logic, Semantics, Metamathematics*, ed. and tr. J. H. Woodger (Oxford, 1956).
E. Tugendhat, "The Meaning of 'Bedeutung' in Frege", *Analysis*, 30 (1969–70), 177–89.
J. Wallace, "On the frame of reference" in *Semantics of Natural Language*, ed. D. Davidson and G. Harman (Dordrecht, 1972).
L. Wittgenstein, *Philosophical Investigations* (Oxford, 1958).
———— *Tractatus Logico-Philosophicus* (London, 1963).
C. J. G. Wright, *Frege's Conception of Numbers as Objects* (Aberdeen, 1983).

INDEX

analysis and decomposition, 221–3
analyticity, 239–40
  and mind-independence of
    Thoughts, 15–18
analytic philosophy, 236–8, 239
analytic/synthetic distinction, 60, 61,
    62
analytic truths, 15–18
anaphoric background, 124
Anscombe, G.E.N., 127n
a priori/a posteriori distinction, 60, 61
arguments (of function), 162–3
argument-place and category, 175
arithmetic, analyticity of, 62–3
assertoric force and predication, 166
atomic propositions, 115

bare acquaintance, 9, 83–4, 87&n, 88,
    89, 90, 91, 93
bare predicates, 134
basic propositions, 118
Bedeutung (*see also* reference), 69–70,
    72n, 98n, 104, 213
  and contemporary use of 'reference',
    64, 73
  and semantic value, 102n
  and truth-value, 188–93
  of predicate, 139
Begriffschrift, 58, 62, 72, 148&n,
    153&n, 196, 197, 198, 199, 206,
    222, 236
Begriffswort, *see* concept-word
belief (*see also* propositional attitudes)
  de re, latitudinarian conception of,
    33n
  necessary conditions, 37–8
  sufficient conditions, 38–9

Bell, D, 192n
Benacerraf, P., 57, 59, 63–7 *passim*
Bestimmungsweisen (modes of
  presentation), 206
Blackburn, S., 81, 108n
'Booles rechnende Logik und die
  Begriffsschrift,' 198, 199, 222
Bradley, F.H., 133
Burge, T., 21n, 31–9, 98, 99&n, 101,
  106n, 107, 108n, 109, 122n

Cantor, G., 58
Carnap, R., 77, 78n, 127
Carruthers, P., 87n
Cartesianism, 29
category and argument-place, 175
Chisholm, R., 33n
Church, A., 127
communication, and mind-
  independence of Thoughts, 7–8
completeness (*see also* saturation), 170,
  176
concepts, 101, 156–7, 206–10, 217–19
  admissibility-for-science, 71
  and judgements, 141, 148, 178–9
  and objects, 171–3, 174
  and properties, 160
  as functions, 198
  definitions, 70
  extension of, 58
  –formation, 222, 224
  functional character of, 144
  identity criteria for, 141
  predicative nature of, 145
  self-identity of, 175
concept-script, 158–83, 216
concept–word, 134, 139

context principle, 240–2
contingency, 217–19
copula, sense of, 133–4
criterial relation, 2–3
Currie, G., 160, 240

Davidson, D., 2n, 107n, 217
Davies, M, 118n, 123
decomposition, 224
   and analysis, 221–3
de dictu propositional attitudes, 34, 35, 36, 39
definition, 59, 64–5, 70–8
   and hints, 74
   and introductory device, 68
   fruitfulness requirement, 65–7
demonstratives, 28–9
de re belief, latitudinarian conception of, 33n
de re/de dictu distinction, 90, 98, 101, 106–7
de re propositional attitudes, 36
de re sense, 98–109 102–3
   and objectivity of thought, 104–6
'Der Gedanke', 191n, 192, 202
'Dialogue with Punjer', 171
'diary' example (Wittgenstein), 93–4
Dingler, H., 192n
direct quotation
   reference of expressions, 185
   sense of expressions, 187
Dudman, V., 129, 132n
Dummett, M., 11n, 40, 41, 42&n, 44, 47, 54, 55, 103n, 106n, 107n, 127, 129, 131–2, 134, 141&n, 144, 146&n, 148, 151n, 154, 156, 189, 227–43

eternal, concepts of, 3
eternality versus timelessness, 4–7
Evans, G., 24n, 28, 29, 83, 87&n, 92, 95–6, 97, 98&n, 100n, 102n, 103n, 104n, 105n, 108n, 123, 128n, 134, 201, 202, 222
evolutionary theory, 136–8
explanation, role of properties, 136
explication, 77–8
expression and language, 214–15
facts, and Thoughts, 155

FAT logic, 115–19
Flew, A., 190n
Fogelin, R., 93n
formal languages and natural languages, 210–12
Foundations of Arithmetic, see *Grundlagen der Arithmetik*
Foundations of Geometry, 72n, 75, 161
Fregean Proper Names, 114, 115, 119, 123
Frege's Atomicity Thesis, 115
French, P., 21n
function and sense, 219–21
'Funktion und Begriff', 190
Furth, M., 127

Gabriel, G., 191n
Geach, P., 114&n, 158–9, 171, 198, 220, 221, 222
Gedanken, see Thoughts
generality and reference, 113–16
geometry, 239–40
grammar, logical, 167, 168
Grossman, R., 151n
Grundgesetze der Arithmetik, 58, 64, 67, 70&n, 72n, 79, 147n, 148, 149, 163, 190, 203, 211, 213, 214
Grundlagen der Arithmetik, 1, 13n, 57, 58, 59, 60, 61, 62, 63, 64, 66, 68&n, 73, 74n, 80, 188, 196, 197, 198, 199, 209, 223, 236, 239, 240, 241

Haack, S., 48n
Hacker, P.M.S., 93n
Heyting, A., 213
Hilbert, D., 68, 177
Hintikka, J., 159n
Husserl, E., 126, 128, 129&n, 206, 240n

incompleteness, 140, 146, 147
indexicality, 9–10
indirect quotation
   reference of expressions, 185–6
   sense of expressions, 187–8
inference, valid, characterisation of, 45–50

INDEX

Intermediate-Value Theorem, 66
'International Platonism', 43
Ishiguro, H., 179–80

judgeable content, 197
judgement(s) (*see also* Thoughts)
  and concepts, 141, 148, 178–9
  and truth, 154, 155

Kant, I., 60–2, 197, 239–40
Kaplan, D., 83n, 100n, 103n, 105n, 106n
Kenny, A., 93n
Kim, J., 83n, 151n
Kitcher, P., 60n
Kleine Schriften, 144n, 145n, 147n
Kripke, S., 35, 80, 122, 227, 231, 232, 233, 234, 235

language
  and expression, 214–15
  centrality for philosophy, 227
Lemmon, E.J., 49n
logic, 216–17
  causal theory, 89
  concept-script and, 161
logical articulation, 163–4
logical categories, 170, 173, 174–5
logical grammar, 168
logical syntax, 111–12
'Logic and Mathematics', 76
'Logic in Mathematics', 65, 66
'Logik', 200
Lotze, H., 191, 191n

McDowell, J., 27, 28, 81, 82, 83, 84, 85, 86, 89, 90, 91, 122, 127n, 234
McGinn, C., 29, 30, 88, 100n, 103, 104n, 108n
McKnight, C., 4n
Marty A., Frege's letter to, 147, 148n, 152, 153n, 192n
meaning, social character of, 96
metaphysical argument, Frege's, 144–57
methodological solipsism, 21–2, 23, 24, 26

Mill, J.S., 73, 127, 235&n
modal logics, 49
mode of presentation, 80, 85, 87–8
'modes of determination (*Bestimmungsweisen*), 206
Moore, G.E., 201, 202, 240, 243
Nachgelassene Schriften, 144n, 145n, 147n, 150, 155, 190, 191n, 200
names
  causal theory, 81–2, 86–7
  'description theory', 80–1
  natural languages and formal languages, 210–12
necessity, 3
  absolute, 3, 6–7
numbers, alternative definitions, 63

objectivity, 13, 14
object-names, admissibility-for-science, 71
object(s)
  and concepts, 171–3, 174
  and singular terms, 52
  as classificatory term, 171
omnitemporality, 3
  of tensed propositions, 10
  of Thoughts, 11
  of truth, 8–12
'On Concept and Object', 131, 134, 143n, 156, 170–1
'On Sense and Reference', 154, 191, 192, 193, 202
ontological nationalism, 44
oratio obliqua, 84–5

past, objectivity about, 13, 14
Peacocke, C., 21n, 24n, 28, 35, 102n, 104n, 106n
Pears, D., 99
Perry, J., 25–31, 28&n, 100, 102n, 104n
'piece of information' and 'sentential role', 25–7
Plato, 133
Platonism, 40–56
  'International', 43
Posthumous Writings, 76, 130, 131, 139, 159–60, 200

predicates (*see also* predication)
  reference, 126–43, 184–5
  sense, 126–43, 186–7
predication (*see also* predicates)
  and assertoric force, 166
  Frege's conception, 139
  regress of, 149–52
primitive truths, 64, 68
proper names
  Fregean, *see* Fregean Proper Names
  reference in contexts of direct use, 184
  sense in contexts of direct use, 186
properties
  and concepts, 160
  in explanations, 136
propositional attitudes (*see also* belief *and under de dictu; de re*), 20–1
propositions, 3
psychological states, narrow and wide, 22–3, 24–5
psychologism, 109n, 240
Putnam, H., 21, 22, 31, 128n

quantification, 114–15
quantity, wild, *see* wild quantity
Quine, W.V.O., 18, 106n, 113, 116

Ramsey, F., 221
realism, 169f, 180–1, 182, 238, 242, 243
recognition, of particulars, 90–1, 92–3
recognition statements, 54
reference (*see also Bedeutung*), 69–70, 71, 72, 73, 203–6, 229–30
  and generality, 113–16
  and semantic value, 134, 205, 208
  and sense, 184–8, 196, 206
  essentially predicative nature of concept, 130
  primary (Sommers), 114
  realistic conception, for singular terms, 54
Resnik, M., 78n
rigid designators, 35
Russell, B., 83n, 107n, 119n, 122–3, 179–80, 236
Russellian propositions, 99&n, 100, 103

Russellian thoughts, 28
Russell's Principle, 87n

saturation (*see also* completeness), 145, 146, 147, 152, 155
Schiffer, S., 109n
Searle, J., 100n, 108n
self-identity, 175, 178
semantic theories, 202–3
semantic value, 134
  and *Bedeutung*, 102n
  and reference, 205, 208
Sen, P.K., 132n
sense, 228, 228–9, 235
  and function, 219–21
  and reference, 184–8, 196, 206
  and truth-conditions, 212–14
  collapsibility of, 165
  de re, 98–109
  eternal existence of, 17
  of name, 80–97
  part-whole doctrine, 156–7
  rich theory of, 91, 92, 97
sentence, unity of, 138–9, 142
sentences
  reference in contexts of direct use, 185
  sense in contexts of direct use, 187
'sentential role' and 'piece of information', 25–7
singular reference, 110–25 *passim*
singular terms, 40, 51
  and objects, 52
  criteria, 41–3, 44–5, 54–5
  realistic conception of reference, 54
Sluga, H., 158, 240
Sober, E., 136–7
solipsism, methodological, 21–2, 23, 24, 26
Sommers, F., 110–25 *passim*
states of affairs, 148–9
Strawson, P.F., 50
subsumption, 142–3, 146, 149–52
synthetic a priori, 61, 239–40

Tarski, A., 46, 117, 118n
tensed propositions, 10
tenseless existence, 4

thought
  laws of, 166
  philosophy of, 237
Thoughts (Frege), 1, 100, 160, 197, 228, 230, 237
  alternative analyses, 221–3
  and concept/object, 157
  and facts, 155
  articulation, 163
  as bearers of unrelativised truth-values, 20
  as psychologically real, 20
  as sense of sentence, 156
  as timeless, 4
  communicability of, 104–6
  criterion of difference for, 30
  identity criterion for, 27n
  identity over time, 14–15
  mind-independence, 2, 3, 7–18
  objectivity of, 104–6
  part-whole doctrine, 144, 147
  supervenience, 2–3, 18
thoughts, Russellian, 28
Tichy, P., 150n
timelessness
  analogy with spacelessness, 6
  versus eternality, 4–7
Translations from the Philosophical Writings of Gottlob Frege, 180
'true' as predicate, 164–6
truth
  as timeless, 9
  objectivity of, and mind-independence of Thoughts, 12–15
  omnitemporality of, and mind-independence of Thoughts, 8–12
truth-conditions, and sense, 212–14
truth-preservation, as regulative principle, 51
truth-value(s), 197
  about past, determinacy of, 13, 14, 15
  and *Bedeutung*, 188–93
  and judgement, 154, 155
  components of, 154, 155, 156
  origin of Frege's use of term, 190–1
Tugendhat, E., 188–9, 191, 204
Twin Earth cases, 22, 23–4, 32–5
type ambiguities, 225–6

'Über die wissenschaftliche Berechtigung einer Begriffsschrift', 192
'Über Sinn und Bedeutung', 154, 191, 192, 193, 202
Uehling, T., 21n
understanding, 199–202
Unex condition, 121, 122, 124
unsaturation, *see* saturation

validity
  -in-English, 49, 50
  language-neutrality of, 50

Wallace, J., 118n
Wettstein, H., 21n
Wiggins, D., 127n
wild quantity, 112, 113, 119–24
Williamson, T., 4n
Winch, P., 179n
Windelband, E., 191, 191n
Wissenschaftlicher Briefwechsel 144n
Wittgenstein, L., 2, 14, 18, 93, 94, 107, 142, 158, 159, 177, 179–80, 181, 183, 194, 212, 237, 238, 242
  and Frege's concept-script, 161–2, 163, 168–9, 170
Woodfield A., 21n, 83n, 99
Wright, C., 2n, 5n, 25, 42n, 43n, 45, 54n, 55n, 242n

1112